T0312019

A CONCISE HISTORY OF ROMANIA

Spanning a period of 2,000 years from the Roman conquest of Dacia to the present day, *A Concise History of Romania* traces the development of a unique nation situated on the border between East and West. In this illuminating new history, Keith Hitchins explores Romania's struggle to find its place amidst two diverse societies: one governed by Eastern Orthodox tradition and spirituality and peasant agriculture and the other by Western rationalism, experimentation, and capitalism. The book charts Romania's advancement through four significant phases of its history: medieval, early modern, modern, and finally the nation's "return to Europe," evaluating all the while Romania's part in European politics, economic and social change, intellectual and cultural renewals, and international entanglements. This is a fascinating history of an East European nation, one which sheds new light on the complex evolution of the Romanians and the identity they have successfully crafted from a unique synthesis of traditions.

KEITH HITCHINS is Professor of History at the University of Illinois, Urbana-Champaign.

CAMBRIDGE CONCISE HISTORIES

This is a series of 'concise histories' of selected individual countries, intended both as university and college textbooks and as general historical introductions for general readers, travellers, and members of the business community.

A full list of titles in the series can be found at:
www.cambridge.org/concisehistories

A Concise History of Romania

KEITH HITCHINS
University of Illinois, Urbana-Champaign

CAMBRIDGE
UNIVERSITY PRESS

CAMBRIDGE
UNIVERSITY PRESS

University Printing House, Cambridge CB2 8BS, United Kingdom

One Liberty Plaza, 20th Floor, New York, NY 10006, USA

477 Williamstown Road, Port Melbourne, VIC 3207, Australia

4843/24, 2nd Floor, Ansari Road, Daryaganj, Delhi - 110002, India

79 Anson Road, #06-04/06, Singapore 079906

Cambridge University Press is part of the University of Cambridge.

It furthers the University's mission by disseminating knowledge in the pursuit of education, learning and research at the highest international levels of excellence.

www.cambridge.org
Information on this title: www.cambridge.org/9780521694131

© Keith Hitchins 2014

First published 2014

A catalogue record for this publication is available from the British Library

Library of Congress Cataloging in Publication data
Hitchins, Keith, 1931–
A concise history of Romania / Keith Hitchins.
pages cm. – (Cambridge concise histories)
Includes bibliographical references and index.
ISBN 978-0-521-87238-6 (hardback) – ISBN 978-0-521-69413-1 (pbk.)
1. Romania–History. I. Title.
DR217.H579 2014
949.8–dc23
2013036670

ISBN 978-0-521-87238-6 Hardback
ISBN 978-0-521-69413-1 Paperback

CONTENTS

ILLUSTRATIONS

MAPS

ACKNOWLEDGMENTS

I am glad for this opportunity to thank colleagues and friends who have contributed much to the present enterprise. Professor Lucian Boia, of the University of Bucharest, and Professor Vasile Puşcaş, of the University of Cluj, have shared with me their knowledge of the Romanian phenomenon through their writings and our conversations over many years. I have benefited, as have many others, from the enthusiasm for history and the critical judgments of Mr. Marcel Popa, the Director of Editura Enciclopedică in Bucharest. The researches and writings of Professor Katherine Verdery and Professor Gail Kligman on fundamental questions of Romanian society and history have constantly expanded my own approach. Two doctoral candidates in history at the University of Illinois, Ms. Pompilia Burcică and Ms. Zsuzsánna Magdó, have lightened the tasks of research immeasurably by their work as research assistants.

"No one is better suited than Professor Keith Hitchins to encompass within a single volume the history of the Romanians and Romania. He knows this country – its language, history, and culture – like no one else. He is also well acquainted with Southeastern and Central Europe, and thus he is able to place Romanian history in a broad European context. The present work offers the reader a full, accurate, and perfectly balanced account of a country situated at the meeting place of East and West which over time had to change direction between opposite poles: this is the idea around which the narrative is structured. For those who wish to know the essentials about this European player the book by Keith Hitchins is by far the best introduction."

LUCIAN BOIA,
Professor, University of Bucharest

"There are two kinds of historians – those who seek to judge and those who seek to understand. Keith Hitchins has paved a path for many younger generations of historians of how to understand empathetically without giving up critical approaches to the past. The historiography on Romania is fortunate to have such an elegant, intellectually astute, and erudite master. The book before you represents the distillation of a lifetime of study, passion, and thoughtful deliberation about the complexities of a land and people at the crossroads between East and West. This book will be of great value to both specialists and a wider audience of readers with an interest in understanding the idea of Europe through this fascinating case study, often marginal to but essentially part of what Europe has evolved to become over the last two millennia."

MARIA BUCUR-DECKARD,
John W. Hill Professor of East European History,
Indiana University

"Keith Hitchins is for most of us the most reliable authority on the history of the Romanians. His erudition is amazingly broad and deep, his discourse is clear and articulate, his narrative is simple and highly objective in a field mined with suspicions and ideological or ethnic biases. We should rejoice to have now a synthesis of his numerous separate studies. It is a fitting monument to a life-long scholarly and creative endeavor."

VIRGIL NEMOIANU,
William J Byron Distinguished Professor of Literature
and Ordinary Professor of Philosophy,
Catholic University of America, Washington DC

Introduction

The 2,000 years of history of a people tempts the writer, and the reader, to seek out long-term trends to provide guidance through complex and contradictory evolutions. So it is with the history of the Romanians. From medieval times to the early twentieth century they followed stages similar to those of other nations in Eastern Europe and even of Europe as a whole: feudalism, of a sort, and a mainly agricultural economy and rural society, until the nineteenth century, and, then, down to the First World War, the transition, slow at the beginning, to an industrial economy and an urban society, where agriculture and the village nonetheless predominated. All the while, from the eighteenth century, the shape of a modern Romanian nation, intellectually at least, was taking form. Then came the interwar period, only twenty years long, when the modernization impulses accelerated, and then, for forty years, came the Communists, who pursued modernization with methods and goals of their own. The post-Communist years offer hints that the Romanians may once again be headed along the path taken two centuries earlier.

What especially may define the Romanians over the long term is their place between East and West. It grants the writer a wide perspective from which to arrange the events of their history. They confronted the dilemma of choice between these two poles from the beginning of their statehood in the fourteenth century, when the principalities of Wallachia and Moldavia were founded. Or, if we are willing to stretch reason a bit, we may say that the East–West

I

encounter began for them even earlier. It came with encounters between the Thracians and Dacians, first with the ancient Greek cities along the Black Sea coast and then with the Romans, the conquerors of Dacia in the early second century. These connections with the West were ethnic, linguistic, and historiographical. Crucial contacts with the East followed, with the Byzantine Empire and the Orthodox world and their Bulgarian and Serbian heirs. The links here were pre-eminently spiritual and cultural, but political, too.

If indeed the Romania that emerged in the twentieth century was a synthesis of East and West, the political contest between the two poles began in earnest in the later fourteenth and fifteenth century, as first the Wallachian and then the Moldavian princes, nobles, and peasants were confronted by the relentless march of the Ottoman Turks north through the Balkans. As the Wallachian and Moldavian princes sought to stem the Muslim advance they thought of themselves as a part of Christian Europe and joined Western crusading armies at Nicopolis (1396) and Varna (1444). But in the same centuries they were forced to defend their countries against aggressive designs from the West, from Roman Catholic Hungary and Poland.

The establishment of Ottoman pre-eminence over the principalities in the fifteenth and sixteenth centuries, which lasted until the early decades of the nineteenth century, could not but draw the Romanians toward the East. Yet, the suzerainty of the sultans, however great the economic burdens and the limitations on sovereignty it imposed, differed significantly from the Ottomans' conquests south of the Danube, which brought the incorporation of the Bulgarian and Serbian medieval states into the very structures of their empire. The Romanians preserved their institutions and social structure and over time exercised greater or lesser degrees of administrative autonomy. Although vassal status prohibited formal relations with foreign powers, neither principality was isolated from the West. From the sixteenth to the eighteenth century they carried on trade and maintained diplomatic contacts, even if indirectly, with Central Europe. They were open to varied cultural and intellectual currents from the West, even though the great movements of ideas such as the Renaissance and the Reformation and the Catholic Reformation would, understandably in Orthodox countries, have modest influence. The Enlightenment was another matter. From the later decades of the eighteenth century until well into the first half of the nineteenth century the Romanian educated classes, especially the younger nobles and the rising middle class, made the idea of progress and the means of achieving it – reason and knowledge and good institutions – their own. Their adaptation of Enlightenment principles is some measure of their approach to Europe. But it is from the era of the 1830s and the Revolution of 1848 and Romanticism that the contest between East and West for the soul and mind of the Romanians was fully joined.

Between the 1860s and the decades between the World Wars, which constitute the "national period," modern Romania took form politically, economically, socially, and culturally, in accordance with the European model. "Europe," the center and west of the continent, established itself as a distinct category in Romanian thought. The concept had a special significance for the Romanians; it meant the modern world, urban and industrial, dynamic and of a high civilization, and turned toward the future. The Europeanization of Romania, if that is the proper term, may be traced from a variety of perspectives: political-administrative, economic, social, and cultural and intellectual. An examination of each leads to the conclusion that Romania was being drawn deeply into the web of European relationships. But such a course was by no means smooth. Nor did it go uncontested. Many Romanians feared that their unique identity would be smothered in the West's embrace; they argued that they should achieve progress by finding models in and drawing inspiration from native sources that had weathered the tests of history.

An abiding preoccupation of Romanian politicians and intellectuals was the crafting of an administrative system that would ensure stability for their young state and enable its people to make progress in every field of human activity. They were inspired by diverse patterns: the French centralization of power, the Belgian assurances of citizens' participation in the political system, and the order and consistency of the English constitutional system, among others. Yet, those Romanians who drew up constitutions and enacted laws did not imitate. They adapted, as they took generous account of their own history and prevailing economic and social conditions and carefully weighed their own ambitions.

The Romanian economy was steadily drawn into the international commercial and financial system beginning in the second half of the nineteenth century as Europeans gradually discovered the value of Romanian agricultural goods and raw materials for their cities and industries, the availability of Romanian markets for their own products, and the profits to be had from investing in Romanian industries and financial institutions. So strong did these Western currents become that by the outbreak of the First World War many branches of the Romanian economy were dependent on European banking and commercial interests. Even the modest farmer of grains was subject to the ups and downs of the international market. The same course of development continued during the interwar period, but Romanian governments were more determined than their predecessors to maintain control over the national economy. Yet in the long run, the chief benefit to Romanians of their integration into the international economic order may have been the incentive to modernize their own economy.

The structures of Romanian society during the nineteenth and twentieth century were also becoming more like those of Western Europe. Such an evolution was largely the consequence of economic development and urbanization and the growing complexities of urban life, but it was no less a response to changes in the mental climate. Most striking perhaps was the rise of the middle class, which in the later decades of the nineteenth century assumed leadership of both the economy and political life and took pride in being modern and European and claimed to represent the interests of the whole nation. The urban working class was also growing, but its role in the broader society remained ill-defined and modest. The peasants, the majority of the population down to the later twentieth century, remained a bulwark of tradition. They were reluctant to change, even under pressure, especially during Communist times. But change they did.

It may be in writing and thinking about themselves from the eighteenth to the twentieth century that the Romanians revealed the true measure of their Europeanness. At the beginning of modern times they were observers of the Center and West. Then they slowly merged their own creativity of the mind and spirit with movements and schools elsewhere in the continent. By the beginning of the twentieth century adaptation gave way to innovation, as Romanian writers, historians, and social thinkers helped to shape continental values and thus expanded the concept of Europe.

For the second half of the twentieth century the question naturally arises about how Romanian Communism fits into the long-term Europeanization of the Romanians. Or we could simply ask if the Communists were Europeanizers. They certainly professed disdain for the private entrepreneurship and market forces prevalent in the West, and they showed no inclination to embrace Western-style multi-party politics and the parliamentary system. They were also intent on wiping away as much of the national tradition as they could, at least at the start of their tenure. They also held up for emulation another model – the Soviet Union and its experience in constructing Communism – and for a decade after coming to power in the late 1940s they dared not deviate from the Soviet-prescribed path. But after the death of Joseph Stalin, as changes occurred in Soviet relations with the East European bloc and with the West, Romanian Communist leaders became bolder and embarked on a project that could be called "national Communism" or, as some would have it, "national Stalinism." In any case, it entailed a re-evaluation of the country's history and certain traditions and suggested the value of at least a partial rapprochement with Europe. Romanian Communists remained Communists, and thus they set boundaries beyond which their vision of Europe could not pass.

The collapse of Communism in 1989 opened the way to a new, genuine reconciliation with Europe. The "return to Europe," as the events of the time are sometimes called, was not at first smooth, as the accretions of four decades of Communism took time to wear away, but the process seems well under way. Perhaps the question to be asked is whether the great experiment of the synthesis of East and West has run its course.

I

Beginnings

Distant origins and the debate about them lie at the heart of Romanian identity. From at least the seventeenth century down to the present, self-identification has engaged the energies of scholars and, not infrequently, of churchmen and politicians, who for their own reasons have been at pains to explain how the Romanians came to be. In their diligence historians, archeologists, and linguists, in particular, have brought to light the most diverse evidence to support the most diverse theories about origins, but sometimes their reasoning has belonged more to myth than to science. Nonetheless, these notions of origins and the interpretations they begot would prove crucial for the image the Romanians gradually formed of themselves and would decisively shape their relationship to "Europe," that is, whether to turn east or west for models and inspiration.

THE DACIANS

Central to the Romanians' long-standing debate about beginnings and identity was the nature of the Roman conquest and settlement of Dacia, the land that was to form the core of modern Romania, both geographically and psychologically. No less important in delineating an acceptable self-image was the fate of the Dacians, the indigenous inhabitants of the land, who were subjected to Roman rule and acculturation for a century and a half.

In the centuries before the Roman conquest of the early second century AD the territory bounded roughly by the Danube, Tisza, and Dniester rivers was home to various Thracian peoples, the most important of whom historically were the Getae and the Dacians. The two were distinct but related peoples, and some historians, from ancient times to the present, have treated them as one, calling them Geto-Dacians. In any case, the Getae inhabited the lower Danube basin and had regular commerce with Greek cities along the Black Sea coast founded as early as the seventh century BC in what is now Dobrudja. The *Histories* of Herodotus, written in the fifth century BC, are one of the earliest narrative sources of information about them and regularly refer to them as a Thracian people. The lands of the Dacians lay in the center of the Carpatho-Danubian basin straddling both sides of the southern Carpathian Mountains. Strabo in the first century BC tells us that the Dacians spoke the same language as the Getae, and Dio Cassius some two centuries later pointed to numerous similarities in their cultures.

The Geto-Dacians, or simply Dacians, as I shall call them, were united into a powerful confederation under a noble, Burebista, who became their "king" in about 82 BC. Ambitious and bold, he assembled a powerful army that enabled him for a time to expand his territory to the middle Danube. His most important conquests, beginning about 55 BC, were the Greek cities on the Black Sea coast, acquisitions that intensified the spread of Greek commerce and technology to the interior of the Dacian lands. Greek artisans and builders were familiar inhabitants of his capital, Sarmizegetusa, which lay in the mountains of present-day southwestern Transylvania.

Burebista inevitably came into conflict with Rome, whose legions had reached the lower Danube by the reign of Augustus (27 BC–AD 14). He was unwise enough to interfere with Roman ambitions and to involve himself in Roman power struggles. He carried out raiding expeditions across the Danube into Thrace, where the Romans had established themselves, and he took the side of Pompey in the civil war which had broken out in 48 BC between him and Julius Caesar mainly because Pompey seems to have recognized his conquests on the Black Sea coast. He had thus made an enemy of Caesar, who was victorious over Pompey and would undoubtedly have mounted a punitive expedition against him, if he had not been assassinated in 44 BC.

Burebista suffered a similar fate at the hands of disaffected nobles at about the same time, and without his forceful leadership his "kingdom" rapidly disintegrated, as tribal chiefs claimed their independence. A succession of rulers asserted their authority from their center in southwestern Transylvania, but not until the accession of Decebal, who united the Dacian tribes, did a Dacian kingdom, somewhat smaller than Burebista's, again take form. The reign of Decebal, which began in about AD 85, witnessed almost continuous warfare between the Dacians and the Roman administration south of the Danube, now organized as the province of Moesia, which extended from the Black Sea to Singindinum (present-day Belgrade). In AD 89 Decebal and the Emperor Domitian (AD 81–96) reached an accord under which Dacia became a client kingdom of Rome and in return received financial subsidies and technological assistance. It brought peace to the region for a decade.

Dacia between the reigns of Burebista and Decebal reveals itself in the written records and in archeological remains to have been a complex society divided into two main classes – aristocracy and commoners. It was from among the former that kings and leading officials and the clergy came, while the mass of the population supplied labor and taxes. This majority was largely rural and lived in village communes, which seem to have had collective responsibility for taxes and such labor services to the king as the maintenance of fortifications. Urban life was, nonetheless, well developed. Sarmizegetusa possessed the attributes of a true city, and it was a significant artisan and commercial center, besides being the seat of royal administration.

The economy was based on agriculture, which provided most of the inhabitants with their main source of income. The main crops were grains – wheat, barley, and millet. But mining, especially of iron, gold, silver, and salt, and artisan crafts, including metals, ceramics, glass, and masonry, were well developed. Dacian artisans thus produced a variety of weapons and tools and products of all kinds for daily life. Influences from both the Roman and Hellenistic worlds were evident in the forms and decorations they chose, influences that were strengthened by a flourishing commerce. In return for processed goods and luxuries such as perfumes and lotions, which were intended for the upper classes, the Dacians sent to the

Danube and Black Sea coastal cities grain and animal products, salt, wood, honey, and wax. This trade seems to have been in the hands of foreign, not Dacian, merchants.

By the reign of Decebal the Dacians had achieved a level of civilization well suited to their needs. In architecture, especially in the some eighty fortresses and the numerous religious sanctuaries that archeologists have identified, they gave evidence of a solid knowledge of mathematics and engineering. They possessed a written language, and in the few specimens that have survived, mainly inscriptions and an occasional word or two from Greek and Latin authors, they used the Greek and Latin alphabets. In religion, according to Herodotus, the Getae practiced the cult of Zamolxis, a priest who, according to tradition, had been a disciple of Pythagoras and had returned to his native land to serve the Dacian supreme god Gebeleizis and preach the immortality of the soul. Other, later sources present Zamolxis as a god himself and suggest that the Getae knew how "to make themselves immortal" through secret rituals. Yet, information about the religion of the Getae and Dacians is so fragmentary that greater precision about beliefs and practices is difficult.

ROMAN DACIA

The Roman conquest of Dacia at the beginning of the second century AD brought an end to the autonomous evolution of Dacian society and civilization. Absorbed henceforth into the cosmopolitan Roman world, both were utterly transformed.

The Emperor Trajan (AD 98–117) initiated a more consistently aggressive policy toward the Dacians than his predecessors had pursued. Shortly after ascending the throne he inspected the imperial frontier along the Danube from Pannonia to Moesia and took immediate measures to strengthen its fortifications. His anxiety about protecting the Roman provinces of Upper and Lower Moesia had been aroused by frequent Dacian attacks across the river during the reign of Domitian, notably the raids into Dobrudja in AD 85–86. Although a peace had been concluded with Decebal in AD 89 which restored a relative calm along the Danube frontier and encouraged a lively trade, Trajan had evidently decided that the Dacians were a permanent menace to the security of Rome's Balkan provinces, especially if they allied themselves with other enemies of Rome such as the Parthians. The mineral wealth and agricultural productivity of Dacia also undoubtedly persuaded him to extend Rome's grasp beyond the Danube.

For the campaign of AD 101–2 Trajan assembled a sizable army to send against Decebal, perhaps two to three times the size of the Dacian force of some 50,000 that opposed him. Two columns of Roman legionaries crossed the Danube at different points, the one at Viminaceum on a bridge formed of river barges where Trajan himself was in command, and the other further east at Dierna. The two columns met at Tibiscum and marched together on Sarmizegetusa, Decebal's capital. At Tapae they encountered the main Dacian army and defeated it, forcing Decebal to sue for peace. Trajan imposed harsh terms with the aim of removing permanently the Dacians' threat to Roman predominance along the Danube. He forced Decebal to withdraw from what is today the Banat and Oltenia, to demolish the walls surrounding the most important Dacian fortresses, to accept the status of a Roman ally, which meant the end of an independent foreign policy, and to receive a Roman garrison in Sarmizegetusa. He may have refrained from destroying the Dacian kingdom in the expectation that it might prove useful in keeping other "barbarian" peoples at bay. Yet, he seems to have thought the peace just achieved merely a truce, his long-term ambition being to transform Dacia into a Roman province. Evidence of his resolve is his commissioning of the architect Apollodorus of Damascus to construct a bridge across the Danube at Drobeta, a project that was begun in AD 102, right after the defeat of the Dacians. The bridge was intended to link the province of Moesia Superior with the newly conquered territories north of the river.

The violations of the terms of peace by Decebal – he did not carry out the required demolition of fortress walls; he sought allies against Rome from all the surrounding peoples and from the Parthians; and he recruited new soldiers – hastened Trajan's resolve to undertake a second campaign against him in AD 105–6. This time after the military victory he showed no restraint: he abolished the Dacian kingdom and, in effect, forced Decebal to choose suicide rather than grace a Roman triumph. Trajan commemorated his conquest of Dacia and at the same time provided a graphic account of the

1 The siege of Sarmizegetusa

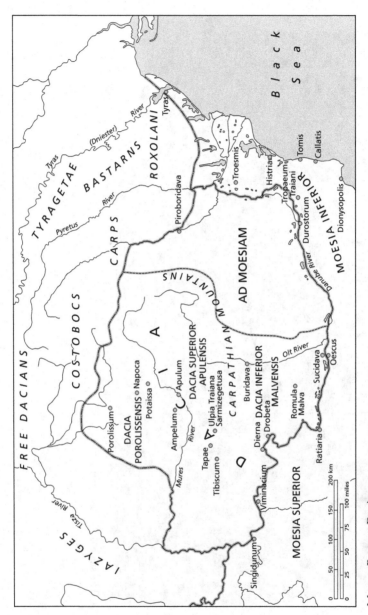

Map 1 Roman Dacia

campaigns in the many panels of the column he had erected in AD 113 in the Forum of Trajan in Rome.

Trajan set about organizing the new province of Dacia even before the defeat of Decebal was complete. By August of AD 106 it had come into being officially by a decree of Trajan delineating its boundaries, setting down the principles that should guide its civil administration and military defense, and specifying the taxes that were to be collected for the imperial treasury. He himself remained in Dacia to oversee the carrying out of his plan and returned to Rome only in the following year. The new province encompassed present-day Oltenia to just east of the Olt River, with the Danube as its southern limit, the Banat as far as the Tisza River, and most of Transylvania. Other territory north of the Danube from the Olt River to the Danube delta and including a part of present-day southern Moldavia was attached to the province of Moesia Inferior. These boundaries remained by and large stable until the withdrawal of the provincial administration and army to south of the Danube in AD 271. Certain significant internal administrative reorganizations did take place in the course of a century and half. Noteworthy was Emperor Hadrian's (AD 117–38) division of Trajan's single province into three: Dacia Porolissensis in the north, Dacia Inferior in the south, and Dacia Superior, the largest, in the center, in order to improve defenses against attacks from Iazyges, Roxolans, and other hostile tribes. Then, in AD 168, also out of concern for defense, Emperor Marcus Aurelius (AD 161–80) centralized the civil and military administration of the three provinces under a single governor with headquarters at Apulum. Roman Dacia remained so until its end.

The province of Dacia underwent a steady Romanization between Trajan's conquest and the withdrawal under Emperor Aurelian (AD 270–75). During these nearly 165 years Dacia was integrated into the complex structures of the Roman Empire. Its institutions of government, its laws and judicial system, all the branches of its civilization, and its Latin language lay at the social and economic foundations and shaped the mental climate of the province.

The chief bearers of this new order of things were the colonists. Ethnically and by social category they were of an almost infinite diversity. First in power and social standing were the governors and the commanders of the legions and their immediate subordinates and the wealthy merchants and businessmen. Next came the artisans and shopkeepers, the legionaries and the veterans, then the farmers and, finally, the laborers and slaves. By the beginning of the third century a sizable minority of the population of Roman Dacia was composed of newcomers. They had arrived from all parts of the Roman world, from Britain to the Near East. Yet, however different their origins, they were united by their sense of belonging to the empire and by their common Latin language.

Dacians formed the majority of the population. They had survived the wars of conquest and lived mainly in the countryside as cultivators of the soil. Some Dacian villages were far removed from centers of Roman civilization, especially those in eastern Dacia, where civil administrators and legionaries were few. But most of the settlements maintained regular contact with urban centers and military camps or were touched by the network of roads that joined together most parts of the province. These rural Dacians could not but be drawn in some degree into the economic system and civilization represented by urban provincial Rome. They thus adopted changes in their way of life, used the official language, Latin, as a *lingua franca*, and even assimilated the gods of the Romans. But Christianity seems to have had few followers, in part because Roman authorities persecuted Christians. In any case, archeological evidence of Christianity in Dacia at this time is fragmentary.

The first century of Roman rule in Dacia was marked by occasional periods of crisis but also by general peace and prosperity, especially between the reigns of Hadrian (AD 117–38) and Marcus Aurelius (AD 161–80). But later, after the reign of Septimius Severus (AD 193–211), insecurity grew and productivity and commerce declined under the constant pressure of attacks by barbarian tribes. At the center, in Rome, the repeated challenges to the authority of the emperors and the consequent undermining of confidence in the integrity of the empire in the middle decades of the third century added to the sense of crisis in far-off Dacia.

Unrelenting attacks against Dacia by the Carps and Goths and the difficulties of defending extended and exposed frontiers led to a partial withdrawal from northern and eastern Dacia under Gallienus (sole emperor, AD 260–68). It brought no improvement in security, and Aurelian at the beginning of his reign, probably in AD 271, moved the army and the civil administration to south of the Danube, which henceforth was to serve as the empire's defensive bulwark protecting its Balkan provinces.

After the official withdrawal from Dacia the Roman character of the province slowly withered as contacts with the empire south of the Danube became increasingly sporadic and as newcomers, this time the barbarian or migratory peoples, arrived for longer or shorter stays. Perhaps most striking in the period between the fourth and sixth centuries was the inexorable decay of urban life. Although cities such as Sarmizegetusa and Apulum continued to exist for a time, they in effect became ruralized, as life there took on the attributes of the surrounding countryside and lost its urban style. Economic activity changed in the same way, as the production of goods and commerce assumed more modest dimensions. There was now a migration from the cities to the villages, which became the centers of economic and social life. Along the Danube cities on the left bank such as Dierna, Drobeta, and Sucidava, which were reintegrated into the empire by Constantine the Great (AD 306–37) and Justinian (AD 527–65), carried on an unpretentious urban way of life until the beginning of the seventh century. To the north, in what would become Transylvania, not only cities but the territory as a whole lost contact with the empire between the fourth and sixth centuries. By this time Roman traditions, rural as well as urban, had been lost.

The fate of the majority of Dacia's population – we may call them "Daco-Romans" – after the departure of the civil administration and legionaries in AD 271 has been a matter of controversy, since the event raises questions about when and where the emergence of the modern Romanians occurred. One issue is clear: for some six centuries after Aurelian's withdrawal old Dacia was occupied by outsiders from the east, the north, and the south. Except for the Slavs, they left few, if any, traces of their presence in the Romanian language, an absence that suggests only intermittent and superficial contacts with the Daco-Roman population, assuming for the moment that it had remained in place after AD 271. The contribution of these outsiders to the ethnic makeup of the later Romanians must have been similarly modest. They came in successive waves.

The Goths moved southward from the Baltic regions and settled in the area between the southern Carpathians and the Danube about AD 332 as auxiliaries of the Romans. They gave way to the Huns, who attacked them in AD 376, forcing them south of the Danube, from where they eventually made their way to Italy, sacking Rome in AD 410. The Huns by AD 420 were well settled in the territory north of the mouths of the Danube and relentlessly extended their control over what would become in the fourteenth century Moldavia and Wallachia and, further to the west, Oltenia. In AD 454 with their center now in Pannonia, they were defeated by a coalition of Germanic tribes, one of which, the Gepids, a branch of the Goths, settled in Transylvania. Then the Avars replaced the Gepids in Transylvania in around AD 567, making numerous settlements along the middle course of the Mureş (Maros) River. The multi-ethnic Avar Khaganate, encompassing Gepids, Slavs, and Romanized populations, covered a vast territory stretching from the steppe north of the Black Sea to the Alps.

Of all these migrations, that of the Slavs left the deepest impression on the Daco-Romans. Coming from the north, they reached the territory east of the Carpathians in the first half of the sixth century and then began to settle in eastern Wallachia and slowly moved westward into Transylvania. Slavic tribes continued to move southward, crossing the Danube into the northern Balkans in AD 602. They were well established between the Danube and the Balkan Mountains when the Bulgarians, a Turkic people, arrived in the region from the steppe north of the Black Sea. In AD 680 they crossed the lower Danube and established their capital at Pliska in present-day northeastern Bulgaria. In the course of the next century the Bulgarian ruling elites underwent a gradual assimilation by the more numerous Slavs, a process sufficiently complete by the tenth century to allow us to speak of "Bulgarians." Of crucial importance was the conversion of Tsar Boris I (AD 852–888) to Christianity in 864. By this time the Bulgarian state had expanded north of the Danube as far as the Tisza River and had absorbed most of present-day Romania, a movement facilitated by the collapse of the Avar realm after defeats by the armies of Charlemagne between AD 791 and 796. This first Bulgarian empire reinforced Slavic influences among the Daco-Romans. But north of the Danube, unlike the course of events to the south, the Slavs were assimilated by the Daco-Romans.

During these "obscure" centuries Christianity established itself among the inhabitants of old Dacia. Yet, the evidence is sparse. Christians were certainly among the colonists and legionaries who came to Dacia after Trajan's conquest, but persecutions to which Roman authorities subjected Christians must have impeded the spread of the new faith and discouraged the organization of communities. The earliest significant archaeological remains attesting to the presence of Christians in Dacia date from the fourth century. Evidence of Christianity in early Dacia also comes from the Romanian language: many words relating to Christianity are of Latin origin, especially those concerning the fundamental ideas of the faith. The extension of the First Bulgarian Empire north of the Danube and across the Carpathians in the ninth century brought formal church institutions, the Byzantine-Slavic rite, and Slavic as the official language of the church, events attested to by the large number of Slavic words in Romanian relating to worship and ecclesiastical organization. The Slavic connection thus established was crucial in turning the Daco-Romans to the East.

CONTINUITY

The scholarly and, often, polemical debate about the continued presence of a Romanized or Daco-Roman population north of the Danube, particularly on the territory of the old Roman province (much of Transylvania, the Banat, and Oltenia) after Aurelian's withdrawal has been clouded by a paucity of firsthand sources and, in modern times, by national passions. The controversy has been wide-ranging and has lasted down to the post-Communist era, though it has assumed an attenuated form as membership in the European Union has softened territorial rivalries between Romania and Hungary. Individual polemicists in the past have differed greatly in their approaches to the matter, but they may, nonetheless, be divided into two broad categories. On one side stand the proponents of continuity, mainly Romanians, who argue that the bulk of the civil population, primarily of the lower classes, stayed in place and tried to carry on their daily lives as before, despite the adverse circumstances. They harbor no doubts that the Romanian ethnic community was formed in Dacia, which they consider the cradle of the nation. On the other side, the opponents of this doctrine of continuity, mainly Hungarians, insist that the evacuation of Dacia in the third century was complete and that the formation of the Romanian people, consequently, took place south of the Danube, in the Balkans. They do not deny the presence of Romanians north of the Danube, even in Transylvania, but they contend that they migrated there from south of the river, perhaps as late as the thirteenth century.

Those who deny continuity cite the "silence of the sources," that is, the lack of credible evidence, either written or archeological, attesting to the presence of a Romanized population in Dacia after the third or fourth century down to the emergence of the Romanian principalities in the fourteenth century. They point out that historians and other writers of the time duly noted the succession of migratory peoples who came to Dacia after the third century, but make no mention of any Romanized inhabitants. The deniers of continuity also use language to buttress their case. They cite similarities between the Albanian and South Slavic languages, on the one hand, and Romanian, on the other, as evidence that the original home of the Romanians could only have been south of the Danube.

The Romanian defenders of continuity are by no means without arguments of their own. They have had recourse to the evidence of archeology to show that a Daco-Roman population inhabited at least parts of old Dacia down to the sixth century. They may acquiesce in the contention of critics that the written sources of the time do not specifically mention the Daco-Romans of Dacia, but they point out that it was the usual practice to note only the leading political or military classes and, hence, the conquerors – the Goths, Huns, Avars, or Bulgarians – but not the Daco-Romans, the conquered. They further insist that the written sources would have recorded such a momentous event as the removal of the whole population of Dacia to south of the Danube, but here, too, they are silent. The "obvious" conclusion they draw is that no migration of such proportions occurred. As for the affinities between the Albanian and Romanian languages, Romanian scholars suggest that the words they share may be a common inheritance from a Dacian or Thracian substratum, although such a theory cannot be verified, as little is known about Dacian or Thracian. They also point out that Slavic borrowings in Romanian could just as easily have occurred in Transylvania through the assimilation of the Slavs as south of the Danube, where they predominated.

Despite serious gaps in our knowledge, the Romanian language, nonetheless, offers intriguing clues about the process of formation of the Romanian people. First of all, Romanian is a Latin language, as its morphology, syntax, and vocabulary of most frequently used words demonstrate. Its Latin character, then, suggests the depths and pervasiveness of Romanization to which the populations north, and also south, of the Danube were subjected. By contrast, the Dacian element in Romanian is modest and, in fact, difficult to measure, since little of the Dacian language has survived. The second most important element in Romanian after Latin is Slavic. Although it had some effect on the structure and phonetics of Romanian, it exercised its greatest influence on the vocabulary. The number of frequently used words in Romanian of Slavic origin suggests that Daco-Romans and Slavs lived together for an extended period before the Romanian language had been fully formed and before the Slavs north of the Danube had been assimilated by the more numerous Daco-Romans. The Slavic element in Romanian was reinforced later by the expansion of the First Bulgarian Empire north of the Danube and across the Carpathians before and after the conversion of Tsar Boris to Christianity in AD 864. It was the form of Slavic brought by the Bulgarians, that is, Medio-Bulgarian, based on the language spoken around Salonika in the ninth century that was the source of numerous Slavic words in Romanian relating to church life, ritual, and the hierarchy. Medio-Bulgarian, using the Cyrillic alphabet, became the official language of the Orthodox Church and of the princely chancelleries in the principalities of Moldavia and Wallachia, when they were formed in the fourteenth century.

Romanian scholars, in general, accept AD 1000 as the date roughly marking the emergence of the Romanian ethnic community, a combination of Roman or Romanized, Slavic, and Dacian populations. They argue that henceforth we may speak of "Romanians."

TRANSYLVANIA

The lands that were to constitute modern Romania continued to receive newcomers well after the arrival of the Slavs, who by the eleventh century had been assimilated into the Daco-Roman population. Of crucial importance for the history of the Romanians was the coming of the Hungarians to Central Europe at the end of the ninth century. From the plains of present-day Hungary they expanded into Transylvania in the first half of the tenth century, taking advantage of the collapse of the Bulgarian Empire after the death of Tsar Simeon in AD 927. As they moved south and east, if we accept the doctrine of Daco-Roman continuity, they encountered a number of Romanian-Slavic political formations, which they brought under their control. These were the "duchies" described by the anonymous chronicler of King Béla II of Hungary (AD 1131–41): those of Menumorut, whose territory lay between the Tisza, Mureş, and Someş rivers and was centered on present-day Bihor; of Glad, which encompassed the region between the Tisza, Mureş, and Danube and the Carpathians; and of Gelu, "a certain Romanian," whose lands lay east of Bihor, beyond the Igfon forest, that is, in "terra Ultrasilvano." In this way Anonymous, as he is known, gave later Romanian proponents of Daco-Roman continuity precious evidence to support their cause. By contrast, Hungarian scholars, in general, have denied the validity of his information, insisting that he was, in fact, describing conditions prevailing several centuries after the settlement of the Hungarians and thus concluding that his account is by no means evidence of an early Romanian presence in Transylvania. In any case, it is clear that the Hungarian tribal leaders who came to Transylvania gradually organized political entities of their own and eventually a principality, which remained separate from Hungary until the beginning of the eleventh century. Even after King Stephen I of Hungary (AD 997–1038) incorporated Transylvania into his kingdom in AD 1002, it preserved a large measure of autonomy.

Old Dacia was host to two more peoples who would greatly affect the history of both Transylvania and the Romanians. The origins of the Szeklers (Székelyek) are still the subject of debate, but there is general agreement that they are closely related to the

Hungarians. The Szeklers may have accompanied them on their migration westward from the Urals and the steppe north of the Black Sea, or they may have come later and joined the Hungarians in the central plains of present-day Hungary in the early part of the tenth century. Their settlement in Transylvania took place in stages, and by the middle of the twelfth century large numbers had settled in eastern Transylvania along the Carpathians, followed by still others in the thirteenth century.

Settlers of another ethnicity – Germans mainly, but not exclusively – came from a territory bounded roughly by the Elbe River in the east and the Rhine and Moselle rivers in the west. Their colonization of Transylvania, mainly in the south, especially in the area of present-day Sibiu (Nagyszeben; Hermannstadt), began in the second half of the twelfth century and continued until the end of the thirteenth. By this time the written sources were referring to these settlers by various names, including *Flandrensi*, *Theutoni*, and *Saxoni*, but in time they all came to be known as Saxons. From King Andrew II of Hungary they received a charter, the *Andreanum*, in AD 1224, which granted them a large measure of self-government in return for an annual payment to the royal treasury and military service.

Transylvania remained a part of the Hungarian kingdom in the middle of the fourteenth century, but its three "nations" (*natio*), Hungarian nobles and Saxon and Szekler upper classes, in process of formation, possessed a large measure of autonomy, which they were determined to preserve. Its destiny was to be markedly different from that of the Wallachian and Moldavian principalities south and east of the Carpathians, which stood in the path of Ottoman Turkish armies of conquest.

2

Between East and West, fourteenth century to 1774

In the four centuries between the founding of the principalities of Wallachia and Moldavia and the first substantial limitation of Ottoman suzerainty over them by a European power, Romanian elites strove to find a secure place for their countries in a neighborhood of competing and never friendly great powers. Princes and nobles, churchmen and intellectuals learned to appreciate early on the advantages of balance and accommodation in international relations. Through often dangerous times they continued to build institutions and fashion a culture that would ensure their identity and survival. At the same time they debated among themselves who they were and where they belonged in Europe. From the beginning they asked themselves whether they should look to the East or to the West for a model. In time, religion and culture inherited from Byzantium and political and economic ties imposed by the Ottoman Empire turned them to the East. Orthodoxy in the broad cultural sense of the term was paramount in establishing their identity and may explain why Roman Catholicism and, later, Protestantism made little headway among them. Yet, the Romanians of the principalities and of Transylvania were never isolated from the West. The educated were always aware of their Roman origins. A shift in their consciousness and aspirations toward the West became palpable in the seventeenth century and gathered momentum in the eighteenth, and thereby they prepared the way for the emergence of the modern Romanian sense of being. Their writings – church books, chronicles, and histories – and their experiments with poetry and artistic prose trace the path they followed from East to West.

FOUNDATIONS

To the south and east of the Carpathians a process of state formation similar to that in Transylvania was underway at least by the thirteenth century. In these territories, over which the kings of Hungary claimed suzerainty, *cnezate*, small regional territorial agglomerations headed by a *cnez* (district prince), were combining into principalities. By the end of the century in the south a new political entity had emerged, Wallachia (Ţara Românească, or the Romanian Land). Under a vigorous Grand Prince (Mare Voievod), Basarab (*c.* 1310–52), it asserted its independence from Hungary by defeating the army of King Charles Robert (1308–42) at the Battle of Posada in 1330. But conflicts between their successors continued, mainly over the control of territory linking Hungary to the mouths of the Danube and the Black Sea. To reinforce his position Nicolae Alexandru (1352–64), Basarab's successor, assumed unprecedented powers as Domn Autocrat (Prince Autocrat) and established the Metropolitanate of Ungrovlachia as a dependency of the Orthodox Patriarchate of Constantinople. These acts, both in 1359, endowed Wallachia with the essential institutions of an independent state in the medieval world – an authoritarian secular power and a single, dominant church. By thus thwarting the ambitions of King Louis of Hungary (1342–82) to impose himself and Roman Catholicism on Wallachia, Nicolae Alexandru set his country on a course of political independence and of spiritual commitment to Eastern Christianity that became touchstones of its evolution down to the nineteenth century. Yet, Prince Vladislav (1364–*c.* 1376), like many of his successors, recognized the virtues of compromise. He accepted Hungarian suzerainty and granted merchants from Braşov (Brassó; Kronstadt) favorable trading privileges at the Black Sea, and, in return, he received from Louis the districts of Severin, on the Danube, and Fogaras (Făgăraş), in Transylvania, as fiefs. But he resisted Louis's efforts to bring his subjects into communion with Rome, a conversion he perceived as simply another means of territorial conquest. To strengthen his ties to the Orthodox East he created a second metropolitanate in Oltenia in 1370, which lasted until *c.* 1403, and he became an active patron of Mt. Athos, founding the monastery of Cutlumuz there in 1369.

To the northeast the principality of Moldavia came into being much like Wallachia. Here, too, local notables resisted the efforts of the King of Hungary to impose his rule over their small principality. An initial revolt in 1359 brought them autonomy under Dragoş, a Romanian military leader from Maramureş, an autonomous region north of Transylvania, and a second revolt in 1364 under Bogdan (*c.* 1359–65), also from Maramureş, led to independence. Like the princes of Wallachia, Bogdan's successors sought to buttress independence from Hungary with outside help, but unlike them they looked first to the Catholic powers rather than to Byzantium and the Eastern Church. Laţcu (1369–77) appealed directly to Rome for support, and Pope Urban V granted him recognition as "Duke" of Moldavia and permission to create a bishopric in his capital to be subject directly to Rome. Prince Petru (*c.* 1377–*c.* 1392) oriented his foreign policy toward Poland, a tendency that would last a century, but in ecclesiastical matters he turned to Constantinople, primarily to counterbalance Hungarian political ambitions, and he established a Metropolitanate in his new capital Suceava about 1386. By the end of the century, when Prince Roman (*c.* 1392–94) extended the principality's borders to the Black Sea, Moldavia had ensured its independence.

By this time, too, political and social structures of a similar kind had taken form in both principalities. The prince had asserted his superiority over the leading noble families by astutely cleaving to the Byzantine tradition of close cooperation between church and state. He had himself anointed by the Metropolitan, an act that separated him from other territorial lords and allowed him to assume the style of the Byzantine *autocrator* and to rule by the grace of God. He also owed his authority to his control of land, the primary source of wealth and power of the time. He not only possessed extensive domains of his own, but he could also dispose of enormous tracts of land not already in the hands of *boiers* (nobles). These he often granted to nobles and ecclesiastics who, in return, pledged their loyalty to him. He could enforce obedience as supreme commander of the principality's army, both the "small army" (*oastea cea mică*), composed of the privileged classes performing obligatory military service, and the "large army" (*oastea cea mare*), formed by all able-bodied men and summoned in times of great peril to the country. He also had the power to tax, for as head of the army he could collect the *bir*, a levy imposed to pay the costs of a campaign or to buy peace through the payment of tribute.

The boiers were the dominant political and social class. Initially, they had been *cnezes* and other local or clan leaders, whose positions of authority had been confirmed by the prince. Others, who had not received such a favor, gradually fell into the ranks of free peasants. After the principalities had come into being other categories of the population achieved boier status through grants of land from the prince or through appointment to high offices, and in time a distinction was made between the great and lesser boiers based on the size of their estates and the importance of the services they rendered the prince.

The mass of the population was composed of peasants. Some, who preserved their personal liberty and their own land, despite the encroachments of boier domains, were free (*moşneni* in Wallachia; *răzeşi* in Moldavia). But the majority were dependent (*vecini* or *rumâni*) because they were obliged to pay tithes or perform labor services for boiers, obligations which, however, do not seem to have been unduly burdensome at this time. Rural communities, whether free or dependent, maintained their traditional form of self-government through elected village councils of "good and old men" (*oameni buni şi bătrîni*).

The prince and the boiers engaged in a continuous competition for political power and economic advantage. The boiers enjoyed limited administrative and judicial immunities on their own estates and were ever vigilant to restrain the extension of power from the center. But the prince still disposed of great expanses of land, which he could use to further his own ambitions. Of some 3,000 villages, only 313 were recorded as benefiting from boier immunities. The rest, in theory at least, were exposed to princely tax collectors and other officials. Yet, despite the inevitable clash of interests, a remarkable degree of cooperation prevailed between prince and boiers, as they recognized the advantages to be had from exploiting the peasants together.

THE OTTOMAN CONNECTION

Hardly had the two principalities taken form than they were confronted by the advance of Ottoman Turkish armies northward toward the Danube in the latter decades of the fourteenth century. Their progress was marked by a victory over Serbian forces at Kosovo in 1389 and by the capture of Turnovo, the capital of the Bulgarian empire, in 1393. Prince Mircea cel Bătrân (the Old) (1386–1418) of Wallachia used a combination of military force, diplomacy, and alliances to keep the formidable adversary at bay. His maneuvering reveals the enormity of the task that his successors were to face in dealing with an enemy that could draw on seemingly unlimited human and material resources. In any case, he thought of his realm as a part of Christian Europe and he looked to the West for support. His first engagement with Ottoman armies came in 1394 when he seized Dobrudja and, in response, Sultan Bayezid I (1389–1402) invaded Wallachia. Mircea successfully parried the thrust at the Battle of Rovine, but he seems now to have paid the tribute (haradj) for the first time as a means of securing peace and did not thereby compromise his country's independence. Then in 1396 he joined with Hungarian, French, and other Christian armies on the lower Danube at Nicopolis, but withdrew in time to avoid the catastrophe that befell the crusaders at the hands of Bayezid. During the Ottoman dynastic crisis following Bayezid's defeat by Tamerlane at the Battle of Ankara in 1402 Mircea supported first one and then another pretender in order to gain favorable terms for coexistence. But after Mehmed I (1413–21) gained the throne he attacked Wallachia in 1417 and forced Mircea to pay the tribute. The calm that followed was only a truce.

It was in this way that Wallachia's contest with the Ottomans began. It was marked by unrelenting pressure from the Ottomans and stubborn resistance by the Wallachian princes. Two turning points measured the progress of this uneven contest. In 1431 Sultan Murad II (1421–44, 1446–51) undertook a campaign north of the Danube which led to the imposition of vassal status on Wallachia. Henceforth, the prince was obliged to pay the tribute annually, render military service when the Sultan demanded it, and send the sons of prominent boiers to Constantinople as hostages. Princes

2 Mircea cel Bătrân (Mircea the Old), Prince of Wallachia,
1382–1418

continued to dispute their vassal status, but when Vlad Ţepeş
(the Impaler) (1456–62) stopped paying the tribute and attacked
Ottoman posts south of the Danube, Mehmed II (1444–46, 1451–
81), the conqueror of Constantinople, drove him from the throne
and installed his brother, Radu cel Frumos (the Handsome) (1462–
75), in his place. Radu did homage to the Sultan and in return was
granted an *ahd-name* (treaty) setting forth the conditions of the

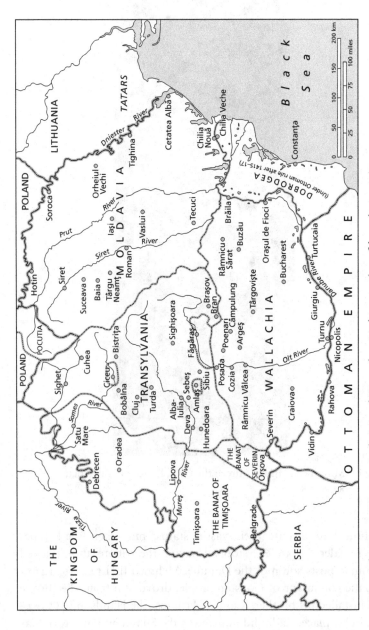

Map 2 The Romanian principalities and Transylvania, fourteenth to fifteenth centuries

principality's autonomy and the duties of its prince. Mehmed's act set a dangerous precedent, for he asserted his right to intervene unilaterally in Wallachian affairs and to choose its prince, though still with the acquiescence of the boiers.

Moldavia, further removed from the main theater of Ottoman military operations than Wallachia and ruled for nearly half a century by the ablest of princes, Ştefan cel Mare (the Great) (1457–1504), resisted Ottoman vassalage until the first half of the sixteenth century. The first serious clash between Moldavian and Ottoman armies occurred in 1420, when the Ottomans unsuccessfully besieged the Moldavian Black Sea port of Cetatea Albă. Peaceful relations generally prevailed afterwards as the Moldavians offered "gifts," which the Ottomans themselves described as *peşkeş*, not *haradj*. But in 1456 Mehmed II demanded *haradj* from Prince Petru Aron (1451–52, 1454–57) for a campaign against Hungary. He paid it, and Moldavia preserved her independence.

Upon his accession to the throne in 1457 Ştefan cel Mare found himself surrounded by aggressive, expansionist neighbors. Besides the Ottomans in the south, there were Hungary to the west and Poland to the north, both of which sought to dominate Moldavia and thus secure control of the lucrative trade routes between the Black Sea and Central Europe. Ştefan's strategy, which he applied with great success, was to balance his enemies off against one another. He paid tribute to the Ottomans, but only when it was advantageous (he ceased doing so between 1473 and 1488); he did homage to King Casimir of Poland as his suzerain when that seemed wise, as in 1459 and 1485; and he resorted to arms when other means failed. He had several notable military successes: in 1467 at the battle at Baia, where he defeated the invading army of King Mathias Corvinus of Hungary, a victory that marked the last large-scale attempt by a King of Hungary to impose his will on Moldavia; and in 1475 at Vaslui, when he defeated a large Ottoman army led by the Beylerbeyi (Governor) of Rumelia. He also appealed repeatedly to the Christian powers of Central and Western Europe to join him in forming a coalition to oppose the advance of the Ottomans, and for his efforts he received from Pope Sixtus IV (1471–84) the title "Athlete of Christ," but it was all in vain. In the latter years of his reign Ottoman pressure was unrelenting, and although his armies still won victories, as in 1497 against King Casimir, he entertained no illusions that he could defeat the Ottomans by arms. Before his death, therefore, he urged his son, Bogdan, to remain on good terms with them as the only way to preserve Moldavia's independence. Bogdan III (1504–17) and his successors maintained a precarious independence until 1538, when Sultan Suleiman I (1520–66) brought Moldavia more firmly under his control. In that year he drove from the throne an unreliable prince, Petru Aron (1527–38, 1541–46), and replaced him with the pliant Ștefan Lăcustă. The new prince did homage to Suleiman as his suzerain, thereby confirming Moldavia's vassal status.

The juridical relationship that evolved between the principalities and the Ottoman state in the fifteenth and sixteenth centuries owed as much to Ottoman pragmatism and legal theory as to the political and social conditions prevailing in Moldavia and Wallachia and the international circumstances of the time. From the perspective of the Islamic law of nations, which the Ottomans observed, the principalities lay in an intermediate zone between *dar al-harb* (the domain of war), that is, territories contested between the Muslim state and its enemies, and *dar al-Islam* (the domain of Islam), territories where their inhabitants were subject to a Muslim ruler and Islamic law. The principalities by the sixteenth century clearly no longer belonged to the former, but they had not entered the latter. Some historians have placed them in *dar al-sulh* (the domain of peace) or *dar al-'ahd*, territory acquired by the Muslim ruler by treaty; still others, in accordance with the Hanafite school of law, which predominated in the Ottoman Empire, have assigned them to *dar al-muvâda'a* (the domain of armistice) or *dar al-dhimma* (the domain of protection and tribute). The latter two terms may represent most accurately the two main phases through which Ottoman–Romanian relations passed, the years 1538–41 marking the dividing line. At the beginning of their encounter, the principalities were vassal states obliged to pay the tribute and render military service, and, then, as the relationship grew tighter, the sultan, for his part, assumed certain responsibilities toward the principalities, notably to give them protection.

The arrangement that thus emerged enabled Moldavia and Wallachia to escape incorporation into the Ottoman political system, as had happened to the Christian states south of the Danube. Various *'ahd-names* and *berāts* (writs of appointment) granted by the sultans allowed the principalities almost full internal autonomy. Thus, the sultan acknowledged the right of the prince and the boiers to rule "in accordance with custom" and forbade Turkish civil and military officials or the Muslim clergy to involve themselves in the internal affairs of the principalities. He allowed the boiers to elect the prince, but reserved to himself the right to approve their choice and to invest the new prince with the insignia of his office. As a consequence of autonomy, the laws and legal system, the social structure, landholding and agrarian relations, cultural and intellectual life, and the status of the Orthodox Church were left unchanged. But the sultan took charge of foreign affairs, prohibiting the princes from maintaining diplomatic contacts with foreign states or conclude treaties with them, and he undertook to defend the principalities against foreign attack.

Despite the extension of their powers over Moldavia and Wallachia, the sultans did not occupy them with their armies and transform them into Ottoman provinces, as they had done with the Serbian, Bulgarian, and other lands south of the Danube and with central Hungary after 1541. The explanation for such restraint lies, first of all, in the evolving contacts between the Ottomans and the principalities. During the early stages of their relations, in the late fourteenth and fifteenth centuries, the sultans tended to regard the principalities as of secondary importance, as they directed their main assault to the west and northwest. They seemed satisfied to keep the princes from joining anti-Ottoman coalitions. Nor did the unity displayed by princes and boiers at crucial moments go unnoticed at the Ottoman court, a unity that deterred military action. Suleiman I, who contemplated appointing *sanjakbeys* (governors) to administer the principalities, was undoubtedly dissuaded from taking such action by the nature of the economic relations that had evolved with the principalities, as they brought large sums of money into the personal treasuries of the sultan and high officials, indispensable quantities of foodstuffs to Constantinople, and supplies of all kinds to the army and navy. Changes in the imperial administration may also have influenced thinking about the status of the principalities. A bureaucracy of professional civil servants was replacing the fief (*timar*)-holders and others, who had sought wealth and power

3 Prince Mihai Viteazul (the Brave)

through war and territorial conquest, as the dominant influence in
high political councils. This new elite promoted fiscal and commercial exploitation of the principalities as more advantageous in the
new international economic order than occupation and direct rule.

Neither the princes nor the sultans respected the engagements they had entered into with one another. In the course of the sixteenth century the sultans were largely successful in reducing the prince to the rank of an Ottoman functionary whom they could treat as they saw fit. Suleiman had no doubts about the extent of his prerogatives. In a letter to King Sigismund I of Poland in 1531 he called the princes his "slaves and tributaries" and claimed that he could dispose of Moldavia and Wallachia simply as his property, "just like Bosnia and Serbia." By the end of the century his successors were treating the principalities as conquered territories and were referring to them as "provinces" (*vilayet*). The princes themselves were conscious of their diminished status. Aron Tiranul (the Tyrant) of Moldavia noted in a letter to the Habsburg Emperor Rudolf II in 1594 that he was merely the "custodian" of his country and dared not make his sentiments known, "so great was the oppression of the Turks." It had become customary for sultans to appoint the prince, although the boiers were occasionally allowed the formality of voting for candidates. The princes could not but acknowledge their dependence. In the past they had customarily styled themselves "rulers by the grace of God," but now they accepted their accession to the throne not as an act of the divine will but as an exercise of the sultan's prerogative.

Despite the tightening of Ottoman control, the essence of the principalities' autonomy remained intact. Political and economic life followed customary patterns. Islamic law was not extended north of the Danube, the boiers retained their lands and privileges, and the princely bureaucracy and local officials continued to exercise their authority as before. Evidence of the principalities' special status was the presence in Constantinople of representatives (*kapukehaya*; Romanian: *capuchehaie*) of the princes, whose main duty was to gain the benevolence of Ottoman officials. They were not unlike diplomatic agents, since they also had dealings with European ambassadors and consuls and thereby enabled the princes to elude the prohibition against relations with foreign powers.

Thus, the princes retained considerable room for maneuver, a position suggesting once again that the relations between vassal and suzerain were fluid. Further evidence of the nature of these links is supplied by events at the end of the sixteenth century, when the

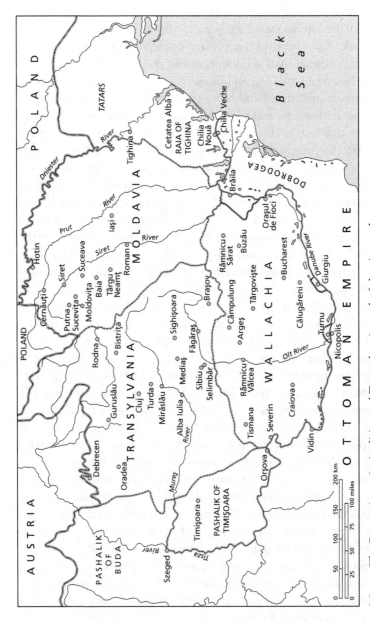

Map 3 The Romanian principalities and Transylvania, end of the sixteenth century

Prince of Wallachia, Mihai Viteazul (the Brave) (1593–1601), made the most serious challenge to Ottoman supremacy since the reign of Ştefan cel Mare.

Mihai, who became prince because of influence in high places in Constantinople, was a gifted military commander and an imaginative state builder. His immediate aim was to free Wallachia from Ottoman control, which complemented plans for an anti-Ottoman crusade being promoted by Pope Clement VIII, the Habsburg Holy Roman Emperor Rudolf II, and Philip II of Spain. Mihai, joined by the princes of Moldavia and Transylvania, gladly adhered to this Holy League, as it came to be called. He raised a revolt against the Ottomans in 1594, and in the following year, with the support of Transylvanian and Moldavian armies, he drove invading Ottoman forces back to the Danube. But allegiances soon became blurred, as the temporary allies pursued ambitions of their own. Yet, in 1600 Mihai briefly united Wallachia, Moldavia, and Transylvania under his rule, a success that marked the high point of his reign. But in achieving his grand design he had made powerful enemies on all sides. Not even the support of Rudolf II could save him. He was assassinated in Transylvania in 1601 by the commander of Habsburg troops, who was determined to be Prince of Transylvania himself. Although Mihai's union of the three principalities was short-lived, his bold stroke became a symbol of Romanian national destiny for generations of patriots in the nineteenth and twentieth centuries.

That Mihai Viteazul could mobilize such widespread support in Moldavia and Wallachia for his initiatives had much to do with the peculiar form that Ottoman domination had assumed in the course of the sixteenth century. It exposed the principalities to a system of fiscal and economic exploitation unmatched in their previous history. First of all, there were the state-to-state obligations specific to the vassal–suzerain relationship. Besides payment of the *haradj*, the amount of which rose steadily, the princes were obliged to support Ottoman military operations by making extraordinary payments to the imperial treasury and by mobilizing and leading armed contingents in the campaign. They also had to oversee the gathering of large quantities of foodstuffs and various other supplies, including timber for the building of warships, and ensure their delivery at designated places on the Danube. Specifically, they were responsible for helping Ottoman and Levantine merchants acquire the necessary quantities of goods at the most favorable prices. The prices paid for these goods and, hence, the compensation received by peasants, who were the ultimate producers of this wealth, fell below what they would have commanded on the international market. So important had this economic connection become by the second half of the sixteenth century that the sultans decided to bring the commerce of the principalities under strict regulation. Suleiman I and his successors thus prohibited the export of certain goods, notably cattle, sheep, wheat, honey, and timber, to other countries until imperial needs had been fully met. Such an arrangement is striking evidence of how dependent the sultan's court and the population of Constantinople had become on the principalities for meat and grain. When in 1578 Cossack raids in Moldavia interrupted the flow of provisions, the Venetian ambassador reported great hardship in the capital and the surrounding area. The long-term consequences of this Ottoman commercial "monopoly" are open to debate. It may well have slowed the development of a native Moldavian and Wallachian middle class, since native merchants could not compete with favored Ottoman merchants and others from the Near East, but at the same time it may also have been a stimulus to agricultural production.

More onerous and in the long run more harmful to the public good than the official obligations of vassalage were the numerous payments, usually designated as "gifts" (*peşkeş*), to the sultan and members of his family and to a multitude of officials from the grand vizier on down. Other gifts, consisting of money and goods, were presented on fixed occasions – the accession of a sultan to the throne or of a prince to his or on certain Islamic and dynastic holidays. Other gifts were unspecified in time and unlimited in amount. They were payments, in effect bribes, which pretenders to the thrones of Moldavia and Wallachia offered the sultan and others of influence at the highest levels of Ottoman society in order to be sure of their support. By the second half of the sixteenth century the office of prince had become the object of a spirited auction in which the prize usually went to the highest bidder, that is, to the candidate who had secured the most influential patrons. It was the peasants, first of all, but also the boiers who bore responsibility for paying the new prince's debts, as they were considered state, not personal obligations. The system of gifts became a regular part of every transaction between princes and his representatives and Ottoman officials of all kinds and could not but lower the moral level of public business.

A MEDIEVAL CULTURE

Intellectual life and literature provide valuable measures of the evolution of the principalities between the fourteenth and the end of the sixteenth century. During this long interval they belonged to a cultural world quite distinct from that represented by Western Europe, one that was dominated by the spiritual and aesthetic ideals of Byzantine Orthodoxy and shared generally by the peoples of Southeastern Europe. The main source of the fundamental works of Christian doctrine and practice, of the *belles-lettres* of the age such as the lives of saints and the "medieval novels" such as Legend of Alexander the Great (*Alexandria*) and *Barlaam and Josaphat*, of juridical works, and of chronicles was Byzantium, although the Romanians adapted them from Bulgarian and, to a lesser extent, Serbian intermediaries, rather than directly from Byzantium.

The attachment of the Romanians to the East is perhaps most visible in the persistence of Slavic or, more precisely, Middle Bulgarian as the language they mainly used for serious writing and other purposes well into the first half of the seventeenth century. The adoption by the Romanians of Slavic as their liturgical language and the language of the princely chancelleries in the fourteenth century was an event of singular importance in their development. Slavic reinforced their ties to the Byzantine cultural and religious world and served as the primary instrument for the transmission of its sacred and secular heritage. The Romanians could accept Slavic as the language of the church because it ranked with Greek, Hebrew, and Latin, and they used it in the affairs of state precisely because of its prestige as a sacred language. But Slavic could not become their religious language in the full sense of the term. Spoken by a part of the clergy, the great boiers, and scholars, it was never the language of the mass of the population, who said their prayers and created a rich folk literature in Romanian.

Monasteries were the major centers of cultural activity in the principalities. Besides spiritual and educational functions, monks were preoccupied between the fifteenth and the first half of the seventeenth century with the copying of Slavic manuscripts, of which some 1,000 have survived. These copyists were thus responsible for preserving the Middle Bulgarian and, to some extent, the Slavo-Serbian versions of the greater part of the Byzantine–Slav religious literary patrimony. Princes were among the most ardent patrons of manuscript copying and embellishment. Ştefan cel Mare was always keenly aware as an Orthodox sovereign of his religious responsibilities to his own people and to the peoples of the Balkans under Ottoman rule and of his role as God's representative on earth, and thus he was a prodigious builder of churches and monasteries and richly endowed them in Moldavia and throughout the Orthodox East with beautiful manuscripts for church services. Although the value of these manuscripts today is scholarly rather than as pieces of original literature, they reveal much about the intellectual and spiritual needs of the upper strata of Romanian society. The manuscripts were mainly religious in content, but their readers were not limited to monks and priests. It is evident from notations on the manuscripts that boiers, chancellery clerks, and the middle class also looked to them for spiritual guidance. The ascetic, mystical view of life was thus not confined to the monastery, but encompassed significant elements of the literate secular society.

Among the relatively few original compositions in Slavic or Slavo-Romanian, as it is often called because of influences of Romanian, were the earliest works of Romanian historiography. Notable among them were the chronicles of three learned Moldavian churchmen of the sixteenth century: Macarie (d. 1558), the Bishop of Roman, whose chronicle covered the history of Moldavia from the reign of Ştefan cel Mare to that of Petru Rareş up to 1542; Eftimie (middle of the sixteenth century), abbot of the monastery of Capriana, who described Moldavia between 1541 and 1554; and Azarie (middle of the sixteenth century), abbot of the monastery of Golia in Iaşi, who continued the chronicle of Moldavia from 1551 to 1574. They all carried on the tradition of the annals and more modest chronicles of the fifteenth century. They wrote in Slavic because it was the language of the church and because they were preoccupied with the same essential religious theme as the church – the exercise of God's will in human society. Macarie expressed the feelings of all three when he lamented the impermanence of things in this world, a condition he ascribed to God's continual testing of his children. They drew heavily on Byzantine chronicles, especially the chronicle in verse of Constantine Manasses (*c.* 1130–*c.* 1187), and did so freely because they thought of their own works as contributions to the general history of the Orthodox commonwealth, not as national histories. Yet, their chronicles marked the end of historiography in Slavic in Moldavia, to be replaced shortly by texts in Romanian. The writing of chronicles followed a similar course in Wallachia, but the Slavic texts have not survived. Traces of them may be found in compilations of chronicles in Romanian made in the second half of the seventeenth century.

The masterpiece of Romanian literature in Slavic is undoubtedly *Învăţăturile lui Neagoe Basarab către fiul său Teodosie* (The advice of Neagoe Basarab to his son Teodosie), composed between 1517 and 1521 by the Prince of Wallachia, Neagoe Basarab (1512–21). He intended it to serve his young son and presumed successor as a comprehensive theoretical and practical guide to a virtuous and successful reign. It is, consequently, many things: a work of moral and religious instruction, a breviary of Orthodox asceticism and mysticism, an exposition of the theory of the divine right of kings, a textbook on the techniques of governing, and an introduction to the art of diplomacy. From beginning to end the work is pervaded by the Christian worldview that dominated medieval Romanian society. Neagoe Basarab wanted his son to understand that a prince reigned by the grace of God in accordance with a contract, which obligated the prince to be a just and merciful ruler under the will of God, who granted him a vicarship over his people.

Even while the most important original works in Slavic were being written, its primacy as the state and literary language was being challenged by Romanian. This shift, gradual but unrelenting, was a response to changes within Romanian society and to powerful influences from outside. In the principalities new social classes that needed a practical and convenient instrument of communication were coming to the fore. The lesser boiers, merchants, government functionaries, and lower clergy had no opportunity to learn Slavic, and even those who did have some knowledge of the language found it inadequate for the purposes of administration and commerce. They stood to gain most from the spread of Romanian and found support in new currents of ideas coming from Central Europe in the sixteenth century. The Protestant Reformation, though it gained few religious converts, deeply affected cultural life and the sense of identity in the principalities and among the Romanians of Transylvania. It offered further evidence that the Romanian medieval worldview was far from being impervious to influences from the West.

The absence of texts in Romanian before the sixteenth century may be attributed to the belief among the literate classes that the spoken language was not as suitable for sacred writings, legal documents, and history as Slavic. It is significant that the oldest text in Romanian that has survived is a private letter about practical matters written by a merchant in Câmpulung, in Wallachia, to the magistrate of Braşov, in Transylvania, warning of the movement of Ottoman troops. It is dated 1521, the same year that Neagoe Basarab completed his "Advice" in Slavic. The differences in the Romanian of the letter from modern Romanian are slight, and the style is polished, evidence that the language had been used in writing for some time in correspondence and even in rough drafts of official documents before their translation into Slavic.

Romanian was introduced as the written language in secular affairs in the second half of the sixteenth century, as the princely chancelleries ceased using Slavic exclusively, Moldavia in 1574 and Wallachia in 1593. The first chronicle in Romanian, an original work, not a translation, dealt with the reign of Mihai Viteazul and was composed in Wallachia about 1597. This and the so-called "Moldavian Chronicle," now lost, composed several decades later, laid the foundations for the flowering of historiography in Romanian beginning in the middle decades of the seventeenth century.

Change came more slowly in the Orthodox Church. It was the most resistant of all to the use of the vernacular and replaced Slavic with Romanian officially only in the second half of the seventeenth century. Before that time it had indeed provided priests with books in Romanian, but only those texts needed for their practical duties, such as a *cazanie*, a book of sermons, or a *trebnic*, a book of prayers. Slavic continued to be used exclusively in the ritual books until 1679, when a *liturghier*, a liturgy book, was translated into Romanian, marking the official introduction of Romanian in the church. The first complete translation of the Bible was published in 1688 in Bucharest.

The printing of books in Romanian, which began in the middle decades of the sixteenth century, contributed enormously to the triumph of the spoken language over Slavic and to the establishment of the norms of a common literary language. Printing had begun in Slavic in the principalities in 1508 with a *liturghier*, only twenty-five years after the printing of the first book in Slavic in Venice. In the meantime, in Transylvania the printing of books in Romanian began under the influence of the Reformation. The Saxons, almost all of whom had embraced Lutheranism, established a printing press in Sibiu, whose products they intended to use to convert the Romanians to their faith. The first Romanian book came from the press in 1544, a Lutheran catechism. It was followed by an *Evanghelier*, the Gospel, between 1551 and 1553, with facing Slavic and Romanian texts. The Romanian translation had circulated in manuscript in Moldavia since at least 1532 and is further evidence of how much the early translations owed to the Reformation.

The Saxons set up a second printing press in Braşov to promote the use of the vernacular in the church. In cooperation with the Romanian community of Şchei, a suburb, they engaged a Romanian cleric and printer, Coresi (d. *c.* 1583), who, beginning with a *Tetraevanghel* (The Four Gospels) in 1561, published nine books in Romanian until his death. Behind his efforts stood the Calvinists, who were determined to convert the Romanians to Calvinism. Coresi's printings had considerable influence on the cultural life of the Romanians on both sides of the Carpathians. They gave a powerful impetus to the use of the spoken language in the church, and they helped to establish the dialect in which they were printed, that of southern Transylvania and northern Wallachia, as the standard form of the written language.

THE SEVENTEENTH CENTURY

The Treaty of Zsitvatorok in 1606 put an end to the so-called Long War between the Habsburg and Ottoman empires, which had begun in 1593 and had encompassed Mihai Viteazul's challenge to the great powers. Peace and relative order enabled the sultans to restore their suzerain powers in Moldavia and Wallachia. Yet, Mihai Viteazul's temporary interruption of their ascendancy persuaded them that a return to the old order as of the latter sixteenth century would not be to their advantage. Thus, rather than resorting to direct, heavy-handed intervention in the principalities' internal affairs, marked by such practices as the arbitrary changes of princes, they chose methods, mostly indirect, suited to the circumstances of the time. One device proved enormously effective over the long term – the migration of upper-class Greeks and Levantines into the principalities in the seventeenth and eighteenth centuries. Its main purpose was to undermine Moldavian and Wallachian autonomy by diluting the solidarity of the boiers, thereby impeding their ability to resist Ottoman pressures. The new, more cautious treatment of the principalities expressed itself also in a moderation of fiscal and economic demands. All in all, then, relations between the principalities and the Ottoman state in the seventeenth century were generally more relaxed than in the previous century. Ottoman military forays were fewer, and prohibitions against interference in the affairs of the principalities by Ottoman civil and military officials, especially along the Danube, were, on the whole, respected. The princes themselves were less constrained than their predecessors in devising and carrying out policies of their own.

The social structures of the two principalities remained essentially the same as earlier. But the boiers, particularly the upper ranks, maintained and even extended their predominance in economic life and strove to gain ascendancy in political affairs by installing a nobiliary regime based largely on the Polish model. But the boiers were by no means a united class. Deep fissures separated the highest ranks from the more numerous lesser boiers, a division that princes were eager to exploit in order to keep their antagonists in line. At the broad base of the social pyramid were the peasants. Some were free and relatively prosperous, but the general trend in the seventeenth century was the deterioration of their legal status and material well-being. High taxes, the provisioning demanded by the Ottomans, and the growing demands of boiers for dues and labor services spurred the enserfment of the peasantry and enabled the boiers to extend their estates at the expense of peasant property. The contest was hardly one of equals, since neither the state nor the church felt obligated to intervene on behalf of peasants. The native middle class was still too small to exert significant influence on the political and economic policies of the state.

Conflict between the princes and boiers dominated the internal political development of the principalities for much of the seventeenth century. The princes were intent on creating a strong, even absolutist, monarchy, while the boiers, mainly the upper ranks, sought a limited monarchy with themselves as the pre-eminent force. A challenge for both princes and boiers was the expanding settlement of Greeks and Levantines in both principalities. The newcomers, using their networks of financial and political patrons in Constantinople, bought landed estates and thereby acquired boier status and soon penetrated the political establishment. Native boiers showed remarkable solidarity in opposing this competition for land and offices. Many held the Ottoman court responsible for the influx of Greeks as a way of establishing a solid power base in the principalities. Occasionally, the boiers won the support of princes, as in 1631 in Wallachia, when they extracted from Prince Leon Tomşa a *hrisov* (charter) ordering the departure of all Greeks who had not been naturalized. Such measures did little to limit the pervasiveness of Greek influence. But the act was a victory for the boiers in other ways. It exempted them from taxation and consolidated their control over their own lands. The boiers of Moldavia obtained similar fiscal and economic concessions in the *aşezământ* (foundation) issued by Prince Miron Barnovschi (1626–29).

In the middle decades of the century two rulers of unusual abilities – Matei Basarab in Wallachia (1632–54) and Vasile Lupu in Moldavia (1634–53) – consolidated princely powers. They achieved success by different paths. Matei Basarab strengthened the center by working with the boiers. He sympathized with their stand against the Greeks and won their support for his own projects by bringing them more fully into the governance of the country through frequent convocations of the Assembly of the Estates. He also extended their control of the land and of those who worked it, in effect, sanctioning the enserfment of the peasants. Vasile Lupu, by contrast, established an authoritarian regime as the necessary instrument for achieving his ambitions to rule over both principalities and to be the chief patron of the Orthodox East. He enlisted the Greek upper classes as his chief allies and ensured their economic advantage by encouraging them to purchase villages and by entrusting them with the farming of state taxes.

The long reigns of Matei Basarab and Vasile Lupu symbolized the significant adjustments that had occurred in the vassal–suzerain relationship. The two sides had become more comfortable with one another, as the princes showed themselves to be loyal and willing to work with the Ottoman bureaucracy in pursuit of mutually advantageous foreign policy goals. Mounting internal political and fiscal difficulties and the more precarious international situation of the Ottoman Empire, especially from the middle of the seventeenth century on, may also have helped loosen Ottoman controls over the princes. These changes were reflected in the willingness of sultans to allow princes chosen by the boiers to ascend the throne and to grant the princes themselves a certain degree of freedom in establishing contacts with foreign states. The intention of the Ottomans to use the principalities as buffers to impede the advance of the Habsburgs southward may also account for their moderation. For their part, the princes to some degree even welcomed the protection offered by their suzerain against aggressive neighbors.

The war that began with the Ottoman siege of Vienna in 1683 and ended with the Peace of Karlowitz in 1699 decisively affected the principalities. The successes of the Austrians and Russians, who joined the conflict in 1687, revealed the extent to which the Ottoman army and government departments had failed to keep pace with their European antagonists. The outcome of the war, which brought about the cession of extensive Ottoman territories in Europe, notably Transylvania, made the Habsburg Monarchy a major player in the affairs of Southeastern Europe. Russia, too, under Peter the Great (1682–1725) increased its involvement in the region and began to elaborate a strategy of aggrandizement that would rely on the support of the Orthodox faithful.

The implications of all these events were not lost on the princes and boiers of Moldavia and Wallachia. Ottoman defeats encouraged strivings for independence, now in harmony with Austrian and Russian ambitions in the region. Prince Şerban Cantacuzino of

Wallachia (1678–88) sought to ensure both his authority in domestic affairs and separation from the Ottoman Empire by concluding an alliance with Austria. Yet, he was wary of Austria's plans for expansion south of the Carpathians and of her promotion of the Roman Catholic resurgence in Eastern Europe, and thus he cultivated closer relations with Russia as a counterpoise to Austria. He died before the treaty with Austria could be signed, but his successor, Constantin Brâncoveanu (1688–1714), continued his initiative. At first, in the dangerous environment of great-power competition that was Southeastern Europe, he was persuaded that the Ottoman Empire alone offered Wallachia the best guarantee of its existence as a separate state. He thus used the sultan's vested interests in the principality to maintain its territorial integrity and, no less important, ensure his own tenure of the throne, even as he negotiated with the Austrians and Russians for a change in the principality's juridical status. But, in the end, particularly after the Peace of Karlowitz, he turned to Russia as the most reliable guarantor of Wallachia's independence and territorial integrity against both Austrian Roman Catholic aggressiveness and an Ottoman resurgence. Yet, caution led him to delay the conclusion of a formal alliance.

The same atmosphere of expectation prevailed in Moldavia, and its princes pursued the same goals as their Wallachian counterparts. Their strivings for independence culminated in the signing in 1711 by Prince Dimitrie Cantemir (1710–11) of a treaty of alliance with Peter the Great, which recognized the independence of Moldavia and established a hereditary monarchy in the Cantemir family. In rejecting the nobiliary regime promoted by the boiers, Cantemir undoubtedly had as his model Peter's absolutist reforms, but he nonetheless sanctioned the privileged position of the boiers in order to ensure their support. The defeat of Peter's army at Stănileşti on the Prut River on July 18–22, 1711 put an abrupt end to Cantemir's and Brâncoveanu's bargaining with Russia and Austria. It led to Cantemir's immediate flight to Russia, to Brâncoveanu's eventual loss of his throne and execution in 1714 at the hands of the Ottomans, and, among long-term consequences, to a resumption of the Ottomans' direct intervention in the principalities' internal affairs and relentless economic exploitation.

TOWARDS MODERNITY

As the seventeenth century progressed writers and intellectuals in the principalities gradually moved away from the medieval foundations of their culture as they absorbed new influences, some coming from traditional sources, but many displaying a distinctly Western origin. Disparate currents which had formed earlier came together in the second half of the century to reveal an embrace by the educated of modern ideas about the world and their place in it and about the ultimate ends of human creativity. The seventeenth century, then, marked a crisis of conscience among both clerical and lay elites not unrelated to the political and economic turmoil that encompassed rulers and boiers. They were all challenged by new intellectual and cultural currents emanating from the West, by the secularization of culture, by new ideas about the purpose of history and literature, and by the replacement of Slavic by Romanian as the language of both and, increasingly, of the church.

Although the bonds between leading Moldavians and Wallachians and the larger Orthodox commonwealth were under strain, tradition had persuasive defenders, especially in the first half of the seventeenth century. A kind of pan-Orthodox consciousness, as opposed to strictly ethnic feelings, was all-pervasive. It was reflected in the deep sense of responsibility Matei Basarab and Vasile Lupu felt toward the Orthodox communities under Ottoman domination. They recognized their unique position as the only Orthodox rulers in Southeastern Europe who had preserved most of the attributes of independence under Ottoman suzerainty; they even saw themselves as the successors of the Byzantine emperors. For these reasons they provided generous financial support to Orthodox churches and monasteries from Mt. Athos to Constantinople and Jerusalem. They welcomed clergy and scholars from all over the Orthodox world and granted them positions of responsibility in education and the church. Romanian churchmen and intellectuals themselves also moved freely within this broader Orthodox community unconstrained by ethnic boundaries and separate languages.

Respect for tradition found eloquent expression in attempts to bring about a revival of Slavic and thereby strengthen links with the sources of Orthodox piety and culture. Two of the most learned men of the time in the principalities devoted their talents to a defense of Orthodoxy, but both were at the same time open to new ideas as they sought to bring about a spiritual renascence. Udrişte Năsturel (*c.* 1596–*c.* 1658), born into an old Moldavian boier family and the holder of numerous important official posts, devoted himself to intellectual pursuits, including the translation of Thomas à Kempis's *De imitatione Christi* into Slavic. He stayed within the cultural community of Eastern Orthodoxy and advocated the use of Slavic as the liturgical and literary language, but he was also equally attracted to the currents of Western humanism. Metropolitan Varlaam of Moldavia (1580–1657), born of a free peasant family, was as staunch a defender of Orthodoxy and its cultural heritage as Năsturel, but he recognized the value of using Romanian when he needed to address a wider audience beyond the elite. For the parish clergy and the literate faithful he composed in 1645 the first original Romanian religious polemical work, *Răspunsul la catehism călvinesc* (Response to the Calvinist catechism) in order to refute the teachings of the Calvinists in Transylvania who were eager to convert the Romanians. He translated into Romanian and supervised the printing of large numbers of copies in 1643 of *Cazania*, a book of sermons, which greatly influenced the development of the Romanian literary language by eliminating the Slavic syntax and creating a flowing, expressive style.

Cultural life in the principalities was open, as before, to a variety of influences from outside. But unlike in previous centuries the contributions of the West steadily grew in importance. The Slavs were still intermediaries, but now they were Poles and Ukrainians, rather than Bulgarians and Serbs, whose role as purveyors of a vigorous culture had diminished greatly as a result of the long Ottoman occupation. Udrişte Năsturel looked to the Kiev of the Metropolitan Peter Mogila (*c.* 1596–1647), who sought to reinvigorate Orthodoxy through the assimilation of the Latin culture of the West as it had been transformed by the Renaissance. The Moldavian historian Miron Costin (1633–91) and the Metropolitan and poet Dosoftei of Moldavia (1624–93) were deeply affected by Polish humanist and baroque literature and had become conscious of the grandeur of classical antiquity in the Polish schools they had attended in their early years. They were not alone in their attraction to the cultural effervescence of seventeenth-century Poland, as a number of boiers looked to Western currents there to offset growing Greek influence at home. Moldavian princes encouraged such intellectual inclinations as a means of strengthening political ties with Poland to relieve Ottoman pressures.

The other major bearers of cultural and literary values were the Greeks, as increasing numbers of clergy and scholars settled in the principalities to escape the uncertainties of life under direct Ottoman rule. They found there a congenial environment in which to pursue their activities, despite political and economic rivalries with native boiers and churchmen. By the end of the century Greek had become one of the languages of cultivated conversation among the upper classes and of higher education, and it was through Greek that Romanian elites expanded their acquaintance with European learning and literature. At the same time Greek spiritual contributions reinforced the sense of a common front in the principalities against both Western Christianity and Islam, a tendency that blurred ethnic and cultural divisions between Romanians and Greeks in favor of allegiance to a common Orthodox community.

Yet, the second half of the seventeenth century marked the triumph of Romanian as the language of the church and, alongside Greek, as the language of intellectual discourse. Greek served the educated upper classes and others such as long-distance merchants as a *lingua franca* throughout the Orthodox world in Eastern Europe, but it by no means replaced Romanian as the chief vehicle for literature and history. Largely through the efforts of such enlightened churchmen as Metropolitan Dosoftei and Metropolitan Antim Ivireanul of Wallachia (1708–16), the fundamental liturgical works in Romanian were introduced into the church. Dosoftei commissioned translations from Greek and published a *Liturghier* (1679), a *Molitvelnic* (Prayer book; 1681), and an *Octoih* (Hymnal; 1683). He persuaded the clergy that performing the church service in the vernacular was not an act of heresy, but was fully in harmony with the traditions of the Orthodox Church. Thus, through his persistence the Romanian Church took an important step toward becoming a truly national church. Antim Ivireanul made no small contribution to this effort by raising the art of preaching in Romanian to a new eloquence through his sermons, which were composed during the reigns of Constantin Brâncoveanu and Ştefan Cantacuzino (1714–16) and published posthumously as *Didahii* (Teachings).

By this time a new type of intellectual had emerged – the lay-man who fostered the secular spirit in culture. He was conscious of Europe, and he measured the political, economic, and cultural state of his own country against the accomplishments of the West and was forced to acknowledge the superiority of the latter, at least in material progress and science. But he and his colleagues were not at all in agreement on how the gap might be closed. Nor did they advocate the wholesale abandonment of traditional spiritual learning and values; they still accepted the Christian explanation of creation and believed in the doctrinal superiority of Orthodoxy over Roman Catholicism and Protestantism. Yet, they displayed a breadth of interests and a spirit of innovation that was distinctly modern and set them apart from their forebears. The thought and writings of Nicolae Milescu and Miron Costin and even of the high churchmen Dosoftei and Antim Ivireanul reveal interests and aspi-rations different from those of their predecessors. They were eager for new knowledge, and in their pursuit of it they discovered clas-sical and contemporary European culture. Their deep admiration for the works of classical antiquity was reflected in the style and spirit of their own works of history and poetry. They also took a new view of the natural world. Although, like earlier generations, they accepted as inevitable the passage from this life to the world beyond, they did not disdain this life as an impediment to spiri-tual completeness. Rather, they expressed deep regret at having to leave it.

Representative of the intellectuals of the second half of the seven-teenth century were Nicolae Milescu and Miron Costin. Milescu (1636–1708) revealed his attachment to the new age by his transla-tion of the Old Testament from Greek, the first complete translation into Romanian. He shunned officially sanctioned texts, choos-ing, instead, the Protestant version of the Septuagint published in Frankfurt in 1597 and kept intact the division of the text made by Martin Luther. In his critical attitude toward sacred writings, in his disregard of ecclesiastical authority in choosing texts and using the best editions available regardless of confession, and in his passion for classical works and philology he displayed those traits peculiar to the humanism of Southeastern Europe of the age. Miron Costin was also a man of his time, as he expressed the melancholy that many of his contemporaries felt as they meditated on the meaning of life. In his philosophical poem, *Viaţa lumii* (The life of the world; 1673), he revealed his skepticism about the illusory nature of this world and his reserve toward the next. His solution to man's existential quandary was neither blind faith nor the renunciation of the supreme divinity. Rather, he recommended that man adjust to this world and use his reason as the most reliable guide to a moral and, hence, satisfying life.

In keeping with the spirit of the age was the new conception of literature entertained by intellectuals as a form of creativity distinct from theological discourse and didactic treatise. Dosoftei laid the foundations of Romanian cultivated poetry; no one before him had tested so keenly the poetical possibilities of the language and fitted it so skillfully to the rhythmic requirements of verse. In his *Psaltirea în versuri* (1671), a translation of the Book of Psalms in verse from Slavic, he proceeded as an artist, continually reworking his texts and striving for perfection in versification and the expression of thought. In a sense, he naturalized the biblical text; rather than being satisfied with a literal rendering of the Slavic version, he introduced allusions to Romanian realities. Miron Costin, usually thought of first of all as a historian, was also the first Romanian writer who consciously undertook to mold the language into a new, flexible means of literary expression. The result of his experiments was *Viaţa lumii*, the first important work of cultivated secular poetry in Romanian. It also contained a preface, which served as the first exposition of prosody in Romanian literature. His thoughts were thoroughly grounded in classical models and represented his search for order in an art form that for Romanians was still spontaneous and inchoate.

The practitioners of history also followed new approaches to their craft. But tradition was strong, as is clear in the writings of the Moldavian Grigore Ureche (*c.* 1590–1647). His great contribution to Romanian culture was *Letopiseţul Ţării Moldovei* (Chronicle of Moldavia). Written toward the end of his life and left unfinished, it

4 Dimitrie Cantemir, Prince of Moldavia, 1710–11

represented a significant advance in imagination and technique over
the work of earlier chroniclers. He displayed a broader vision than
they by extending his purview beyond the events of his own principality to include thoughts about the origins of the Romanians, and
he took care to give his information artistic form. But, on the whole,
he accepted the didactic role of history and attributed the general
course of human affairs to the intervention of the Almighty. Miron

Costin, by contrast, while acknowledging the value of history as a guide for future generations, viewed life as the continuous unfolding of the human condition, for which men themselves, not solely the workings of Providence, were responsible. His *Letopiseţul Ţării Moldovei* (1675), which covered the history of the principality from 1595 to 1661, provided valuable information and a methodology for his successors and is a work of literature which surpassed in narrative technique and descriptive richness all previous Romanian historical works. His masterpiece, *De neamul Moldovenilor* (On the Moldavians; 1686), which dealt with a single theme – the origins of the Romanians and of their language – and assumed a polemical tone, was the first modern Romanian historical work. Both Ureche and Costin represented a trend that would come to dominate Romanian historiography down to the present: their work was becoming national, especially as they meditated on the common Roman origins of the Romanians, and thus they signaled a clear break with the pan-Orthodox stance of the sixteenth-century chroniclers.

Dimitrie Cantemir, Prince of Moldavia (1673–1723), provides an illuminating link between the latter half of the seventeenth century and the new intellectual horizons of the eighteenth. The works he wrote are, on the one hand, the crowning achievements of old Romanian literature and, on the other, harbingers of the modern in Romanian learned writing and *belles-lettres*. His *Istoria ieroglifică* (Hieroglyphic history; 1705), the first original composition in Romanian that was neither a religious work nor a chronicle, shows the range of his interests; it is at once a novel, an autobiography, a history, a political tract, and a philosophical meditation on the nature of man and his place in the world. It reveals the new mentality that had taken hold among a small circle of intellectuals at the end of the seventeenth century. They looked to the future with confidence. Gone was the apprehension of "terrible times" and the sublime melancholy of Miron Costin. Their place had been taken by a new dynamism and a sense of liberation from the symmetrical and static forms of life that pervaded the chronicles and religious writings of earlier generations.

In another, earlier work of philosophy, *Divanul sau gâlceava Înţeleptului cu Lumea* (The council, or the quarrel of the wise man with the world; 1698), Cantemir made the first attempt by a Romanian at philosophizing as a method of examining fundamental questions about the nature of the world. It places him midway between two ages and two worlds, as it interweaves traditional spirituality and rationalism, Eastern and Western thought. The Wise Man argues that reason, to be adequate, needed the "light of faith," for only in this way could reason, inherently imperfect, be good and just. Yet clearly, Cantemir, without renouncing faith, is on the side of reason and is thus close to the thinking of his intended audience because the Wise Man, in the end, conceives of man as a rational being and admits the power of reason in acquiring knowledge. Cantemir, then, while defending the prerogatives of faith, departs from traditional Orthodox thought, which emphasized the immediate intuition of essences as superior to rational processes.

Besides philosophy and literature, Cantemir pursued careers as the first Romanian orientalist and as a historian of modern inclinations. He spent a large portion of his youth in Constantinople as an official hostage in order to ensure the loyalty of his father, Constantin Cantemir, Prince of Moldavia (1685–93). In the imperial capital he eagerly acquainted himself with all aspects of its politics and society and religion. One of his best known works was a history of the Ottoman Empire, *Incrementa atque decrementa aulae othomanicae*, which he completed in 1716 and wrote, in part, to awaken the European powers to the weaknesses of the empire and thereby encourage them to undertake the liberation of the subject Christian peoples in Southeastern Europe. Published in English in 1734–35 as *The History of the Growth and Decay of the Othman Empire*, it was for a long time the standard work for scholars in the field. He also wrote *Curanus*, an analysis of the Koran and the Muslim religious tradition, which was published in Russian in St. Petersburg in 1722. His devotion to Christianity is evident, as he rejects the divine mission of Mohammed and denies the revealed character of the Koran. Yet, he approached Islamic civilization with a full appreciation of its achievements. He rejected completely the idea of the inherent inferiority of the East and the natural superiority of Western civilization. He also wrote a sophisticated study of Turkish music, probably completed in Constantinople in 1704, for which he devised an original system of notation.

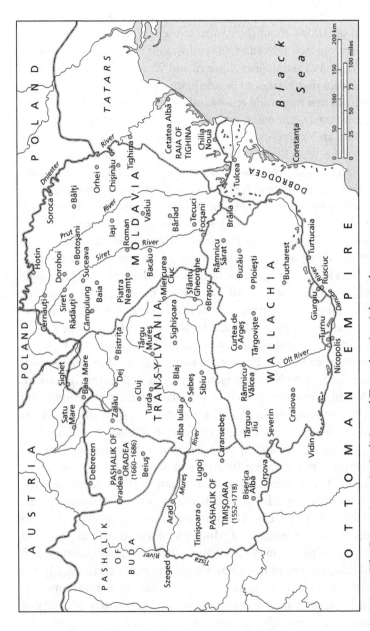

Map 4 The Romanian principalities and Transylvania, eighteenth century

Cantemir approached the study of history as a philosopher in the broad humanist sense of the term. He thought of a work of history, like every work of culture, first of all, as a kind of meditation on the essential nature of the world and on the human condition. His approach, then, was much like that of the modern philosophers of culture who sought the general and the universal in the phenomena they studied. Although he believed that the existing order in the world had been imposed by divine reason, which ultimately determined change in all human matters, he was equally certain that the world was subject to a process of evolution. The life of states, in particular, as revealed in history, offered striking evidence of continuous change, as they passed through a cycle of growth, maturity, and decay. From his vantage point in Constantinople he had become convinced that no human power could interrupt the inexorable decomposition of the Ottoman state. His crowning achievement as a philosopher of history was *Hronicul vechimii a romano-moldo-vlahilor* (The chronicle of the antiquity of the Romanians), perhaps the most impressive work of erudition of old Romanian literature. He planned to write a comprehensive history of the Romanians from their origins to his own day, but he completed only the first part, in 1717, which brought events down to the formation of the principalities of Wallachia and Moldavia. His sources exceeded in variety and quantity those used by his predecessors and included Greek and Roman authors, historians writing in German, French, Italian, and Polish, numerous oriental works, and Russian and Serbian chronicles. In a long introduction where he discussed the purpose of history and the general problems of historical research he urged objectivity on all practitioners of the craft. But he found it difficult to follow his own advice. In this first critical history of all the Romanians he was intent on proving a thesis: that the Romanians were of pure Roman descent and had dwelled in ancient Dacia without interruption since its conquest by Trajan.

THE PHANARIOT REGIME, TO 1774

The Ottoman court countered Russian and Austrian ambitions in the principalities and met the disloyalty of their princes by turning to a community that had rendered invaluable diplomatic and financial services to the empire for more than a century – the wealthy Greek families of the Phanar district of Constantinople. The sultans chose the new princes from among them expressly to oppose the spread of Russian and Austrian influence in Moldavia and Wallachia and to further the principalities' political and economic integration into the empire. The resulting partnership formed the basis of the so-called Phanariot regime, which began in Moldavia in 1711 and in Wallachia in 1716 and was to remain in place until 1821.

Ottoman economic and fiscal demands rose continuously as the exploitation of the principalities exceeded the level of the late sixteenth century. The quantities of supplies of all kinds delivered to Constantinople and the fortresses along the Danube knew practically no bounds and took the form of a tightened commercial monopoly that, as before, required Ottoman needs to be satisfied before the principalities could export their sheep, grains, and other goods to foreign countries. Whenever supplies grew short, as in 1761 and 1764, the sultan would suspend exports on short notice. In any case, the prices paid to peasants and other producers by Ottoman merchants, who had the responsibility of buying what was needed, were, as earlier, invariably lower than prevailing market prices. Of the state-to-state obligations, the amounts of the tribute and of the "gifts" that accompanied every official negotiation grew enormously. To these payments were added the sums that candidates for the two thrones paid to the sultan's treasury and to officials of all ranks to gain their good will and win the coveted appointment. Competition for the throne was such good business for the Ottoman elite that the sultan changed princes frequently. Efficient administration suffered, as Wallachia had eighteen princes between 1730 and 1768, and Moldavia seventeen between 1733 and 1769. Nonetheless, a certain continuity of government was ensured, as some princes were shifted between Bucharest and Iaşi: Constantin Mavrocordat during this period was prince of Wallachia six times and of Moldavia four times.

Manipulations and abuses of the office of prince should not obscure the high qualities and solid accomplishments of a number of Phanariot princes. Constantin Mavrocordat (Wallachia and Moldavia, 1730–69) used his considerable experience to carry out a program of reforms in both principalities, which was in harmony with the enlightened tendencies of the age in Central Europe. In a lengthy *hrisov* in 1741 he set out a plan for the rationalization of government administration, the fiscal system, and the judiciary, which aimed at creating a strong monarchy reinforced by bodies representing the privileged classes. Noteworthy was his intention to expand the power of the state to regulate landholding and the relations between the two main classes who were responsible for production – the boier masters of the land and the peasants. He was especially concerned with the excessive mobility of the peasants, caused by their efforts to escape the dues and labor burdens imposed on them by landlords. Thus, in order to bring a certain degree of stability to agriculture and ensure payment of state taxes he abolished serfdom in Wallachia in 1746 and in Moldavia in 1749. All these undertakings were approved by the Ottoman court, which had as its own goals peace and order in the countryside and the expanded production and delivery of goods. Vassal–suzerain relations thus achieved a certain equilibrium down to the later decades of the century.

THE CHURCH UNION IN TRANSYLVANIA

The eighteenth century was a time of profound change for the Romanians of Transylvania. The acquisition of the principality by the Habsburgs, part of the spoils from the victorious war against the Ottomans, which was confirmed by the Peace of Karlowitz in 1699, drew the Romanians more directly than ever before into the cultural currents and political rivalries of Central Europe. Habsburg rulers and statesmen were engaged in a bold project to centralize political authority in Vienna, bring reason and efficiency to state administration, and infuse a spirit of enterprise and innovation into economic and intellectual life. As a result, the main segments of Romanian society, from the clerical elite to the mass of the peasants, found their essentially Eastern way of life and world of ideas gravely challenged. But the shaking of the old order in Transylvania brought both elites and masses closer to the modern world.

The Habsburgs in Transylvania were confronted by institutions and mentalities that slowed the absorption of the principality into the general structures of the empire. To succeed, then, they would have to undermine those autonomies that had arisen since the era of settlement by the Hungarians, Saxons, and Szeklers and had taken form in the so-called Union of the Three Nations in 1438. The Union evolved into a monopoly of power and privilege imposed by the Hungarian nobility, the Saxon urban patriciate, and the upper classes among the Szeklers. They were the three nations. Social class, not ethnicity, determined membership, and, thus, the masses of Hungarian, Saxon, and Szekler peasants and others were excluded. The three nations in the fifteenth century were, naturally, Roman Catholic, but in the sixteenth century the Protestant Reformation made many converts among the Hungarians (Calvinist and Unitarian), Saxons (Lutheran), and Szeklers (Calvinist). The new Protestants and the remaining Roman Catholics eventually reached an understanding, and adherence to one of their churches became a condition of political privilege, that is, of membership in one of the nations. The three nations and four churches formed the backbone of Transylvania's autonomy when the Habsburgs arrived. The Romanians, who composed perhaps half the population of Transylvania in the early eighteenth century, were not a part of this system. They were excluded because they were Orthodox and overwhelmingly peasant.

During these centuries the Romanian Orthodox Church had led a precarious existence as merely tolerated by the three nations, but had, nonetheless, been able to maintain an administrative organization and a hierarchy presided over by a Metropolitan in the sixteenth and seventeenth centuries. In the seventeenth century the church was subject to heavy pressure from the Calvinist princes who were determined to convert the Orthodox clergy and faithful to Calvinism. György Rákóczi I (1630–48) was especially zealous. He had printed in 1642 in Alba Iulia (Gyulafehérvár; Karlsburg) a Calvinist catechism in Romanian and demanded that the Metropolitan disseminate Calvinist teachings among his flock. Prince Mihály Apafi (1661–90) intervened directly in the affairs of the Orthodox Church and had Metropolitan Sava Brancovici (1656–59, 1662–80) imprisoned because of his sturdy opposition to Calvinist proselytism. Two of his successors, Teofil (1692–97) and Atanasie (1697–1701), were attracted to a Church Union with Rome, which was sponsored by the newly arrived Habsburgs, in order to protect their church from Calvinist coercion and obtain full legal status for it.

Circumstances created an unlikely community of interests between the Habsburgs and the leading element of Romanian society – the upper clergy. In search of allies for their campaign to overturn the dominance of the three nations the Habsburgs looked to the Romanians, who could hardly be defenders of a political and social order that disdained them as outsiders. They recognized the inconvenience of the Romanians' Orthodoxy, but they had at hand a stratagem that had proved effective among the Ruthenians in the seventeenth century – the Church Union with Rome based on the principles enunciated at the synod of Ferrara-Florence in 1439, which had temporarily ended the schism between the Byzantine and Western churches. The Church Union with the Romanians would serve perfectly the purposes of the Habsburgs, who were intent on using the Roman Catholic Church as one of the instruments for holding together the empire's diverse territories. Thus, under the supervision of the Roman Catholic Primate of Hungary, Cardinal Leopold Kollonich, negotiations with the Romanian Orthodox bishop and his archpriests, which were conducted by the Jesuits, who returned to Transylvania with Habsburg armies, resulted in the Act of Union of 1701. Under its terms the Orthodox clergy and faithful acknowledged the Pope of Rome as the visible head of the Christian Church and accepted the use of unleavened bread in the Communion, the existence of Purgatory, and the procession of the Holy Spirit from the Father and the Son. But all other matters, including canon law, ritual, and practices such as a married parish clergy, remained untouched. In return the Romanian clergy were to enjoy the same rights and privileges as the members of the three nations among whom they lived. In this way the Habsburgs gained the good will of an influential elite, who could, if they chose, foster imperial aims among the large rural population. In time, so the Habsburgs and Kollonich reasoned, the Romanian clergy would come to see the Church Union as a step toward conversion to Roman Catholicism. The now Greek Catholic, or Uniate, clergy acquired, or at least were promised, social and political benefits befitting their station. The Court of Vienna chose to believe that the actions of the clergy also signified the acceptance of the Union by the mass of Romanian peasants, and thus it regarded the Orthodox Church as having ceased to exist.

The Church Union with Rome marked a turning point in the history of the Romanians of Transylvania. It opened to them Western cultural and intellectual influences of the most diverse sorts by providing the new Greek Catholic clergy with unprecedented opportunities for higher education in Roman Catholic lyceums in Transylvania and universities in Rome, Vienna, and Trnava (Nagyszombat). The aim of the Habsburgs and Kollonich was to form a well-educated and devoted Greek Catholic clergy that would be inspired to gain adherents for the Union among the mass of the rural population. But events were to take a different course. In time, rare (for Romanians) educational opportunities and the experience of Central Europe enabled the Greek Catholic clergy to assume political as well as spiritual leadership of the Romanians as they organized the struggle to end discrimination against Romanians and raise themselves to the rank of a fourth nation.

No less important a consequence of the Union was the sense of identity which it fostered and which by mid-century the clerical elite had transformed into a new idea of nation. Inspired by their bishop Ion Inochentie Micu-Klein (bishop, 1729–44), who was conscious of Roman origins and regarded his church as a bridge between East and West, they conceived of nation in ways that differed fundamentally from the privileged communities represented by the three nations. The nation the clergy served was ethnic, and it encompassed all Romanians, even if social distinctions remained strong. They accepted without debate their descent from the Roman conquerors of Dacia and the Latin origins of their language, but they were not modern nationalists, as they did not go so far as to make either history or language, that is, ethnicity, the justification for equality with the three nations. Rather, they still depended on the diplomas of emperors and kings and other authoritative juridical documents for that purpose. Yet, they conceived of the Church Union as significant beyond the bounds of religion. It was for them a return to Rome, to the ethnic origins that ultimately defined them. At the same time, they expressed devotion to their Eastern cultural and religious heritage and were utterly opposed to making their Greek Catholic Church more Latin.

The mass of the peasants reacted to the Church Union very differently from the clerical elite. They resisted it with all their being, an obstinacy that reveals a mental climate in the villages beholden to tradition and a sense of community defined by religion. The Greek Catholic clergy, who were trained to be missionaries of the Union in the countryside, in fact did little. They were deeply aware of how devoted the peasants were to Orthodox rituals and practices, and even though the Union made no changes in either, they were anxious to avoid the upheaval they knew even the mention of Rome and the Pope would cause. The great majority of peasants, therefore, did not know that the clergy had accepted the Union and that they, too, were considered Uniates.

The relative calm of the countryside in southern Transylvania was shattered in 1744 by a Serbian Orthodox monk, Visarion Sarai, who claimed to have been sent by God to preach the truths of Orthodoxy. In response to his warnings of eternal damnation for all those who had received the sacraments from Greek Catholic priests whole villages and districts rose up to demand priests of their own choosing and freedom to worship as they saw fit. They shunned priests and families who had become Uniates and declared a true kinship only with Greeks and Russians because they shared the same faith. The tumult died down after Visarion's arrest, but violence broke out with full force again in 1759, when a Romanian monk, Sofronie of Cioară, reignited passions about the Union and its threat to salvation. Order was restored only after Empress Maria Theresa agreed in the same year to restore the Orthodox Church in Transylvania by appointing a new bishop.

By the middle of the eighteenth century, then, both the principalities of Moldavia and Wallachia and the Romanians of Transylvania stood at the threshold of the modern world. The political, economic, and intellectual elites in the principalities and the Greek Catholic clerical elite in Transylvania were being drawn toward European currents of ideas and models of behavior. Yet, tradition proved tenacious and would subject successive generations of elites to severe challenges as they strove to reconcile their Eastern heritage with Western innovation.

3

From East to West, 1774–1866

Even if the year 1774 does not by itself mark a sharp turn in the history of the Romanians, significant events, nonetheless, occurred then and within a few years of this date that signaled the advent of the modern era in their development as a nation. Between the latter decades of the eighteenth and the middle of the nineteenth century the social and political structures of the two principalities underwent fundamental change, promoted by enlightened princes, by several generations of "patriotic" or "reforming" boiers, and then, in the decade before and after the Revolution of 1848, by intellectuals beholden to Western thought and example. In international relations, Russia emerged as the foremost challenger of Ottoman supremacy in the principalities and repeatedly drew concessions from sultans to expand their autonomy. Even more important in some ways were changes in the way educated Romanians thought about who they were and what their relationship to Europe should be. A little book of prayers, *Carte de rogacioni*, published in 1779 by a Romanian priest in Transylvania, revealed the progress of this shift in mentality. It was printed in Latin, rather than Cyrillic, characters and was thus meant to be a statement of ethnic distinctiveness and a confirmation of the bonds with Europe.

Perhaps the most striking feature of these nearly nine decades was the gradual linkage of Moldavia and Wallachia to Europe. It was primarily an effort at adaptation rather than imitation, since those who had placed themselves in the forefront of this process by no means intended to abandon the essence of their ethnic identity. Nonetheless, the reformers, as we may call them, could not but feel anxiety at the enormous disparity they perceived between the material progress and intellectual dynamism of the West and the heavy burdens of tradition at home. These impressions were all the more forceful because now they came not only from books but from personal experience, as travel between the principalities and Central and Western Europe steadily grew, especially from the 1830s on. As the reformers pursued their agenda of modernization they slowly relegated their Eastern heritage further to the margins of public life. Thus, their approach to the problems of society, essentially pragmatic and urban, gradually separated them from the traditional beliefs and aspirations of the rural world. These differences gave rise to a spiritual and material division between the city and the village and, hence, between small social and economic elites and the mass of the population – the peasants.

The main characteristic of political life during the period was the continuous rationalization of public administration. The reformers, both princes and boiers, joined by the still modest but growing middle class, strove to unify the legal system by replacing the many varieties of customary law with a single code, to separate executive, legislative, and judicial functions, to put public finances on a solid foundation with annual budgets, and to entrust all these matters to a well-trained, professional civil service. Although these measures in time brought greater order and efficiency to the management of public business, they also increased the powers of the prince and the central bureaucracy at the expense of local government and local initiative. Yet, this concentration of power in the capitals – Bucharest in Wallachia and Iaşi in Moldavia – was not without its benefits, as like-minded individuals, united by both class and principle, formed groups and incipient parties, which were to become the engines of political life in the second half of the nineteenth century.

The structure of society was also undergoing fundamental change. The great boiers, who had dominated the old regime politically and economically because of their control of land, slowly gave way to the middle class, as economic life became more diverse and the means to wealth and higher social position were multiplied accordingly. Important merchants and businessmen together with the growing professional class became the chief innovators and entrepreneurs in both economic and political life and were thus in harmony with the new spirit of the time. Social differentiation was also taking place within the peasantry, caused mainly by the effects of an essentially urban, capitalist economic development. A small number of peasants took advantage of the new opportunities to improve their status, but the great majority continued to lack even the bare necessities of life. Standing somewhat outside the traditional class system were the intellectuals, many of whom were the sons of boiers, while others came from the middle class. Together with the entrepreneurial classes they formed the nucleus of a new elite who looked to the West for economic and intellectual guidance and who over time became the decisive force in public life. Women as a social category lacked full legal standing and civic rights and were thus, in effect, excluded from political life. On the very margins of society were the Gypsies, whose status was that of slaves.

The intellectual elite espoused a new idea of community, which was to affect profoundly the course of modern Romanian history. Until the second half of the eighteenth century Romanians had generally defined themselves by membership in the broader Eastern Orthodox community and were still affected in many ways by the Byzantine legacy. But now Romanian intellectuals, and others, began to use such terms as "nation" and "fatherland," both with ethnic connotations, as they contemplated new forms of political and social organization. Their sense of ethnic identity grew stronger as their contacts with Western and Central Europe deepened, and by the decade preceding the Revolution of 1848 the idea of the ethnic nation gave moral certainty to their public ambitions, and the struggle to achieve the independence and union of Moldavia and Wallachia absorbed their energies. The new united Romania that the majority envisioned was to be secular and the embodiment of the liberal ideas predominant in Western Europe of the time.

Economic change did not keep pace with the innovations in political organization and social thought. The cultivation of the land and the relations between the peasants and the masters of the land remained largely as they had been a century earlier: peasants supplied the labor and the tools and even made the decisions about what to plant; the boiers provided land and received rents and services, but generally lacked the entrepreneurial spirit. Yet, changes were coming, as the old order of the communal village gave way to private property and as Romanian agriculture became more and more closely linked to the international market, especially in grains. In cities and towns the traditional artisan crafts and their guild organizations faltered under the mounting pressure of imports from Central Europe and slowly yielded to new forms of production that eventually became the modern factory. Infusing life into these new forms were changing attitudes toward profit and investment, which suggest the advent of capitalism.

Of lasting effect on the internal development of the principalities were changes in their international status. As each of the great powers sought its own predominance in the region as a replacement for the weakened Ottoman Empire, the Romanian political and intellectual elite sought ways to take advantage of their rivalries to promote autonomy and eventually achieve independence. In time, largely through their efforts, the fate of Moldavia and Wallachia became a distinct aspect of the larger Eastern Question. The growing political and economic concern of the powers with the principalities, in turn, loosened the Romanians' links to the Ottoman state and, no less, to the traditional Orthodox cultural world, and in the process hastened their approach to the West. These events deeply affected the ways educated Romanians thought about themselves and about the paths of development their nation should follow. Their awareness of the differences between East and West and the need they felt to choose between these two poles lay at the heart of Romanian history from the 1770s to the 1860s.

THE POLITICAL ORDER, TO 1821

Political power in Moldavia and Wallachia, at least until the Greek War for Independence, was in the hands of an oligarchy formed of the prince and the great boiers. The prince was the key figure in the system largely because he was the agent of the Ottoman state and had been chosen by the sultan to promote imperial ambitions. His powers, accordingly, were extensive, as the formulation and carrying out of internal policies lay mainly with him. As long as he fulfilled his duty toward the sultan to maintain domestic peace and order and ensure the payment of the tribute and the delivery of supplies and, just as crucial, satisfied the needs of a host of officials by providing the sums required to obtain and hold his office, he could exercise his own discretion in domestic matters. Yet, he could not hope to achieve all these goals without the support of leading boiers, nor, in effect, could they achieve theirs without some degree of cooperation with him. Thus, even though tension between them was constant, they were united by a common determination to maintain the existing social and economic order and pass on to the peasantry the main responsibility of bearing public burdens.

A number of princes were highly talented, and, despite the process by which they were selected, they contributed significantly to the well-being of their respective principality. Noteworthy among them was Alexandru Ipsilanti, a Greek from one of the most important Phanar families who was Prince of Wallachia, 1774–82 and 1796–97, and of Moldavia, 1786–88. He belongs in the company of the enlightened despots of the age because of his comprehensive reform of Wallachia's government and judicial system, intended to put them on rational foundations. His effort to codify Wallachian law was a notable success, and he recognized the vital importance of higher education for the general progress of society. He was equally intent on enhancing his own powers and relentlessly concentrated authority in his own hands at the expense of the provincial boiers. To accomplish his goals he relied increasingly on a bureaucracy and high boier functionaries who owed their first allegiance to him.

A notable aspect of political life was the frailty of representative institutions. One cause may have been the decline in status of the boiers. By the middle of the eighteenth century they had lost the right to elect the prince, while the body that had represented their interests, the Assembly of the Estates (Adunarea de Stări), had yielded to the General Council (Sfatul de Obște), made up of a small number of great boiers appointed by the prince. Representative bodies suffered also from the absence of a robust middle class, which typically had an interest in promoting limited, efficient government. Perhaps the main cause of their weakness lay ultimately with the sultan and the Ottoman bureaucracy. They supported the prince precisely because he was their man in the principalities and they had no interest in institutionalizing opposition to him, even though on occasion they might use boier grievances to pressure him.

The Orthodox Church may well be included in an overview of the political system because of the long-standing intertwined relations between state and church. The fortunes of the church had been closely bound up with the political destiny of the two principalities ever since their founding. Their relationship was in keeping with the Byzantine tradition. The higher clergy did not conceive of the state as separate from the church and did not engage the prince and boiers in a contest for supremacy. Nor did they promote political and social policies distinct from those of the prince. Rather, they perceived church and state to be engaged in complementary missions, the one spiritual and the other secular: the church gave the state moral support, while the state ensured respect for the church and its clergy, all intended to foster the well-being of the Christian community that both served. Princes and boiers shared this view, at least in theory.

The traditional relationship between church and state manifested itself across the entire range of political, economic, and social life. The higher clergy sat alongside the great boiers on the highest councils of state, while princes and boiers had a decisive role in choosing metropolitans and bishops. The church contributed substantially to the economic welfare of the state, since the monasteries together were the largest landholders, and their production made it possible for the princes to fulfill their economic obligations to the sultan. The church also provided the general population with important services – education, care for the sick and poor, and the keeping of vital statistics – at a time when these tasks were not considered the responsibility of the state.

The Moldavian and Wallachian churches continued to serve as an essential link to the Eastern Orthodox world. They were, to be sure, national churches in the sense that they were autocephalous, but they maintained the canonical links with the Patriarchate of Constantinople established in the fourteenth century. These bonds had been further strengthened in the latter seventeenth and eighteenth centuries by the advent of the Phanariot princes and the occupation by Greeks of high ecclesiastical offices. The Moldavian and Wallachian churches had also committed themselves to the East through their material support of Orthodox churches throughout the Ottoman Empire. The "dedicated monasteries" in both principalities, so called because a part of their incomes were set aside for good works in the East, contributed crucial resources to the defense of Orthodoxy under Muslim rule.

THE ROMANIAN QUESTION

As the Ottoman Empire continued to display weakness the great powers considered various possibilities of dividing up its still vast territory. Inevitably, the Romanian principalities, because of their geography, became the special object of attention of at least two of the powers – Russia, which was intent on replacing the Ottoman Empire as the dominant force in the region, and Austria, which had been advancing into Southeastern Europe since the end of the seventeenth century.

Russia was the more aggressive. It fought three victorious wars against the Ottomans – 1768–74, 1787–92, and 1806–12 – and thereby extended its influence in the principalities to the point of exercising an informal protectorate over them. The creation of stable links to Russia became a prime objective of its rulers and statesmen, as Catherine the Great made clear in her "Greek Project" of the 1770s and 1780s. As she contemplated the expulsion of the Turks from Europe and even a revival of the Byzantine Empire, she proposed as part of a reorganization of their territory the union of Moldavia and Wallachia into the "Kingdom of Dacia." According to one version of this plan, it would be ruled by a prince acceptable to Russia and would serve as a neutral zone between Russia, Austria, and the Ottoman Empire.

Peace treaties and diplomacy as well as wars greatly enhanced Russia's position in the principalities. The Treaty of Kuchuk Kainardji in 1774 laid the juridical foundation for Russia's peacetime intervention in the principalities' affairs by granting its ambassador in Constantinople the right to bring to the attention of the sultan any violations of their autonomy by Ottoman officials. Of crucial importance in expanding Russia's authority and prestige in the principalities was the appointment of a Russian consul in Bucharest in 1782 and a vice-consul in Iaşi in 1784, who became the chief agents of Russian policy in the principalities. Then, the Treaty of Iaşi in 1792 brought Russia for the first time to the

5 Prince Alexandru Moruzi receives Sir Robert Ainslie, English ambassador to Constantinople, at his residence in Bucharest, July 19, 1794

frontier of Moldavia by sanctioning her acquisition of the territory between the Bug and Dniester rivers. Two decades later, in 1812, by the Treaty of Bucharest Russia advanced to the Danube by annexing the part of Moldavia lying between the Dniester and Prut rivers, later known as Bessarabia. Because of these successes and Russia's contribution to the defeat of Napoleon, Russian prestige in the principalities after the Congress of Vienna in 1815 was at its height, and Moldavians and Wallachians naturally looked to the east for their liberation.

By comparison to Russia, the other great powers played but modest roles in the principalities. Austria nurtured projects for territorial and economic expansion beyond the Carpathians, especially the opening of the lower Danube and the Black Sea to its commerce, but Austrian rulers and statesmen were primarily concerned with the affairs of Central Europe and, particularly, the upheavals caused by the French Revolution and Napoleon. French interest in the principalities intensified with the advent of Napoleon, but he thought of them mainly as bargaining chips as he pursued his broader European goals. Great Britain also viewed the principalities from the perspective of shifting European alliances and as a means of furthering its ambitions in the Near East. Political rather than economic interests in the principalities were paramount, as British statesmen thought of them as barriers to Russian penetration of the Ottoman Empire and thus as defenders of British interests in the region.

THE IDEA OF NATION

Among educated Romanians a new sense of community was emerging that was ethnic rather than social or religious and was rooted in history and language. The same idea was manifest on both sides of the Carpathians – in Transylvania as well as Moldavia and Wallachia – but the precise form it took reflected differences in historical development.

Intellectuals in Moldavia and Wallachia in the latter decades of the eighteenth and the early nineteenth century had as one of their preoccupations their identity and its historical origins. Their sense of ethnic distinctiveness was based, in part, on a Byzantine–Orthodox political and cultural heritage going back at least to the founding of the principalities. But far more attractive in the cultural and political environment of the eighteenth century were the theory of Roman origins and, implicitly, the innate Europeanness of the Romanians.

Intellectuals did not limit the idea of the Romanness of the Romanians merely to learned treatises, but used it as a political and diplomatic weapon. During the war between Russia and the Ottoman Empire in 1768–74 the boiers in memorandum after memorandum to Russian officials called themselves Roman colonists, an appeal to noble ancestry intended to gain a place for themselves at the peace conference that would decide their fate. Much later, in a memorandum in 1807 an anonymous author tried to persuade Napoleon to support an independent Moldavia by citing the inhabitants' Roman origins: he described the Roman conquest and the Romanization of Dacia and insisted on the continuity of Roman settlements there after the Emperor Aurelian's withdrawal of the legions. A number of other writers also referred to Roman lineage as a reason to re-Europeanize the Romanians and stressed the urgency of the matter by contrasting their present dismal state under Ottoman domination with the glorious age of their Roman ancestors. These authors by no means invented the idea of Roman origins; Moldavian and Wallachian chroniclers of the seventeenth century, notably Grigore Ureche and Miron Costin, as we have seen, had described it as a fact beyond challenge. But the intellectuals of the eighteenth and early nineteenth century were, nonetheless, innovators because they used the idea to further their political agenda and inspire a national revival.

A few intellectuals went beyond Rome in exploring the sources of Romanian identity. They allowed the Dacians a role, and, in so doing, they moved closer to modern thinking about the Romanian ethnic nation. They emphasized the importance of territory in establishing an identity and used Dacian ancestry to claim that the Romanians were the oldest inhabitants of ancient Dacia and had resided there without interruption for 2,000 years. This Dacian sentiment was the creation of the eighteenth century and was perhaps nurtured by the currents of Romanticism. In any case, it contrasts sharply with the attitude of the seventeenth-century chroniclers and many intellectuals of the eighteenth century, who dismissed the Dacians as uncivilized.

At the heart of this flourishing ethnic consciousness lay the recognition that the Romanians belonged to Europe. Intellectuals accepted the long-held thesis that the principalities had stood for centuries as the defenders of Europe against the Ottoman invaders. They thus viewed their own subjection to Ottoman rule as a calamitous break with Europe, which they thought was in large measure responsible for their decline. Their goal was to restore their links to Europe, which was for them the model of civilization and material well-being. As early as 1733 the Orthodox Metropolitan of Moldavia had for the first time in writing described Europe as the source of culture and light, but after 1800 such appraisals became common. Some writers went so far as to see Europe and the East as fundamentally different worlds, the former a paragon of dynamism and progress, the latter weighed down by lethargy and routine. In such a dichotomy they found an irrefutable argument in favor of ending Ottoman domination of the principalities. How, they wondered, could the structures of an oriental civilization ensure the well-being and progress of a European people?

Beyond the Carpathians, in Transylvania, other Romanian intellectuals were engaged in similar explorations of identity. Almost all of them were Greek Catholic priests and had studied in Roman Catholic or Greek Catholic lyceums in Transylvania and universities in Rome, Vienna, and Trnava. They maintained their commitment to the doctrines and practices of Eastern Orthodoxy, except in a few particulars, but their cultural orientation and ambitions were broadly European. They placed themselves within the currents of the European Enlightenment, in its Central European incarnation, through their respect for reason and learning and their promotion of education. They were European also in their embrace of Rome and Roman civilization, thereby joining in the revival of the classical tradition characteristic of eighteenth-century Europe. They were encyclopedic in their interests – history, philosophy, theology, language, pedagogy – and unconstrained in applying their learning as priests, teachers, writers and translators, and political activists. What gave direction to their diverse enterprises was the idea of nation. It was ethnic and was grounded in the evidence provided by history and language, and it found eloquent expression in the theory of Daco-Roman continuity.

The first to present the theory in detail was Samuil Micu (1745–1806) in a series of historical works, notably his four-volume *Istoria şi lucrurile şi întîmplările Românilor* (The history and the concerns and the events of the Romanians). In it he argued that the Romanians of his day were the pure descendants of the Romans who had settled in Dacia after Trajan's conquest and had all come from Italy. He was certain that there were no other inhabitants of Dacia when they arrived because the Roman legions had conducted a war of attrition against the Dacians. When Aurelian withdrew the army and administration from Dacia, Micu insisted that the majority of the population stayed behind and during the centuries of barbarian invasions survived by taking refuge in the mountains. It was these Roman descendants organized in independent duchies whom the Hungarians encountered when they entered Transylvania in the tenth century and with whom they concluded an alliance of equals to govern the territory. Yet, the history of the Romanians from that time down to the eighteenth century, he lamented, was one of inexorable decline, as they were unable to resist the united forces of the other three nations: the Hungarian nobility, the Saxons, and the Szeklers.

Such an account of events does not stand up to critical scrutiny, as suggested earlier. Micu was strongly influenced by prevailing political and social circumstances and by his own determination to restore the Romanians to their rightful place as the equals of the other three nations. In an age when nobility, or quality, rather than numbers was the primary criterion of social and political standing, he felt compelled to prove beyond any doubt the direct descent of the Romanians from the masters of the ancient world. All his Romanian contemporaries on both sides of the Carpathians shared his views.

Micu and his colleagues also used language to demonstrate the Roman origins of the Romanians. He and Gheorghe Şincai (1754–1816), a fellow priest and historian, published a scholarly grammar of Romanian, *Elementa linguae Daco-Romanae sive Valachicae*, in Vienna in 1780. In it they argued that Romanian was simply a distorted form of Classical Latin and could easily be restored to its original purity if foreign accretions were removed. They shunned the Cyrillic alphabet in favor of Latin characters in order to reveal the true nature of their language, and they used the system of transliteration devised by Micu for his book of prayers, *Carte de rogacioni*, published the previous year. Another colleague, Petru Maior (1760–1821), the author of the polemical defense of continuity, *Istoria pentru începutul Românilor în Dachia* (The history of the origins of the Romanians in Dacia), reinforced the Latinist argument by compiling the first etymological dictionary of Romanian, *Lexicon Valachico-Latino-Hungarico-Germanicum*, which was published in Buda in 1825. In the preface he contributed a significant correction to the Micu–Şincai thesis by pointing out that Romanian was descended from spoken, not Classical, Latin.

These scholar-priests were activists who presented their case to the highest authority in Vienna in 1792, when they submitted an imposing statement of national identity and aspirations, the *Supplex libellus Valachorum*, to Emperor Leopold II (1790–92). Here they set forth the theory of Daco-Roman continuity with detailed references from numerous sources as just grounds for claiming full equality for the Romanian nation with their privileged neighbors in Transylvania. Their use of the term "nation" itself is striking. They had in view all the Romanians of Transylvania – peasants as well as upper class, Orthodox as well as Greek Catholic – and thus they abandoned the narrow sense of the term that stipulated class and religion as the criteria for enjoying privileges and rights. But their erudition and logic moved neither the imperial court in Vienna nor the authorities in Transylvania to grant their request, and these continued to be formidable defenders of the old order and discouraged any organized Romanian political activity for the next half-century.

AUTONOMY

If Moldavia and Wallachia survived in a dangerous neighborhood of great-power rivalries it was, in part, because their leading classes shared a sense of solidarity nourished by a sturdy historical consciousness of their distinctive identity, both ethnic and Christian. As we have seen, intellectuals made crucial contributions to the formation of this sense of community. To be sure, the inability of the powers to agree for long on a division of territory or the delineation of spheres of influence was a boon for the principalities, but activism on the part of the Moldavians and Wallachians themselves was the key to their survival.

The chief defenders of the principalities' autonomy came from the ranks of the great and middle boiers, joined occasionally by a public-spirited prince and members of the growing middle class. The patriotic boiers, as they are sometimes called, led the effort to persuade the Russian, Austrian, and Ottoman imperial courts that the principalities had never renounced their autonomy and that peace and order in the region could be had only if it were respected. Their defense of autonomy never took violent forms; it was limited to informing the representatives of the great powers of the true state of things and reasoning with them, especially with Russian diplomats, whom they regarded as the most sympathetic to their cause. They continually insisted that the earliest agreements between the Moldavian and Wallachian princes and the sultans had never compromised the principalities' independence and had set clear limits to the obligations they owed their suzerain. They thus demanded that the violations of the *ahd-names* that had accumulated over time be annulled and that their "ancient rights" be restored. A characteristic statement of principle came from Iordache Rosetti-Rosnovanu, a great boier and High Treasurer of Moldavia, in a memorandum to the Russian ambassador in Constantinople in 1818. He urged that Moldavia's myriad obligations to the Ottoman state be limited to an annual "gift" and that the principality no longer have to suffer Ottoman interference in its political and economic life but be allowed to govern itself as an independent state.

None of these arguments carried much weight at the Ottoman court. As the strategic importance and economic contributions of the principalities grew in the latter eighteenth and early nineteenth century, Ottoman officials became less willing than ever, despite Russian victories in war and heavy diplomatic pressure, to hear of the election of princes by the boiers, freedom of commerce, diplomatic relations with Western Europe, and the revival of national armies. The sultans were loath to make such concessions because the principalities had become the first line of defense against Russia and Austria and were the indispensable granaries of Constantinople. They were anxious lest the loosening of the bonds with Moldavia and Wallachia become the beginning of the end of the empire in Europe.

The patriotic boiers were undaunted by failure. By the time the Phanariot era ended in 1821 they had committed themselves irrevocably to the cause of independence. But they were at the same time realists. Convinced that they could not be successful by themselves, they sought the "protection" of Russia. The patronage of the tsars did, in fact, help to bring Ottoman domination to an end much sooner than they could have expected.

1821

The Greek War for Independence, which broke out in 1821, set in motion a series of events over the next half-century that thoroughly undid the status quo. Between this war and the Revolution of 1848 the contours of modern Romania gradually took form. Moldavia and Wallachia moved closer to union and independence through the perseverance of an elite formed of boiers and the middle class and through the intervention of the great powers. Institutional changes carried out during these three decades brought order to government administration, led to experiments with representative assemblies, and stimulated the formation of political groupings, now separated from one another as much by ideology as by social status. Society itself became more cosmopolitan and complex as cities grew in number and size and as social differentiation and mobility accelerated under the impress of changing economic and cultural patterns. In the economy production increased in both industry and agriculture, but their structures continued to resist innovation. Underlying these economic and social changes were bourgeoning contacts with the West. No significant aspect of the public and private life of the elite and of those who aspired to join it was left untouched by "Europe."

From the outbreak of the Revolution of 1848 to the promulgation of the Constitution of 1866 the shaping of modern Romania accelerated. Romanian political leaders, taking advantage of conflicting ambitions among the great powers, achieved the union of the principalities and ensured their independence. They gained these objectives in the way foreseen by an earlier generation – through a collective international guarantee in place of single-power protection. At home during this time political institutions gradually assumed European forms and political thought reached new levels of complexity in confrontations between liberals and conservatives. Divergent ideologies increasingly had Europe as their touchstone. To liberals, the West was a source of inspiration, to the conservatives a cause of anxiety, as both sides warmed to the debate over national identity and paths of development. In the meantime, the role of the state in both public and private life expanded relentlessly, as ministries and bureaucracies assumed primary responsibility for education, took over civil functions and social services long exercised by the Orthodox Church, and became active promoters of economic growth.

To return to the spring of 1821, Wallachia was the scene of a complex social and national movement. A large-scale, mainly peasant, uprising, originating in Oltenia, encompassed most of the principality. Its causes lay partly in the unbearable conditions on the land and partly in the fiscal and administrative abuses of local officials. At another level a number of boiers sought to bring an end to Ottoman

6 Tudor Vladimirescu in 1821

suzerainty, while others concentrated on driving out the Phanariots. Their actions were the overt responses to the strong sense of patriotism and a national consciousness which had already found theoretical expression in the projects of the reforming boiers. The economic and social demands of the peasants and the political aspirations of the boiers intersected in the movement led by Tudor Vladimirescu, one of the major figures of early modern Romanian history.

Vladimirescu, the peasants, and the boiers were stirred to action by the general rising against Ottoman rule in Southeastern Europe initiated by Greeks united in a secret organization, the Philike Hetairia (Friendly Society). Its leaders intended to free the Greeks from Ottoman rule by leading a general uprising of Christians in Southeastern Europe. Alexandru Ipsilanti, the leader of the Hetairia, was well placed to accomplish its goals. As the son of Prince Constantin Ipsilanti of Wallachia (1802–7) he could draw on connections with Romanian boiers, and as a major-general in the Russian army he seemed a reliable guarantor of Russian aid. He and his colleagues had no doubt that the great boiers in Moldavia and Wallachia would support them because culturally, they, too, belonged to the Greek world. Thus, the principalities would provide a reservoir of men and supplies for the advance southward to Greece.

Events were to show that the Hetairia had seriously misjudged the mood in the principalities. Although some prominent boiers and high churchmen welcomed the Greek insurrection as a means of throwing off Ottoman domination, they were equally determined to abolish the Phanariot regime and eliminate Greek competition for political office and economic advantages.

The initiative for an armed uprising on the Romanian side did not come from the great boiers but from a provincial leader of modest social origins, Tudor Vladimirescu (*c.* 1780–1821). Born into a family of free peasants in Oltenia, he had become well known to the people of his region as a local official, the head of a corps of volunteers in service with the Russian army in the Russo-Turkish War of 1806–12, a merchant, and an owner of land, which admitted him to the ranks of the lesser boiers. He was drawn into the planning of the Greek uprising in the principalities by Iordache Olimpiotul, the commander of the Prince of Wallachia's guard, whom he had met during the Russo-Turkish War, and by the great boier Constantin Samurcaş, the prince's high commissioner in Oltenia. They considered Vladimirescu the most able Wallachian military commander. But he himself had no intention of being merely the instrument of others, as he had his own agenda – to free Wallachia from Ottoman rule and to bring about political and economic changes to benefit the lesser boiers and the peasants. His pursuit of these goals brought him into a fateful conflict with the Greeks and great boiers.

In January 1821, Vladimirescu was engaged in organizing an army and gathering supplies in his native Oltenia. To rally support among the peasants he issued a general proclamation promising all who joined his army membership in *Adunarea Norodului* (Assembly of the People), which he conceived of as a representative body empowered to act for the common good. He also promised the peasants an end to the "abuses" of officials and the "tyranny" of boiers, but he said nothing specific about the abolition of labor services or the granting to them of property rights over the land they worked. Yet, even the promise of reform was enough to bring peasants from all over Oltenia to his side.

Moldavia was the scene of decisive events at the beginning of March. On the 6th Alexandru Ipsilanti and a small force of Hetairists crossed the Prut River from Bessarabia and entered Iaşi. Ipsilanti immediately issued a proclamation announcing the start of a general war to liberate all the Christians of Southeastern Europe from Ottoman rule and promising the Moldavians peace and security. Prince Mihai Suţu (1819–21) and a few boiers and high clergymen welcomed him because they thought that Russian military intervention was at hand. Ipsilanti with a small army of about 2,000 men set out for Bucharest, where he planned to join forces with Tudor Vladimirescu. But support for his cause had already begun to crumble, as word spread that the Tsar had condemned Ipsilanti's actions and thus was unlikely to protect Moldavia from Ottoman retribution.

Tudor Vladimirescu, upon learning of Ispilanti's arrival in Moldavia, set off from Oltenia for Bucharest with an army of some 8,000 men. He was determined not only to throw off Ottoman suzerainty, but also to put an end to the century-long predominance of the Phanariots, a goal he made clear in his promise to assist Ipsilanti and his army to move south of the Danube as quickly as possible. He was obviously relying upon the intervention of the Russian army. Yet, he had no intention of turning the principality into a Russian dependency, for once Wallachia had been liberated he wanted the Russians to withdraw across the Prut River and let the Wallachians be masters in their own house.

By the time Vladimirescu had reached the outskirts of Bucharest on March 28 the balance of forces had drastically changed. All hopes for the Tsar's intervention had by now vanished. To present a united front to both Greeks and Turks he came to an understanding with the boiers. But he had another motive, too: he aspired to become prince and he was intent on ascending the throne in the traditional manner, elected by the boiers and blessed by the church, not as a revolutionary.

In the end, Vladimirescu achieved none of his objectives. Ottoman armies marched into Wallachia and Moldavia on May 25, and the Tsar gave his approval for the "restoration of order" in both principalities. By now hostility between Ipsilanti and Vladimirescu had come to a head. Ipsilanti, wrongly suspecting Vladimirescu of forming an alliance with the Turks against the Greeks, ordered his arrest, trial, and execution on June 8. Almost at once Vladimirescu's army disintegrated, and shortly afterward the end also came for Ipsilanti's movement. On June 19 his small force was defeated by the Turks, and a few days later he himself crossed the border into Transylvania, where he was interned.

Although Vladimirescu's movement had been short-lived, the goals he sought to achieve were firmly rooted in the Romanians' recent historical experience. His proclamation of the right of self-determination embodied the general will to be free from Turkish and Phanariot domination; his promises to relieve the peasant of intolerable burdens to landlord and tax-collector and the enthusiastic response he stirred revealed the depths of the agrarian problem; and his proposals to ease restrictions on commerce and abolish the privileges of foreign merchants spoke to the ambitions of the rising middle class. His defeat by no means discouraged the movement for independence or stifled the aspirations to political and economic reform.

POLITICS, 1821–1848

The Ottoman military occupation of the principalities was of short duration. Yielding to pressure from Britain and France, the Ottoman government and Romanian boiers reached an agreement in 1822 which preserved Ottoman suzerainty, but ended the occupation and restored native princes to the thrones of both principalities.

Yet, these changes did not resolve fundamental constitutional issues. The new princes, Grigore Ghica of Wallachia (1822–28) and Ioan Sandu Sturdza of Moldavia (1822–28), both able men, were determined to expand their prerogatives, a goal which set them at odds with the boiers, who thought they deserved a greater share of power. The long-standing conflict between princes and boiers was thus extended into the post-Phanariot period.

Another unresolved problem was the role of Russia. The new Tsar, Nicholas I (1825–55), was determined to pursue Russia's interests in the principalities vigorously, and in 1826, he forced the sultan to accept the Convention of Akkerman. It reasserted Russia's prerogatives as the "protecting power" and required the princes, the boiers, and the Ottoman government to take into account the "observations" of the Russian ambassador in Constantinople concerning the principalities.

Fundamental disagreements with the Ottomans over the principalities, Greece, and the Caucasus nonetheless persisted and led to a Russian declaration of war in April 1828. Russian armies occupied Wallachia and Moldavia in order to ensure the passage of troops and supplies to the front south of the Danube. By August 1829 they had broken through Ottoman defenses in eastern Thrace and stood ready to march on Constantinople. The Ottoman government recognized the hopelessness of its situation and accepted Russian terms for peace.

The Treaty of Adrianople, signed on September 14, 1829, proved to be a milestone in the political and economic development of the principalities. The sultan agreed to the administrative autonomy of Moldavia and Wallachia and returned to Wallachia the Turkish fortresses at Turnu, Giurgiu, and Brăila on the Danube. The economic terms of the treaty eventually proved a strong stimulus to agriculture and trade because they relieved the principalities of the obligation to provision Constantinople and opened them to international markets. The Ottoman government also agreed to the drawing up of new administrative statutes for the principalities under Russian supervision and to accept a Russian occupation of the principalities until it had paid a huge war indemnity. Now only remnants of Ottoman suzerainty remained: the annual tribute and the sultan's right to confirm the election of the princes.

The Russian occupation brought substantial modernization to public life in the principalities. Of crucial importance was the introduction of a new fundamental law for each, the Organic Statutes, which established a framework for orderly and efficient government. But the motives of Russian officials were hardly altruistic. They promoted order and efficiency, to be maintained by the possessing classes, as the most effective way of achieving their own long-term goals of predominance in the principalities.

Tsar Nicholas entrusted the carrying out of the provisions of the Treaty of Adrianople to an energetic officer and administrator, Pavel Kiselev, who assumed his duties as prince, in fact if not in name, of both principalities in November 1829. Until his departure in April 1834 he exercised almost unlimited powers in reorganizing political and economic life. Although many contemporaries thought his acts revolutionary, he had no intention of overturning the established social order. He sought, rather, to perpetuate it by defining precisely the rights and obligations of all classes and by providing the administrative and legal machinery to enforce them. Undoubtedly, his most important accomplishment was the elaboration of a fundamental law for each principality. The Organic Statutes were the product of close cooperation between Russian authorities and Romanian boiers.

The Statutes ensured the continued dominance of the boiers in political life by recognizing their exclusive right to be represented in the new legislature, by according them the leading positions in the central administration, by exempting them from taxes, and by confirming their property rights over their estates. But the authors of the Statutes also felt constrained to accept at least a limited participation of the middle class in the conduct of each principality's affairs and saw the wisdom in creating a more favorable climate for economic development. Such indulgence did not, however, extend to the peasantry, the majority of whom remained in as precarious a social and economic condition as before. The Statutes also introduced drastic changes in every branch of government in the principalities. Old practices and institutions were modified or abolished, as the political, judicial, and fiscal functions of government became more orderly and systematic. This was true especially of fiscal affairs, as an annual budget was adopted based on projected revenues and expenditures and drawn up by the prince and approved by the legislature.

The Organic Statutes imposed a series of essential innovations in public administration. One guiding principle was the separation of powers among the executive, legislative, and judicial branches of government. At the same time, the Statutes preserved the tradition of a strong executive. Thus, despite new powers granted the legislature, the prince remained the key figure in the political system. Another general principle evident in the Statutes was centralization, which was reflected in the supervision of village affairs and urban administration by officials appointed by and responsible to the central government. They also expanded the supervisory authority of the state over the Orthodox Church and drastically reduced the role of the clergy in civil affairs, notably its keeping of vital statistics, all signs of the growing secularization of society.

All in all, the Organic Statutes hastened the modernization of the principalities. They enhanced the predictability of government, especially in fiscal matters, and thus offered more reliable guarantees for investments and contracts, indispensable conditions for economic progress. They also brought the union of Moldavia and Wallachia closer by endowing them with almost identical political institutions and granting their inhabitants joint citizenship. Yet, despite these innovations, the Statutes did not constitute a sudden break with the past. Rather, in many areas of public life they expanded upon earlier ideas and projects, such as the rational management of the finances, which the reforming boiers had advocated in the preceding decades. The concentration of power in the hands of the prince and the expansion of the central bureaucracy at the expense of regional and local administration also fitted in with trends already underway.

Russian armies continued to occupy the principalities after the sultan had approved the Organic Statutes because the Tsar wished to keep Kiselev in place to supervise their implementation. The Russian government had sponsored the Statutes in the first place to gain the support of the boiers and thereby consolidate Russia's pre-eminence in the principalities. When the Tsar finally ended the occupation in 1834 it was because of improved relations with the Ottoman Empire and the certainty in St. Petersburg that Russia's position in the principalities had been made secure.

Between the end of the Russian occupation and the outbreak of revolution in 1848 Romanian society was in a state of flux. It was a period of curious juxtapositions. Remnants of Ottoman suzerainty survived alongside the surge toward independence; representative government won new ground even as Russian interference intensified; and Eastern tradition continued to clash with Western innovation. Striking contrasts were everywhere manifest – in dress, language, and customs.

The political life of the period bore witness to pervasive restlessness and expectation. The princes found themselves constantly at odds with the boiers and the Russian consuls in Bucharest and Iaşi, whose primary function was to persuade both the boiers and the princes to act in accordance with Russia's best interests. Indeed, the activities of the consuls became so obtrusive as to nourish anti-Russian feelings among the influential classes and lay the foundations of suspicion and ill will that were to characterize Romanian–Russian relations to the end of the twentieth century, while boier discontents were one of the issues princes who reigned under the Organic Statutes had constantly to keep in mind. In Wallachia Alexandru Ghica (1834–42) was anxious to be a national monarch standing above parties, but his idea of a strong ruler made cooperation with the liberal and patriotic boiers in the legislature impossible. His successor, Gheorghe Bibescu (1842–48), was equally unsuccessful in mollifying the boiers, who accused him of authoritarian ambitions.

In Moldavia Prince Mihai Sturdza faced opposition similar to that of his colleagues in Wallachia, but he was more successful in overcoming it. He steadfastly pursued two objectives during his long reign (1834–49): the increase of his own authority and the maintenance of good relations with Russia. Despite his own good intentions and considerable powers, which included the manipulation of elections and a strict censorship, Sturdza could not stem the growing restlessness among the boier and middle-class elite. The incomprehension between him and the young, mainly Western-educated sons of boiers grew into open conflict, as the latter saw in Sturdza only the defender of the old order and of the humiliating deference paid to a foreign power.

SOCIETY AND THE ECONOMY, 1821–1848

Between Tudor Vladimirescu's movement and the Revolution of 1848 Moldavian and Wallachian society moved further away from eighteenth-century social and economic norms toward those that were to characterize the united national state of the later decades of the nineteenth century. Two events occurred which were to have profound consequences for the development of modern Romania: accelerated demographic change and the expansion of economic ties with Western Europe. Perhaps the most striking social development of the period was the growth of population, a European-wide phenomenon that began later in the principalities than in the West. It was characterized, in particular, by a more than twofold increase in the urban population during the first half of the nineteenth century. The continuous movement of people from the countryside to the cities and towns and expanded immigration from foreign countries, all directed primarily toward urban centers, was unrelenting.

These changes over time undermined the social equilibrium that had prevailed in the eighteenth century. They also opened the way to a restructuring of the economy by stimulating the exploitation of the country's raw materials and expanding its productive capacity. The pressure of population was felt most keenly in agriculture. At the beginning of the century the land available for farming had been adequate to feed the existing population even with traditional methods of cultivation, since the amount of arable land seemed inexhaustible. But by the middle of the century, as forests and other reserves dwindled, it became apparent that without sweeping changes in its organization and methods agriculture could no longer satisfy the needs of a growing population or meet the increasing demands of the international market, upon which the economies of both principalities had increasingly come to depend.

Demographic change was everywhere evident. The population of Moldavia rose from 1,115,325 in 1826 to 1,463,927 in 1859 and that of Wallachia from 1,920,590 in 1831 to 2,400,000 in 1860. The exact causes of the increase of population remain obscure, because of insufficient data. Undoubtedly, the main cause was the decline of the death rate, owing in part to an end of warfare on

Romanian soil and to modest improvements in health and sanitation. Accelerated economic activity and greater fiscal stability may also have played a part: they offered many people new hope for the future and thus may have encouraged them to have larger families. Immigration, especially of Jews into Moldavia, also contributed to the growth of population. The increase of population was particularly evident in cities. The causes of this unprecedented urban growth were diverse, but natural increase was not among them, since in many cities such as Iaşi and Galaţi mortality exceeded the birth rate. Rather, urban population grew primarily because of the constant flow of people from the countryside. This migration was, in turn, the result of population increases in rural areas, the consequent decrease of available cropland and pasture, and the growing labor and fiscal burdens on peasants resulting from the steady commercialization of agriculture.

The social structure of the two principalities was also undergoing significant change as a result of population growth and economic expansion. By the 1840s the middle class had become the most dynamic force behind the development of cities. Merchants, artisans, and members of the liberal professions formed its essential components, but they did not constitute a unified class. For many, boier status was the ideal to which they aspired, and thus the consolidation of a true bourgeoisie, marked by a heightened sense of class consciousness, was to come about only in the second half of the century.

Important modifications were taking place in the social composition of the boier class. Even as the Organic Statutes had consolidated the political power of the great boiers, social and economic forces were at work undermining their predominance. In the first place, the boier class as a whole was losing its exclusive character, as the number of boiers steadily increased, mainly through the purchase of offices by merchants and government functionaries. Differences of outlook between the new and the old boiers were often striking. The former were turned toward the future and maintained at best a tenuous link to the values of the old regime, whereas the majority of the great boiers continued to extol the virtues of the aristocratic style. Within the narrow circle of the great boiers itself an unbridgeable generation gap had appeared. Many of the sons of boiers who had returned home after study and travel in Western Europe could no longer accept the leisurely style of their fathers' way of life.

The process of embourgeoisement already evident before 1821 accelerated in the 1830s and 1840s. The boiers of the lower ranks who managed their own properties were eager to develop commerce and improve agriculture. Many invested in small business enterprises. Nor were such interests foreign to the great boiers. But it was the lesser boiers who stood closest to middle-class values and aspirations and who contributed to the foundation of that liberal bourgeoisie which successfully challenged the ascendancy of the great boiers in the second half of the century.

Industry was of modest dimensions in the 1830s and 1840s. Although the volume of production grew and technological improvements were introduced, the organization of production remained largely what it had been in previous decades. Capital accumulation was small and was used mainly to finance commerce and provide individuals with loans for personal needs and, especially, the purchase of land. To invest in "factories" was still considered risky, and the preservation of the guild system discouraged innovation. Although the Organic Statutes had proclaimed the principle of economic liberty, the guild system with its myriad regulations remained powerful.

The exchanges of goods intensified, but few modifications in the organization of commerce occurred. Fairs retained their importance on both the local and international level, and in the cities and larger towns, merchants carried on largely as before, but the professionalization of the merchant class was nonetheless well underway as the state's regulation of their activities became more systematic. Yet, many of the old impediments to internal commerce remained in place. The weak purchasing power of the mass of the population, inadequate communications and transport, and elementary banking and credit facilities hindered the growth of the domestic market.

The most dramatic economic development in the principalities at this time was undoubtedly the expansion of foreign trade. Britain and France now joined in the competition for Romanian raw materials and markets alongside the Ottoman Empire and Austria, which until then had dominated the commerce of the principalities. Romanian exports to the West were, of course, agricultural, primarily grain and animals. Imports consisted mainly of consumer goods destined for the wealthy such as textiles, glassware, and furs; they contributed little to the development of domestic industry or to the strengthening of the general economic foundations of the principalities.

Two generations of intellectuals, those who adhered to the traditions of the Enlightenment and the classical style of the previous century and the Romantics and revolutionaries, who looked to the future, placed their stamp on cultural life and political thought between the Treaty of Adrianople of 1829 and the outbreak of the Revolution of 1848. The boundaries between them were hardly rigid, as both were energetic and ready to confront any challenge. Their often naive enthusiasm and strong sense of patriotism, their grandiose projects and encyclopedic ambitions were beholden to the spirit of the time, a kind of liberalism, which after the revolution came to be known as Forty-Eightism (*paşoptism*). They were inspired by a single, all-encompassing goal: to raise the Romanian nation out of its backwardness and to bring it into communion with the modern world, which, to them, meant Western Europe.

Literature faithfully reflected the spirit of the time. Poetry and prose were subordinated to the ideals of national unity and independence, to sympathy for the lower classes, especially the peasantry, and to efforts to nativize inspiration by directing it toward history, folklore, and the local landscape. Much of the writing of this period was also inspired by a belief inherited from the Enlightenment that literature had an inherently didactic purpose, and thus authors emphasized the useful over the aesthetic and thought first of the general good rather than of personal gratification. These were characteristic liberal tenets of the time, which Romanian intellectuals shared with their counterparts throughout East Central Europe.

A new element intruded upon the literary scene after 1830: the reading public. It was still small, but it was increasingly democratic in its composition, as merchants, artisans, state functionaries, and village intellectuals (priests, schoolteachers, notaries) joined the great and middle boiers. The readers of newspapers came mainly from the middle class. In 1834 there were 200 subscribers to *Curierul*

Românesc (The Romanian courier), which had been founded in Bucharest in 1829 by Ion Heliade Rădulescu (1802–72), the leading literary figure of the period. Although their number was modest by later standards, they were a presence to be reckoned with. Even men like Heliade Rădulescu, whose motivation was not primarily commercial, had, nonetheless, to take into account their readers' tastes, which were often unsophisticated, in order to preserve their newspapers and printing houses for their real work of education and enlightenment, especially the publication of books.

Of all the currents that affected cultural and intellectual life, Romanticism exerted the strongest influence. Its salient characteristic in both Moldavia and Wallachia was an overriding concern for nation. The idea of nation itself was different from what it had been in the eighteenth century. An earlier generation of scholars had spoken with pride about the Roman, and sometimes of the Dacian, origins of the Romanians and had used such an association as a measure of their own character and nobility. But in the works of writers after 1800 the idea of nation began to assume modern contours. For Naum Râmniceanu (1764–1838), a learned cleric and historian, membership in the Romanian nation was determined by ethnicity and religion (Orthodoxy), and, hence, it transcended political boundaries to include Romanians everywhere. In the memoranda which the lesser boiers drew up after 1821 to persuade the great boiers to share political power with them they pointed out that they all belonged to the same nation. Their claim, put simply, was that equal political rights followed naturally from the sharing of a common history and membership in the same ethnic community. By the 1840s such thoughts had lost their novelty. The old juridical conception of nation, based on privileges which set one social class above all others and thus ensured the political and social ascendancy of the boiers, had given way to an ethnic conception which embraced all social classes, even peasants. The young generation of intellectuals, in particular, no longer used rank or wealth as criteria for membership in the nation. For them, all-encompassing ethnic communities had become the primary cells of human society.

The writing of history in the 1830s and 1840s was also influenced by Romanticism and the new idea of nation. Historians continued to study national origins in order to add to the evidence of

Roman descent, although the theory was by now generally accepted among the educated. But an equally compelling attraction of history was the mystery of beginnings and the thrill of deciphering the past through ruins and inscriptions that had survived almost as a miracle. Historians were also drawn to ages of glory. The focusing of attention on Prince Mihai Viteazul, who had briefly united Moldavia, Wallachia, and Transylvania under his rule in 1600, was by no means accidental, but mirrored perfectly the heightened preoccupation with national unity and independence. In the hands of its best practitioners history became the story not simply of rulers and heroes but of all the people. The outstanding example of the new history was *Histoire de la Valachie, de la Moldavie et des Valaques Transdanubiens*, published in Berlin in 1837 by Mihail Kogălniceanu (1817–91), who had studied history at the University of Berlin and who was to occupy a central place in Romanian public life for the next four decades. The idea of nation had made a powerful impression on him. He thus conceived of history as the creation of a whole people, not just of their leaders, and, hence, he argued, it was essential to undertake a many-sided investigation of the past in order to reveal fully the accomplishments of peoples, and, especially, to grasp the spirit that guided them.

The task of fashioning the disparate strands of thought about history and literary creativity into a coherent cultural doctrine was taken up by the writers gathered around *Dacia Literară* (Literary Dacia), a review founded by Mihail Kogălniceanu in Iaşi in 1840. Its title was symbolic of his and his colleagues' aims: to promote a sense of unity and purpose among all Romanians living within the historical boundaries of ancient Dacia by cultivating a genuinely national literature. To be national, Kogălniceanu insisted, literature had to reflect the distinctive traits of the Romanian people as revealed in their history and folklore, and had to have as its principal sources of inspiration the historical experiences and the contemporary aspirations of Romanians.

The institutionalization of culture was also characteristic of the time. Societies and associations of all kinds sprang up, bringing likeminded individuals together to promote a multitude of causes. They made the theater a regular part of social and literary life; they laid the foundations of a modern educational system from the village

7 Mihail Kogălniceanu

primary school to the university; and they endowed the newspaper with its mission to mold public opinion and stir a sense of civic responsibility.

The "generation of 1848," then, stood for a new, comprehensive vision of nation, and they were determined to place their theory before an audience well beyond their own limited circles. In so doing, they moved much closer to "the people" than any previous generation and thus gave a distinctly modern turn to the idea of nation. The first great test of this new nation came during the springtime of peoples in 1848.

THE ROMANIAN 1848

For Romanian intellectuals, the spring of 1848 signified the triumph of the idea of nation. In both the principalities and the Habsburg Monarchy they justified demands for independence or political autonomy by invoking the inherent right of the ethnic community to self-determination. In Moldavia and Wallachia they sought to throw off the Russian protectorate and to restore the historical equilibrium with the Ottoman Empire, and in Transylvania, the adjoining Banat region, and Bukovina they undertook to unite all Romanians in a single, autonomous duchy. They even contemplated a union of all Romanians on both sides of the Carpathians, for they felt strongly the bonds of ethnicity, language, and culture. But such thoughts were fleeting, as political realities, notably the absolutism of Russia and Austria, constantly intruded upon hypotheses and reveries. Yet, the idealism of the Forty-Eighters persisted, never more so than in the bonds of solidarity they felt with the other small nations of Europe struggling to free themselves from the rule of others. This particular sense of community owed much to Western thought and example, and, thus, 1848 also serves as a measure of the Romanians' integration into Europe.

The Revolution of 1848 in the Romanian principalities was primarily the work of liberal intellectuals. It was they who initiated it, defined its goals, and gave it direction. The generation of 1848 was set apart from its predecessors especially by its firsthand acquaintance with Western Europe. The majority had gone to France to complete their studies, and a few, like Mihail Kogălniceanu had taken their degrees at a German university. In any case, their spiritual second home was Paris, and they felt themselves to be a part of Europe. They recognized the West as a political and cultural model for their own part of Europe and had few doubts that its pattern of development was applicable to the principalities.

Their ideas about political forms and economic progress thus owed much to the liberalism of the day. They were attracted to liberal ideas, in part, because they judged them to be the most far-sighted and creative of the period in that portion of Europe – the West – which they had adopted as their model. They were eager to place themselves at the head of a movement for beneficial, forward-looking change like those figures in France and other Western countries whom they admired and wished to emulate. At a more practical and immediate level the triumph of liberal ideas promised them freedom from foreign domination by offering them, the elites, and, in time, all Romanians, the right to determine their own destiny. Liberal ideas were attractive to them as advocates of individual freedom and constitutional government precisely because these principles called into question the legitimacy of the surrounding conservative empires, which they perceived as the prime obstacles to national self-determination.

Despite their admiration for the West, the Forty-Eighters, as we may call them, were not social engineers who were intent on imposing institutions that had little relation to their people's historical experience. On the contrary, they were keenly aware of conditions at home and were highly selective in their application of Western theory and practice. But the striking contrasts between home and the West made them impatient to begin the work of reform and make up for lost time. A typical statement of the high principles that guided them and a revealing insight into their notion of how society (and nations) could be changed for the better was the draft of a constitution for Wallachia drawn up in 1838 by Ion Câmpineanu (1798–1863), head of Partida Naţională (the National Party) between 1835 and 1840 and a minister in the Wallachian provisional government in 1848. He set down in the first article the general principle that Wallachia was a land of liberty for all who lived there, and in the second article he declared all Wallachians equal before the law, all eligible to hold civil and military office, and all subject to taxation. He then proclaimed guarantees of individual liberty, specifying that no one could be prosecuted or arrested except as determined by law. Other provisions limited the powers of the sovereign to legislate, reserving this prime political function to a general assembly, which alone could levy new taxes and approve the annual budget. Câmpineanu was thus engaged in laying the foundations of an ideal form of government and in the process betrayed his own belief that good ideas and good institutions could transform society and lead to the emergence of a just a prosperous commonwealth. The fervent idealism he expressed caught perfectly the mood of the times.

The aspirations of the generation of 1848 reflected the deep dissatisfaction all classes felt with existing political and economic conditions. Many boiers objected to the authoritarian ways of the princes and sought a greater share of power for themselves, while others advocated moderate reforms in agriculture and public administration; the growing middle class resented the high taxes it paid to the state and its continued exclusion from political power; and the peasants were desperate to escape mounting labor services and dues owed landlords.

Events in Western Europe – the overthrow of King Louis-Philippe of France in February 1848 and the rapid spread of revolution to Vienna, Buda-Pest, and German cities – roused Romanian intellectuals to action. Students in Paris reacted immediately to events and hastened home to Iaşi and Bucharest to support and, in some cases, lead movements for liberal political and social change. In Iaşi at the beginning of April, boiers and members of the urban classes drew up a statement of grievances which called for the installation of a moderate liberal political system and measures to stimulate economic development. But they had no thought of overturning existing political and social structures, that is, of acting like revolutionaries. In any case, their experiment was of short duration. Prince Mihai Sturdza met their demands with force, and after brief clashes many leading reformers were forced into exile.

In Wallachia, the reformers were more revolutionary. Liberal, Western-educated boiers led the assault on the old regime, and in March C. A. Rosetti, a radical liberal, and Ion Ghica, a moderate, helped form a revolutionary committee to organize an armed uprising. Nicolae Bălcescu (1819–52), the revolutionary spirit among Romanian students in Paris, joined the committee in April. On June 21 at Islaz, on the Danube, they put their plan into operation with the issuance of a proclamation setting forth their goals. It represented the culmination of two ideas which had gained wide currency among the educated since the second half of the eighteenth century: that membership in the Romanian nation depended

8 The 1848 generation in Wallachia

upon ethnicity, not social rank, and that the principality of
Wallachia was entitled by international treaty to exercise internal
sovereignty and be independent of foreign domination. The committee declared its intention to respect all existing treaties with the
Ottoman Empire, but it could not conceal its hostility to Russia
and demanded an end to the regime instituted by the Organic
Statutes. It then enumerated the principles it intended to follow

in setting the country on a new course, echoing Ion Câmpineanu's draft constitution: equality of rights for all citizens, an equitable sharing of public burdens through a progressive income tax, broad participation in public life through an expanded franchise, freedom of the press, speech, and assembly, the abolition of forced labor services by peasants with an indemnity to landowners, an expanded school system and equal and free instruction for everyone in accordance with his intellectual abilities, an end to all ranks and titles of nobility, and the election of the prince from any category of the population for a five-year term.

The proclamation of Islaz was a characteristic program of the European liberal intellectuals of 1848, with its emphasis on individual liberties, its faith in good institutions, and its provision for an increased role for the citizenry in public affairs. But these were not simply borrowings by the Romanians from Western European experience. The evolution of the principles which the revolutionary committee expressed so forcefully may be traced back through the memoranda of the reforming boiers, the proclamations of Tudor Vladimirescu, the plans of the circle around *Dacia Literară*, and the aspirations of liberal boiers of the 1840s.

The main theater of action was Bucharest, where on June 26 the Forty-Eighters replaced Prince Gheorghe Bibescu with a provisional government, composed mainly of young liberal intellectuals. The new government undertook at once to introduce reforms and create new institutions. One of its first acts was to provide for its own defense by forming an army. It also set about the delicate task of agrarian reform, but because liberals and conservatives were deeply divided over the measures to be taken and because all sides feared that rapid changes in existing conditions on the land would bring economic catastrophe to the country nothing substantial was accomplished. It was no more successful in other attempts to carry out the promises it had made at Islaz. It judged the elaboration of a fundamental law an essential first step and made plans for the election of a constituent assembly to draft a constitution to replace the Organic Statutes. But foreign intervention cut short the life of the provisional government.

Its differences with Russia were fundamental and, in the end, proved irreconcilable. The Tsar had already revealed his determination to maintain the protectorate over the principalities by sending his army across the Prut on July 7 to occupy Moldavia. He also intended to suppress the revolution in Wallachia, but preferred to do so in alliance with Ottoman authorities in order to avoid international complications. In its own defense, the provisional government sought to parry the danger from the east by seeking support from France and Britain, but to no avail.

Cooperation between the Russian and Ottoman governments meant the end of the provisional government's hopes of survival by playing one enemy off against the other. With the Tsar's approval an Ottoman army moved into Wallachia in September. It met fierce resistance when it entered Bucharest on the 25th, but its superior numbers prevailed, and members of the provisional government and many supporters fled into exile. When Ottoman authorities seemed to slacken in their pursuit of revolutionaries, the Tsar ordered his army to occupy Wallachia on September 27.

In the Habsburg Monarchy, too, Romanian intellectuals responded immediately and enthusiastically to events in Western and Central Europe in the spring of 1848. As the old order collapsed they were stirred to action by expectations of achieving long-sought national goals. They were liberals, but they saw in civil liberties and representative institutions, first of all, guarantees of national political autonomy. Their aspirations and successes varied from province to province: in Transylvania these aspirations ran counter to the efforts of Hungarian leaders to bring about the union of Transylvania with Hungary; in the Banat and the adjoining area of Crişana, or Bihor, antagonism between Romanians and Hungarians proved less acute, but Romanians stoutly opposed Serbian domination of the Orthodox Church and its schools; and in Bukovina Romanian leaders attempted to preserve the historical ethnic character of the province, but were unable to rally the Orthodox Church or the mass of the population to their cause.

The Romanian Revolution of 1848 in Transylvania was, as in the principalities, a revolution of the intellectuals. It was they who formulated its goals and devised a strategy to achieve them. Their objectives were grounded in the world of ideas specific to the evolution of Romanian society in Transylvania, and thus they gave priority to national emancipation. But they were also idealists. They believed wholeheartedly in human progress, in the unlimited ability of men to improve their condition through the reform of their institutions. Like their counterparts elsewhere in Europe, they professed faith in the swift and glorious transformation of society. But, as events were to show, they misjudged the rhythm of change in history and thus they foresaw the death of the old regime before its time had come.

Romanian leaders found themselves in a quandary. On the one hand, they had welcomed the political reforms and civil rights which Hungarian liberals in Hungary advocated and promised to extend to Transylvania, but, on the other hand, they wanted to ensure the existence and progress of their own nation. The immediate focus of their concern was the union of Transylvania with Hungary as demanded by Hungarian liberals in both Transylvania and Hungary. Some Romanians, notably George Bariţiu (1812–93), the editor of *Gazeta de Transilvania* (The gazette of Transylvania), since 1838 the main voice of Romanian intellectuals, were willing to accept the union in return for political and civil rights and guarantees for the Romanian language and culture. Simion Bărnuţiu (1808–64), a lawyer and a staunch defender of Romanian national rights, took a decidedly different view of events. He made the preservation of Romanian nationality the paramount issue of the day, and he warned his compatriots against accepting the union until they had ensured their full rights as a nation. He rejected Hungarian promises of universal suffrage and other freedoms because the price would be the renunciation of nationality. He pointed out that these benefits were offered to the Romanians only as individual citizens of Greater Hungary, not as a corporate entity, a nation, with its own destiny to fulfill. Thus, he concluded, liberty had no meaning unless it was national, and only in an autonomous Transylvania, where they formed a majority of the population, could the Romanians hope to preserve their most precious possession – their nationality.

All parties among the Romanians succeeded in reaching agreement on general principles and a program of action, which they presented to a national assembly held at Blaj on May 15 and attended by some 40,000 persons. At the head of their program was a declaration of the independence of the Romanian nation and of its equality with the other nations of Transylvania and a promise to defend its newly acquired rights by establishing a political system based on the liberal principles of the time.

Romanian opposition to the union of Transylvania with Hungary proved unsuccessful. On May 30 the Diet of Cluj, which was dominated by Hungarians, overwhelmingly voted for union. From this time on relations between Romanian leaders and Hungarian authorities steadily deteriorated. By fall, Bărnuţiu, Bariţiu, and their supporters had sided with the Court of Vienna to oppose Hungarian national claims. The Romanians thus found themselves in the incongruous position of supporting the conservative reaction led by the Habsburg court against fellow liberals, the Hungarians, because of the clash of national aspirations.

Romanians elsewhere in the Habsburg Monarchy had also mobilized to defend their interests, and by the end of 1848 they had joined with the Romanians in Transylvania to seek the support of the Court of Vienna for their program. Delegations from all three provinces – Transylvania, the Banat, and Bukovina – gathered in Olműtz, in Bohemia, where the Court had established itself after a revolutionary outbreak in Vienna. Under the leadership of Bishop Andrei Şaguna, head of the Orthodox Church in Transylvania, they presented a new national program to the Emperor Francis Joseph on February 25, 1849, in which they called for the political union and autonomy of all the Romanians of the Monarchy in a "duchy" of their own. Never before had the Romanians expressed so clearly their ideal of ethnic solidarity within the Monarchy. They also signaled their conviction that federalism was the solution to the Monarchy's nationality problems.

The Romanians failed to achieve their objectives either in Olműtz or at home. The Court of Vienna implicitly rejected their proposal for union and autonomy in the new imperial constitution which it promulgated on March 4; it re-established the historical Crown lands and made no mention of federalism, let alone rights for the separate nationalities. Then, in April, it admonished the Romanians directly to remain loyal to the Emperor as the only course that could ensure their future well-being.

Between April and July 1849 Nicolae Bălcescu, in a desperate move to save the liberal and national revolution in Central Europe, tried to bring about a reconciliation between the now independent Hungarian government in Buda-Pest and the Romanians in Transylvania. He met with Lajos Kossuth, who was the leader of independent Hungary, and with Avram Iancu, who commanded a Romanian military force in Transylvania, and was encouraged by the willingness of both sides to come to an understanding. But events on the battlefield overtook him. In the middle of August Austrian and Russian armies forced the main Hungarian field army to surrender, and by the end of the month all organized resistance to the Habsburg restoration had ceased.

The suppression of independent Hungary dashed Romanian hopes of a united, autonomous duchy. The fragile alliance of necessity between the Romanians and the Court of Vienna, already strained by the former's aspirations to self-determination, on the one side, and by the imperial revival, on the other, disintegrated. In Transylvania, a host of Austrian officials descended upon the principality with instructions to restore it to the status of an imperial province subject to Vienna as quickly as possible. The Banat and Bukovina underwent a similar process. Everywhere the new bureaucracy expected the Romanians to resume their places as loyal, and anonymous, subjects of the emperor.

THE UNION OF THE PRINCIPALITIES, 1850–1859

A restoration of sorts also took place east and south of the Carpathians. The Convention of Balta Liman of May 1, 1849 between Russia and the Ottoman Empire established a joint protectorate over the Romanian principalities, with Russia as the senior partner. The two powers chose new princes – Barbu Ştirbei in Wallachia and Grigore Ghica in Moldavia – and closely monitored their activities to ensure that liberalism and nationalism made no recovery. Ştirbei was the more conservative of the two and aspired to rule as an absolute, if enlightened, monarch. Ghica was more sympathetic to the moderate liberal agenda of 1848 and allowed a number of Forty-Eighters to return from exile and even brought some of them into his government. Both princes promoted economic development and education and were far from being docile instruments of Russian and Ottoman policy.

A new international crisis, which led to war between Russia and the Ottoman Empire in 1853 and the involvement of France and Britain a year later, brought the union and independence of the principalities nearer to fulfillment than the Forty-Eighters could have imagined. Although the powers intended to settle the issues raised by the Crimean War in their own interests, now for the first time in a modern international negotiation the Romanians themselves played a significant role in determining their future.

The Treaty of Paris of March 30, 1856, which the three victorious allies imposed on Russia at the end of the war, decisively affected the political fortunes of the principalities. Although they remained under Ottoman suzerainty, they benefited from the collective oversight of the powers, who forbade any single power to interfere in their internal affairs. All the signatories, including the Ottoman Empire, recognized the administrative independence of the principalities, the right of each to maintain a national army, to legislate, and to engage freely in commerce with other countries. The powers created a special commission of inquiry to go to Bucharest to gather information and draw up recommendations on the future form of government of the principalities. In a striking departure from their usual treatment of the principalities the powers allowed the election of a special advisory assembly, a so-called *adunare ad-hoc* (ad hoc assembly), in each principality, which was to inform the commission about public opinion on all the important issues before it. All the information thus gathered was to be presented to a conference of the powers in Paris, where final decisions would be made and communicated to the principalities in the form of a decree promulgated by the Sultan.

Fateful for the future course of Romanian–Russian relations was the article in the Treaty of Paris by which Russia ceded three southern districts of Bessarabia to Moldavia. The area in question amounted to only 5,000 square kilometers and was of modest economic importance. But now Russia no longer bordered the Danube, and, most serious of all, the Tsar felt the loss of this territory as a personal affront and was committed to recovering it.

Russia's cession of southern Bessarabia to Moldavia added to the existing strains in Russo-Romanian relations. Although the protectorate of the 1830s and 1840s and role in the suppression of liberal movements in 1848 were the most immediate causes of animosity toward Russia, neither Moldavians nor Wallachians had reconciled themselves to the annexation of Bessarabia in 1812. Boiers

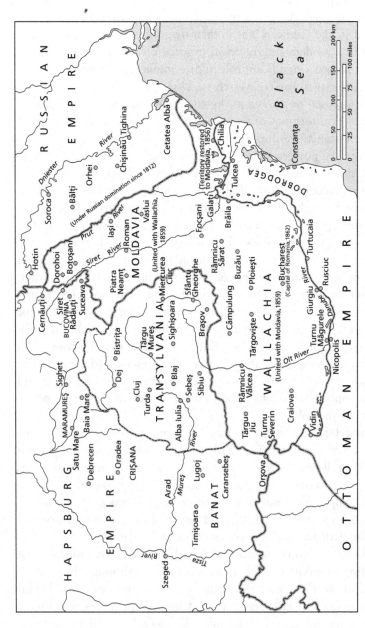

Map 5 Romania and Transylvania after 1856

and intellectuals were painfully aware of the relentless Russification
to which an authoritarian, centralizing regime had subjected the
Orthodox Church, education, and cultural life, but they had no
means of reversing the integration of the province into the Russian
Empire.

The decisions reached at Paris spurred the activities of those who
demanded the union of the principalities. In Iaşi and Bucharest they
feverishly organized their supporters in anticipation of the elections to the *adunări ad-hoc*. They were heartened by the return of
many Forty-Eighters from exile, notably the liberal radicals C. A.
Rosetti and Ion C. Brătianu. Despite the hostility of Austria and the
Ottoman Empire and the obstructionist tactics of the *caimacami*,
temporary regents who had replaced princes Ştirbei and Ghica, the
unionists won the elections to the *adunări ad-hoc* in both principalities. The two assemblies met in October 1857 and immediately
passed resolutions calling for union and autonomy and a collective
guarantee of the new order by the powers. Large majorities in both
assemblies took a liberal stand on such matters as fundamental
civil rights and government reform, but they showed little inclination to engage in social experiments such as agrarian reform. The
Wallachian assembly finished its work on December 22, 1857, the
Moldavian on January 2, 1858.

The focus of attention now shifted to Paris. On April 7, 1858 the
commission of inquiry, as instructed, issued its report to the powers on the wishes of the Romanians as expressed in the *adunări
ad-hoc*. After lengthy debate the powers signed the Convention
of Paris on August 19, whose main purpose was to endow the
principalities with a definitive political organization. Although the
powers stopped short of granting union to the principalities and
left them under Ottoman suzerainty, they agreed that the United
Principalities of Moldavia and Wallachia, as they were now called,
should henceforth administer themselves freely and without interference from the Ottoman government. They had still to pay the
tribute, and the princes had still to be invested by the sultan, but all
the parties to the agreement knew that these obligations were now
mere formalities. Yet the Convention was much more than a treaty
regulating the international status of the principalities. In setting
forth the fundamental rights of citizens and the qualifications and

duties of political leaders, it took on the attributes of a constitution, and those who drafted it were clearly sympathetic to the
liberal ideas they had encountered in Bucharest. Thus it provided
for: a legislative assembly for each principality elected for a seven-
year term, and a Central Commission meeting periodically at
Focşani, on the Moldavian–Wallachian border, to consider laws
of common concern; a prince for each principality, to be elected
by the assembly for life; a council of ministers responsible to the
assembly; separate national armies, but with a single commander-
in-chief appointed alternately by the two princes; the irremovabil-
ity of judges and their independence of the executive power; and
a common Court of Cassation at Focşani. The Convention also
abolished the boier ranks and privileges and proclaimed equality before the law and the principle of public office open to every
citizen on the basis of merit. But it set such high property qualifications for voting that the number of electors was limited to
a few thousand persons, mainly large landowners and the upper
middle class. The restricted franchise was contradictory, for it was
certain to impede the passage of liberal political and economic
reforms, particularly a new law governing landlord–peasant relations, which the Convention itself had recommended as urgent.
Finally, the powers placed the government of each principality in
the hands of a provisional commission of three *caimacami* until
the election of the princes.

The main function of the provisional commissions was to oversee the election of new legislative assemblies, which, in turn, were
to choose the princes. A spirited electoral campaign in Moldavia
resulted in an assembly favorable to union. There were many candidates for prince, but the liberals ultimately carried the day by
securing the election of a Forty-Eighter, Alexandru Cuza, a sup-
porter of union, on January 17, 1859. In Wallachia the assembly
was dominated by conservatives, but they were deeply divided
among themselves. When it became apparent that no faction could
elect its own candidate, the deputies decided to proclaim their support for union by electing Alexandru Cuza as prince. The vote for
him on February 5 was unanimous. The Romanians, then, by themselves had achieved *de facto* union by adhering to the letter of the
Convention of Paris.

THE REIGN OF ALEXANDRU CUZA, 1859–1866

The new prince of the United Principalities was descended from a family of service nobles, who had held important positions in the central and district administration of Moldavia since the seventeenth century, but were not among the great boier families. Alexandru Cuza was born on March 20, 1820 and like many boys of his class had received his schooling at a French boarding school in Iaşi and then had been sent to Paris for further study. At home he took part in the reform movement in Iaşi in 1848 and was briefly exiled. In the 1850s he occupied various administrative posts and rose steadily in rank in the army. At the time of his election as prince he was commander of the Moldavian militia. He undoubtedly owed his election to his long patriotic service, his consistent unionist position, and his liberal, though not radical, political and social ideas.

The powers duly reassembled in Paris to consider the new turn of events. Although Austria and the Ottoman Empire raised objections, the powers as a whole were little inclined to reopen the "Romanian question" and voted on September 7, 1859 to accept the double election of Alexandru Cuza. In effect, they recognized that the momentum toward the union of Moldavia and Wallachia was irreversible.

Final recognition of the union of the principalities required further negotiations between the Ottoman Empire and the powers. But the course of events in the principalities themselves made the outcome all but certain as institutions and public services in the two countries merged. Their armies had, in effect, already been unified under a single command. Now the currency, the telegraph lines, and the customs services were fused into one. Officials in the two capitals maintained contact with one another directly without going through their respective foreign ministers, and the Central Commission at Focşani worked feverishly to unify laws and administrative procedures.

Formal recognition of the union by the powers was not long in coming. At the Conference of Constantinople they persuaded the Sultan to issue a *firman* (decree) to that effect on December 4, 1861. Alexandru Cuza moved swiftly to take advantage of the favorable moment, on the 23rd proclaiming the union completed. The final act in the creation of the new unified state was the law of February

9 Prince Alexandru Cuza

21, 1862, which abolished the Central Commission at Focşani. The
name "Romania," which had been frequently, if unofficially, used
in the 1850s to refer to a unified state between the Black Sea and
the Carpathians, now became the common name for the United

Principalities and beginning in 1862 it was used in the country's official acts.

During the critical period before and after the administrative union of the principalities a modern political system gradually took form. The institutions of a national state were created, replacing the superstructure founded upon a monopoly of power by a single class, the boiers. Political parties, then in process of formation, became indispensable machinery for the functioning of these institutions, and the free flow of ideas served as a powerful catalyst of change. Political thought, previously repressed or censored, rose to the surface of public life in all its vitality as individuals and groups vigorously expressed their preferences. The clash of ideas, in turn, encouraged the like-minded to unite to defend high principles and achieve more worldly social and economic goals. Their conviction that success would depend upon consistency of thought and unity of purpose led eventually to the formation of political parties and the emergence of the party system.

The two main political tendencies of Cuza's reign were, broadly speaking, liberalism and conservatism. The former represented a synthesis of the ideas of the reforming boiers during the period of the Organic Statutes, the ideology of 1848, and the more radical aspirations of the later 1850s. The majority of liberal leaders had striven for reform in 1848 and accepted social and economic change as being in the natural order of things. Conservatism, on the other hand, was the heir to the traditions and privileges of the pre-1848 era. Its representatives were anxious to preserve existing social and economic structures and to restrict the franchise and reserve public office to the propertied classes. Moderate and radical liberals generally looked to Western Europe to provide a model for political and economic progress, while conservatives tended to be wary of that model and insisted that development be compatible, first of all, with the historical character and immediate needs of Romanian society.

After the administrative union of the principalities in 1862 a division of forces within liberalism occurred. It was deeper in Wallachia than in Moldavia. In Wallachia a radical group, dubbed "the reds" by their opponents, broke away from the moderates. They had been the most revolutionary of the Forty-Eighters and the most committed of the unionists and were led by C. A. Rosetti and Ion C. Brătianu, and they were well organized. They had a central club or committee in Bucharest, which served as the headquarters for a network of similar clubs in cities and towns throughout Wallachia, and they used their newspaper *Românul* (The Romanian) to spread their ideas and maintain party discipline. They introduced a number of innovations into Romanian politics by mobilizing the masses in the cities as a means of overcoming the political advantages of wealthy conservatives. Large public gatherings and street demonstrations were among their favorite weapons, which, moreover, became a regular feature of election campaigns. Moderate liberals, who were especially strong in Moldavia, also stood for political and economic reform, but they drew back from the rapid pace of change promoted by the radicals. Their leading figure was Mihail Kogălniceanu, whose ideas and personality ensured cohesion for Moldavian liberalism during its formative period.

Relations between Cuza and the legislative assembly were tense almost from the beginning of the new national administration. The causes were complex, partly ideological, involving differing agendas for reform, and partly political, arising from Cuza's determination to lead and unwillingness to tolerate obstruction of his projects.

Cuza had much in common with the liberals. Like them, he was intent on bringing about fundamental changes in the social, economic, and political organization of the country. He was closer to the moderates on political reform and somewhat more radical than they when it came to social innovation. Nevertheless, he preferred to work with the moderates rather than the radicals, and in the early years of his reign he hoped to create a strong center party with which to push his program quickly through the legislature. He was suspicious of the radicals because of their past secret revolutionary activity and their avowed intention to democratize the political system by, among other means, diminishing the powers of the prince. In particular, he objected to their efforts to arouse the masses, the kind of ferment he thought harmful to a new state that was undergoing a thorough transformation and was continually threatened by foreign intervention.

As time passed, Cuza became frustrated at the assembly's stubborn opposition to his program, particularly electoral reform and a new agrarian law, which he thought essential if the country was to join the ranks of modern states. Matters came to a head in the spring of 1864. Disenchanted by the course parliamentary government had taken, he dissolved the assembly on May 14, 1864.

To consolidate his authority Cuza promulgated a new electoral law and constitution (*Statut*). Despite liberal provisions in both, they were not primarily liberal documents. Although the electoral law increased the number of voters, the system of electoral colleges and the indirect election of deputies it endorsed continued to dilute the voting strength of the majority, particularly the peasants. The new law was not a profession of faith by Cuza in the democratic process. It was, rather, an attempt to reconcile the democratic spirit, representing his ideal, with an authoritarian executive power, a concession on his part to the demands of practical politics. The *Statut* also reflected Cuza's disenchantment with representative assemblies and thus brought about a fundamental change in the relationship between the executive and legislative branches of government. The new constitution made the legislature subordinate to the prince, for it granted him such far-reaching powers as the sole right to initiate legislation and an absolute veto over bills passed by the assembly.

Cuza's coup of May 14 cleared the way for him to move swiftly in carrying out his economic and social program. The centerpiece was the so-called rural law of August 26, 1864, which instituted an extensive redistribution of land. It recognized the full property rights of dependent peasants to the land they already possessed in accordance with previous laws, which had made allotments on the basis of the productive capacity of the individual peasant household. The law limited the amount of land available to peasants to two-thirds of the landlord's estate. But forests, which were essential for the economic well-being of many households, did not enter into these calculations. The law also abolished for all time compulsory labor services and the tithe and other dues which the peasants had owed the landlord for centuries. But the peasants had to assume the largest share of the compensation payments due landlords.

Of the immediate consequences of the rural law, the most obvious was the granting of 1,801,311 hectares of land to 463,554 peasant families, or roughly an average of 4 hectares per family.

Some 60,000 of these families, however, received only enough for a house and garden. Although a substantial amount of land thus changed hands, large landholding had by no means disappeared. After the reform landlords together with the state still held about 70 percent of the arable land and pastures, while peasant property made up the rest.

Cuza was eager to develop other branches of the economy besides agriculture, but he lacked the necessary financial resources, since the bulk of state revenues continued to come from taxes that fell heaviest on those classes least able to pay. Thus forced to turn to foreign loans, he was quickly disabused of the notion that the Western powers, who had placed Romania under their collective protection, would feel obligated to provide financial aid. When he granted an Anglo-French consortium the concession to establish Banca României (The Bank of Romania) in 1865, he was certain that it would funnel large amounts of capital into the country. But he was to be sorely disappointed.

Cuza drew up ambitious plans to endow the new state with modern institutions. He gave particular attention to the judicial system, which he was eager to reorganize in accordance with the needs of a modern European state. Notable was the promulgation of a new civil code in 1864, which assured the individual of personal freedoms, guaranteed the equality of all citizens before the law, and safeguarded private property. In order to create an informed and productive citizenry he proposed to bring education within the reach of all classes and to make certain that it satisfied the genuine needs of Romanian society. To that end he promulgated the comprehensive education law of 1864, which regulated instruction at all levels and gave special attention to primary education, establishing the principle that it be free and compulsory.

Manifest in all Cuza's legislation was the tendency of the central government to increase its control over all institutions, old and new. Laws concerning the Orthodox Church are a striking example. From the beginning of his reign Cuza had shown himself to be a zealous partisan of the secular state. He was determined to bring the Orthodox Church fully under the supervision of the state in all but strictly religious matters, a goal he in large measure accomplished. In particular, a series of laws severely curtailed the role of the church in civil affairs and enhanced the state's oversight of its administrative system. From an economic standpoint the most important of Cuza's church laws had to do with the secularization of monastery lands, which represented roughly a quarter of the country's territory. The law, which was enacted in 1863, brought extensive agricultural lands under the control of the state and thus ended the substantial role that monasteries had played in the economic life of the country since the Middle Ages.

Despite Cuza's success in carrying out his ambitious reforms and institution-building and his tight control of the government bureaucracy, his position was gradually undermined. His enemies on both the right and the left came together in a "monstrous coalition" composed of such otherwise incompatible elements as conservatives and radical liberals. The conservatives condemned him as being too liberal and could not forgive him for his agrarian and electoral reforms; the radicals abandoned him because he was not liberal enough. Both groups were put on guard by his cavalier treatment of the legislature, that is, themselves. They could thus put aside their differences for the moment in order to remove Cuza from the throne and replace him with a foreign prince. Isolated politically and ill, Cuza himself was contemplating abdication, as he intimated in his message to the assembly in December 1865. All these signs of weakness encouraged the plotters to proceed.

Led by the radical liberals with Ion C. Brătianu and C. A. Rosetti at their head, Cuza's opponents decided to carry out their coup swiftly in order to avoid public disorder and the foreign intervention that had previously accompanied internal troubles. They won over key elements of the army, who arrested Cuza on the night of February 23, 1866. The prince offered no resistance and signed the abdication papers immediately. Shortly afterward he was allowed to leave the country for Austria, where he lived until his death in 1873. His departure into exile symbolized the end of an era, which had had its origins in the eighteenth century with enlightened princes and the reforming boiers. It just as dramatically marked the beginning of another era, which was to last until the Second World War.

4

The national state, 1866–1919

The year 1866 marks a significant date in the political fortunes
of modern Romania. By this time its institutional structures were
largely in place and its mental climate clarified. The union of
Moldavia and Wallachia was accomplished, and the independence of the United Principalities was all but assured. The political foundations of "Romania," as the Romanians now called their
country, had been laid: a constitution adopted in 1866 would serve
as the fundamental law, with occasional modifications down to
1923; a new dynasty, a branch of the Hohenzollerns, ascended
the princely throne in the same year and enhanced the prospects
for political stability; administrative principles – a strong executive and a centralized bureaucracy – had been codified; and the
dominant philosophies of the age – liberalism and conservatism –
found expression in new political parties in process of formation.
By this time, too, the country's political and intellectual elites had
embraced the idea of nation as a moral compass, and they welcomed the duty it laid upon them to redraw the country's political
boundaries in accordance with ethnic patterns. By the mid 1860s,
contacts with Western Europe had become customary and were
viewed as crucial to national progress. The West, or "Europe" as
many Romanians continued to call it, presented the elites with a
permanent model of development, to be followed or rejected as
they saw fit, but never to be ignored.

INDEPENDENCE, 1866–1881

Those liberals and conservatives who overthrew Alexandru Cuza lost no time in installing a provisional government and filling the vacancy on the throne. The majority of them favored a foreign prince as the most effective way of diminishing internal rivalries for power and thus of ensuring political and social stability. They finally offered the throne to Karl of Hohenzollern-Sigmaringen (1839–1914), who accepted it and reached Bucharest on May 7, 1866.

The new prince, who belonged to the Catholic branch of the family that ruled Prussia, had but a modest acquaintance with the country he had been invited to rule, and it was only by trial and error that he was to learn the fine points of Romanian politics. A measure of his success was the longevity of his reign and his key role in public affairs. From the very beginning he made foreign and military affairs his special province and in time, as his acquaintance with issues matured, he became a decisive force in internal political life as well. The great powers accepted the Romanian fait accompli, as they had done with the overthrow of Cuza. The Sultan also recognized Karl (now Carol) as hereditary prince in October 1866, but he clung to the fanciful notion that the United Principalities would remain an integral part of the Ottoman Empire.

In the meantime, a Constituent Assembly adopted the draft of a new constitution on July 11, and Carol promulgated it the following day. It was the work of those who had overthrown Cuza. Although the conservatives, representing mainly the large land-owners, had won most of the battles in the Constituent Assembly, the Constitution of 1866 was essentially a liberal document. It limited the powers of the prince to those of a constitutional monarch, provided for representative government, made ministers responsible for their acts, and reinforced the principle of the separation of powers. It also set down at length the rights and liberties of the citizenry, who were henceforth guaranteed equality before the law, complete freedom of conscience, of the press, and of public meetings, the right of association, and the protection of one's domicile and person against arbitrary search and arrest. The exercise of these rights, despite occasional infringements by government officials, over time brought somewhat larger numbers of people into the political process and by assuring a free exchange of ideas, especially through the press, contributed greatly to the formation of a democratic public opinion. The constitution also guaranteed property owners full rights of possession, declaring property to be sacred and inviolable and promising that the only cause of expropriation would be the general welfare. The main purpose of these stipulations was to protect the great estates against further agrarian reforms, but article 20 made clear that the land given to the peasants by the rural law of 1864 must never be touched.

Immediately evident in the parliamentary system instituted in 1866 was the enhanced position of the legislature. Composed of two houses, a Chamber of Deputies and a Senate, it became almost an equal partner with the prince in making laws, and it gained the right to question ministers about policies and abuses of power and even to subject them to parliamentary investigations. The constitution also limited the prince's authority: he could exercise only those powers expressly granted to him, and, thus, rule by decree, as practiced by Cuza, was no longer possible. Yet his powers were considerable, and if he were skillful and determined, he could manipulate the political machinery to his advantage. He retained a decisive role in the legislative process, as he could submit his own bills to parliament and he could veto bills, action which could not be overridden by the legislature.

The Constitution of 1866 thus resembled in many respects liberal fundamental laws in place in Western Europe. The similarity between them was one of the main consequences of that opening of the West to Romanians, which had begun in the 1830s and 1840s. The main source from which authors of the Constitution drew was the Belgian Constitution of 1831, both in form and in substance. Yet it was by no means a simple imitation of others, since those who drafted it took account of specifically Romanian conditions when dealing with such matters as property, education, and local government.

A fundamental question arises: was the Constitution of 1866 suited to the social realities of the principalities? At first glance, it would seem not to be, for it was in essence a middle-class document prepared for a country whose middle class formed only a thin layer of the population. At the top of the social scale remained the boiers, who were intent on maintaining their political and economic predominance. At the other end of the scale was a peasantry who composed over 80 percent of the population and had had few opportunities to gain any political experience. A broad, enlightened public opinion and an experienced citizenry capable of making the sophisticated political system operate as its authors intended were for the time being largely absent. As a result, the real world did not always accord with the written text, and high principle was often compromised in order to maintain the structures (and the fictions) of constitutionalism.

The formation of the two large, dominant political parties in the decade after the adoption of the Constitution of 1866 largely completed the political superstructure of the pre-World War era. With the National Liberal Party and the Conservative Party in place, the parliamentary system came fully into being.

The authors of the Constitution and the founders of political parties gave no notice specifically to women. That women should play an active role in the new political system as a distinct social group or could even have issues of their own requiring political debate, let alone legislative action, struck the majority of political leaders as highly novel ideas. Thus the Constitution of 1866 and subsequent parliamentary acts left women in a juridical status that could be traced back to the law codes of Matei Basarab and Vasile Lupu in the middle of the seventeenth century. They stipulated the legal dependence of the wife on the husband in all matters, making her position essentially that of a minor. Thus, down to the First World War, in accordance with the Civil Code of 1866, women could not be a party to any legal arrangement without the consent of her husband or a judge and could not freely dispose of their inheritance or other wealth acquired during marriage. Discrimination in public employment was widespread. Certain professions were closed even to women with university degrees, and those with legal training were not allowed to plead cases in court on the grounds that they did not enjoy political rights. Women were, indeed, deprived of political rights, and the general mood of the time made any significant change unlikely. When several members of the Chamber of Deputies, including C. A. Rosetti, during the debate on the revision of the Constitution in 1884 proposed that married women who met the financial requirements for the ballot be allowed to vote directly for candidates, the response from many colleagues was laughter.

Another category of society also had formidable obstacles to overcome in order to gain civil rights. Gypsies had been slaves since their arrival in the Romanian principalities from south of the Danube in the fourteenth century. They were subject to various labor services and payments, depending upon whether their masters were princes, boiers, or clergy and whether they themselves were settled or nomadic. Even though they contributed much to the economies of the principalities through their labor in agriculture and as craftsmen, they occupied the margins of Romanian society, since their style of life was fundamentally different. Support for their emancipation came from many sides, especially liberals. Mihail Kogălniceanu wrote *Esquisse sur l'histoire, les moeurs et la language des Cigains* (1837) in order to acquaint the political and cultural elites with their condition and spur reform, and Ion Câmpineanu freed his own slaves. Through the efforts of reformers the Gypsies achieved full emancipation in Moldavia in 1855 and in Wallachia in 1856. In the half-century down to the First World War some of the 200,000 to 250,000 Gypsies settled on land the state made available to them or moved to cities, while many continued their nomadic way of life. In any case, the great majority remained outsiders.

In foreign policy, both Liberals and Conservatives realized that Romania could not achieve independence or become a regional power if it stood alone. The Liberals, at first, preferred to work with neighboring peoples in Southeastern Europe rather than be dependent upon the great powers, who, they rightly supposed, cared only about achieving their own aims in the region. But the Conservatives, who were in power between 1871 and 1875, thought it wiser to secure a reliable patron from among the great powers.

International complications precipitated by uprisings in Bosnia and Herzegovina against Ottoman rule in the summer of 1875 showed the wisdom of such an approach. While the crisis offered Romanian leaders the opportunity to bring their struggle for independence to a successful conclusion, efforts on their own in the spring and summer of 1876 to accelerate matters by threatening dire consequences unless the Ottoman government immediately recognized Romania's independence failed because they lacked great-power support. A new government headed by the Liberal leader,

Ion C. Brătianu, returned to a stance of neutrality, but aligned its policies with those of Austria-Hungary and Russia.

As relations between Russia and the Ottoman Empire deteriorated in the latter part of 1876, the Romanian government decided that an understanding with Russia was imperative. In the ensuing negotiations, Prince Carol and Brătianu insisted on a general treaty not only covering military questions but also recognizing Romania's independence and guaranteeing her territorial integrity. But the Tsar and his ministers were interested only in a limited understanding that would allow Russian armies to cross Romanian territory to reach the Danube and would avoid political commitments. As war between Russia and the Ottoman Empire became imminent the two sides composed their differences. On April 16, 1877, Romania granted the Russian army the right of transit across its territory, but obliged the new partner to respect the country's "political rights" and "existing integrity." The Romanian parliament ratified the agreement and declared war on the Ottoman Empire. The Liberal majority and public opinion demanded an immediate declaration of independence. In response, Mihail Kogălniceanu, the foreign minister, declared that the ratification of the convention with Russia had dissolved all existing links to the Ottoman Empire, and on May 21 parliament made the break formal by proclaiming the country's "absolute independence."

Relations between Romania and Russia during military operations against Ottoman armies south of the Danube were continually strained. Carol wanted the Romanian army to participate fully in the campaign, thereby securing for the country the status of a co-belligerent and recognition of its independence. But the Tsar and his military commanders professed to have no need of Romanian military assistance and did not modify their stand until August 1877, when Ottoman armies stopped the Russian advance at Plevna, in northern Bulgaria. The Tsar and Russian commanders appealed for Romanian troops and accepted Carol's conditions that his army have its own base of operations and separate command. In the ensuing fighting and siege of Plevna from September to December, the Romanian army contributed decisively to the defeat of Ottoman forces, which opened the way for the rapid advance of Russian troops southward toward Constantinople and an end to hostilities.

Russia's manner of making peace brought relations with Romania to the breaking point. The Ottoman government accepted Russian terms for an armistice on January 31, 1878, but Romanian representatives were not invited to take part in the negotiations. The Russian side followed the same procedure in drawing up the Treaty of San Stefano of March 3, which compounded the dismay and bitterness in Bucharest. To be sure, the treaty recognized the independence of Romania, but it also required the return of southern Bessarabia to Russia. Even though Russia offered Dobrudja and the Danube delta as compensation, Prince Carol and Brătianu accused Russian officials of breaking pledges to respect the territorial integrity of their country. The Russians replied simply that the guarantee had been directed against the Ottoman Empire and argued, disingenuously, that, in any case, the southern districts of Bessarabia had been ceded to Moldavia, not Romania, in 1856. Not surprisingly, Romania joined the major European powers in demanding a revision of the treaty.

At the Congress of Berlin, which opened on June 13, 1878, the Western powers forced a revision of the Treaty of San Stefano in order to diminish Russia's influence in Southeastern Europe, but they left intact the provisions relating to Romania. Thus the final treaty, signed on July 13, recognized the independence of Romania, but set two conditions: it must eliminate the religious restrictions on the exercise of civil and political rights contained in article 7 of the Constitution of 1866, a matter primarily of concern to Jews, and it must accept the "return" of southern Bessarabia to Russia. As compensation, they granted Romania the Danube delta and Dobrudja as far as a line drawn from east of Silistria on the Danube to south of Mangalia on the Black Sea.

The negotiations over Romania's independence at the Congress of Berlin brought to the fore the situation of the Jews. The steady growth of the Jewish population of Moldavia and Wallachia mainly through immigration from Austrian Galicia and the Russian Empire beginning in the 1830s reached 133,000, or roughly 3.6 percent of the country's population of 3,725,000. From the beginning the Romanians in general treated them as foreigners, but in 1848 and during the reign of Alexandru Cuza liberals made attempts to grant them civil equality. They failed, mainly because the leading classes were intent on creating an independent nation-state that could only

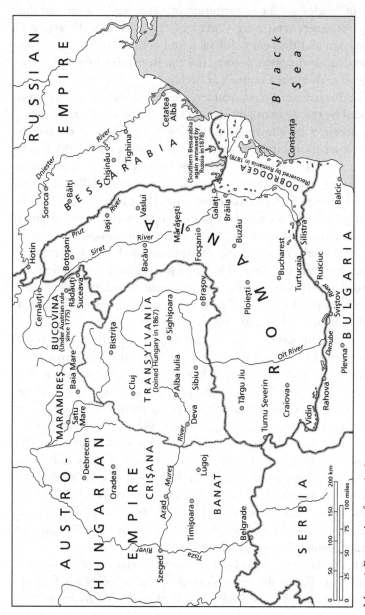

Map 6 Romania after 1878

be Romanian and Christian. This principle found forceful expression in article 7 of the Constitution of 1866, which stipulated that only foreigners who were Christians could acquire the status of Romanian and thus enjoy full civil and political rights. It was this issue that set the great powers and the Romanian Liberal government at odds at the Congress of Berlin.

The Romanian government eventually yielded to the pressure exerted by the Western powers. In October 1879 parliament modified article 7 by allowing any foreigner regardless of religion to become a citizen, but it did so grudgingly. Except for the 888 Jewish veterans of the War for Independence, who were granted citizenship as a group, naturalization was declared to be an individual matter. The person seeking citizenship would first have to reside in the country for ten years and show himself to be "useful" to the country, submit a formal application, and then await the passage of a special law by parliament approving the application. Under this cumbersome procedure only several hundred Jews became citizens down to 1919. The civil status of the rest remained technically unchanged, but they entered all areas of economic life and the professions, and, to this extent, they became a part of the larger society.

The most important result of the Congress of Berlin for Romania was clearly the recognition of independence. It finally severed the juridical link with the Ottoman Empire which had lasted some four centuries. Although Ottoman suzerainty had become largely nominal since 1829, its formal termination gave a powerful boost to national pride. In a practical way, independence allowed Romanian politicians and intellectuals to devote full attention to nation-building. Yet despite the enthusiasm of the moment, they remained realists. They understood that a small country in the pursuit of even modest foreign policy objectives and eager to create a modern national economy could ill afford to ignore the interests of the great powers. In any case, they reinforced independence and raised the country's prestige by proclaiming Romania a kingdom and Carol as king on March 26, 1881. The event seems to have taken the population of the country by surprise. The public celebrations in Bucharest following the proclamation reflected the organizing skill of local officials rather than the enthusiasm of the public as Carol remained for them a cold, distant figure. The great powers raised no serious objections.

MODELS OF DEVELOPMENT

The events of the preceding fifteen years had brought Romanian politicians, economists, and social thinkers face to face with all the problems of national development. The specific issues were many, but two strikingly different paths lay before them. One, the "Europeanist," drawing upon Western experience, would lead to industrialization and urbanization and would bring radical changes to every facet of Romanian society; the other, "traditionalist," based upon Romania's agricultural past, would require the preservation of social structures and cultural values as nurtured for centuries in the rural world. The ensuing national debate over identity and development was to last until the Second World War.

The first coherent criticism of the direction modern Romania had taken came from a group of young men in Iaşi who had studied at universities in Western Europe and were eager to raise Romanian intellectual and cultural life to a European level. They argued that after the Treaty of Adrianople in 1829, which had ended Ottoman control of their foreign trade, the Romanian principalities had embraced the European economic and cultural world too eagerly and had "opened their doors too widely" to innovations of all kinds. Young Westernizers of the 1848 generation, they complained, borrowed and imitated recklessly, ignoring long-established customs and experience. The inevitable result, so their indictment ran, was that contact with Europe had touched only the upper surface of Romanian society, while the great bulk of the population remained beholden to the past. Such ideas lay at the heart of traditionalist currents of thought about development for almost three-quarters of a century. But these early critics were not, in fact, traditionalists. Rather, they had been nourished on the very ideas that would bring Romanians into closer communion with Europe. Filled with optimism about the future of their country in the aftermath of the union of the principalities and imbued with confidence in their own ability to set it on a proper course, these young, Western-educated intellectuals formed a society in 1863 to propagate their ideas and turn public opinion in their favor. They called it "Junimea" (Youth).

The dominant figure of the society from its beginnings until its end at the turn of the century was the philosopher and literary critic

Titu Maiorescu (1840–1917), one of the stalwarts of Romanian conservatism. The influence of Junimea on Romanian cultural life owed much to his intellectual brilliance and his skills as an organizer and manager. He was seconded by other outstanding figures. Petre Carp (1837–1919), the descendant of an old Moldavian boier family, contributed substantially to the creation of the distinctive Junimea spirit, a mixture of critical intensity, erudition, and conviviality. Others who contributed to the influence of Junimea were the historian and economist Alexandru D. Xenopol and the materialist philosopher Vasile Conta. The great creators of modern Romanian literature in the second half of the century – the Romantic poet Mihai Eminescu, who brought Romanian poetic language to its height, the prose writer Ion Creangă, who revealed the true spirit of the village, and the dramatist Ion Luca Caragiale, who satirized the imperfections of a middle class still unsure of itself – drew inspiration from the intellectual and spiritual values promoted by Junimea.

It was, above all, Maiorescu who gave critical expression to the Junimists' reservations about the course modern Romania was following, reservations which he summed up in his famous dictum, "formă fără fond" (form without substance). He had discovered a fundamental incongruity between the institutions and the social structure of contemporary Romania. For him, there were only two classes in Romanian society – landowners and peasants; he denied the existence of a third class – the middle class. Yet it was also evident to him that prevailing cultural and political forms had been imported and simply placed on top of the ancestral customs and patriarchal spiritual life of the great mass of the population. These forms, he argued, introduced haphazardly, did not at all correspond to the prevailing social conditions in Romania; they were, rather, suited to those profound changes in the West that had brought the bourgeoisie to power. But, Maiorescu insisted, Romania had no bourgeoisie, and that was why, he complained, Romanian institutions, especially the constitutional system, all designed for a bourgeoisie, could hardly function effectively in a largely rural society

The second generation of Junimists expanded upon Maiorescu's doctrine of "form without substance" and brought it closer to other indigenist currents. Characteristic of their thought were the ideas of Constantin Rădulescu-Motru (1868–1957), a student of

Maiorescu's and a professor of philosophy and psychology at the University of Bucharest after 1904. Like many Romanian intellectuals of the time he was preoccupied with the identity and future of the Romanian nation. He wrestled with the complexities of the issue in a small book, *Cultura română și politicianismul* (Romanian culture and politics for its own sake; 1904), where he drew a sharp distinction between a civilization and a culture. Deeply influenced by German philosophical and sociological thought, he expanded upon Maiorescu's ideas about the uniqueness of the Romanians' evolution by focusing on the village. It was here in this world of the "organic forms of social life" and of "natural links" between the members of the community, in this culture, rather than in the cold, mechanical relationships of the city, in the civilization that was "Europe," that he was certain the Romanians could be themselves and prosper. It was an idea that many intellectuals embraced in the decades to come.

Certain agrarian currents that rose to prominence toward the end of the century shared the ideas of Rădulescu-Motru and other Junimists about how societies developed and how change should occur within them. The most dynamic of these currents was Sămănătorism (Sowerism), animated by the contributors to a weekly cultural review, *Sămănătorul* (The sower), which began publication in Bucharest in 1901. Like the Junimists, they held that Romania had been diverted onto a false path of Western capitalism and bourgeois liberalism that was wholly unsuited to its character.

The chief theorist of Sămănătorism was the historian and polymath Nicolae Iorga (1871–1940). He had already achieved prominence in Romanian cultural life as professor of history at the University of Bucharest at the age of twenty-four and as a skilled polemicist in cultural matters. At the heart of his theory of social development lay his belief that change, to be beneficial, must be gradual, evolutionary. His extensive studies of world history had persuaded him that mankind, and especially ethnic nations, had followed an essentially organic development. As a result, he insisted, any break with tradition could only be at a nation's peril, since every people could only pursue a course of development determined by the "national spirit," which had formed gradually over many centuries. Under no circumstances, he argued, could a people abandon its heritage by imitating foreign models or by indulging in abstract social experiments.

Iorga was unrestrained in his sympathy for the peasant because he was convinced that the village was the place where the laws of social change operated in their purest form. For him, the village was the preserver of a way of life built up over the centuries where organic structures were "fully respected." He admired the village especially as the locus of high moral values, and he drew a sharp distinction between it and the modern industrial city, where, he warned, impersonal mechanical relationships created a sterile environment.

The city, then, was for Iorga, a symbol of everything that had gone wrong in the evolution of nineteenth-century Romania. He identified it as the place where capitalist industry flourished and where a new economic and social order was growing that undermined the moral foundations of traditional society. The whole process, political as well as economic, by which modern Romania had come into being struck him as artificial, an "exercise in ideology" imposed arbitrarily upon a people who until then had followed a natural, organic evolution. Completely odious, in his eyes, had been the attempt of the generation of 1848 to integrate Romania into the general currents of European civilization, an act that could only compromise the morals of a patriarchal society. He was even harder on those who had fashioned the Constitution of 1866. He called it a calamity and the work of ideologues following abstract notions of state-building, which had nothing to do with the previous course of Romanian political development.

Yet despite his admiration for the rural world and his hostility to the new social and economic forms, he was resigned to the impossibility of returning to some earlier age. In a public lecture in 1907 on the relationship of the village to the city, he accepted the latter as characteristic of the modern age and even admitted that it would eventually dominate the village. As a historian he could not but recognize the inevitability of change; all he asked was that the forms of social life inherited from the past be replaced with care by other forms that were neither false nor foreign.

Contemporary with Sămănătorism was Poporanism (Populism). Its advocates shared with the Sămănătorists certain assumptions about the inherent agrarian character of Romanian society, about the deviations that had occurred in their country's development in the nineteenth century, and about the need to return to the earlier sources of organic growth. But unlike the Sămănătorists, they were not satisfied merely to speculate on the relative merits of this or that civilization and to issue calls for a moral revival. Instead, they were committed to a far-reaching reform of agrarian structures and sought to achieve immediate political and economic goals.

The leading theorist of Poporanism was Constantin Stere (1865–1936), who had been born in Bessarabia and had been deeply influenced by Russian Populism. He devoted special attention to the peasantry and defined Poporanism as love for the people, as the defense of their interests, and as unremitting labor to raise them to a level of a conscious and independent social force. He (and the Poporanists in general) thought of development mainly in economic terms, unlike the Junimists and Sămănătorists, who accorded pride of place to ideas and culture. Underlying his theory, which he elaborated in his famous polemic with the socialists, *Social-democratism sau Poporanism?* (Social democracy or populism?), a series of articles he published in 1907 and 1908 in *Viaţa Românească* (Romanian life), the most prestigious cultural review of the period and a monthly he had helped found in 1906, was the rejection of the notion that every country was destined to follow the same path as Western Europe. He declared Romania to be a country of peasants, and he conceived of its economic and social future as being inextricably linked to small, self-sufficient peasant holdings.

On the left a different vision of Romania's future emerged. The leaders of the fledgling socialist movement were, in a sense, Europeanists, since they argued that Romania could never be isolated from the broader currents of European economic and social development. They were thus certain that industry, not agriculture, held the key to Romania's future.

The pre-eminent socialist theorist of Romania's development was Constantin Dobrogeanu-Gherea (1855–1920), who had been born in the Russian Empire and had settled in Romania in 1875. Like the Sămănătorists and Poporanists, he acknowledged Romania's economic backwardness, but he rejected their formulas for making the best of underdevelopment. Instead, he was intent on sweeping away the network of economic and social structures which stood in the way of the full flowering of Western-style liberal political institutions and capitalist economic forms. The existing structures he called "neoiobăgia" (neoserfdom), and in a work of that title in 1910, he investigated the unique features of Romania's social evolution in the nineteenth century and identified the main obstacles to the country's future progress.

As a Marxist, Gherea felt a special obligation to show why Romania was not destined to remain forever agricultural, and he was at some pains to justify the need for industry and a proletariat. He by no means denied the importance of agriculture or minimized the gravity of the agrarian problem, but he had no doubt that the future of Romania, that is, its ability to overcome economic underdevelopment, would depend primarily on industrialization. For Romania, he warned, it was a question of "to be or not to be."

Romanian economists, unlike the philosophers of culture, approached the problems of development in a pragmatic way, and they armed themselves with statistics and the evidence gleaned from their experience in the field. The relative merits of agriculture and industry lay at the core of their ideas about economic progress. A national economy based on a strong agriculture had many passionate advocates, such as Ion Strat (1836–79), a professor at the University of Bucharest, who was certain that Romania was destined for the foreseeable future to remain an agricultural country. A convinced free-trader, he thought that economic activity was governed by natural forces such as population and climate, and should, therefore, be free of all constraints, including those imposed by the state. For the same reasons he opposed forced industrialization sponsored by the state. For the time being he saw no possibility of industry developing in Romania because the conditions which he deemed essential were totally lacking.

Equally forceful and influential were the proponents of industrialization. Petre S. Aurelian (1833–1909), an agronomist by training and a leading figure in the Liberal Party, was typical. He likened international economic competition to a war, in which the great industrial powers were on one side and the agrarian countries on the other. The only salvation for the latter in this unequal contest, as he saw it, lay in industrialization. He warned his fellow countrymen that Romania could defend her independence only by following the same path of development as the West – industrialization and its complement, urbanization.

This debate among economists and philosophers of culture was by no means merely an academic exercise. The polemics moved from the realm of theory to practical application when political parties adopted the arguments of one side or the other. Agrarian economic interests and traditional social values were reflected in the policies of Conservative governments, while the Liberal Party, representing the rising middle class, pressed forward with the building of a national economy inspired by the Western model. But the key matters at issue were not easily resolved; they continued to generate controversy well into the twentieth century.

THE ART OF POLITICS

The political structure of the Romanian kingdom between 1881 and 1914 remained essentially that of the principality, as the Constitution of 1866 continued to provide the general framework for political activity. The engines that drove the complex machinery of government were political parties. There were two of consequence – the Conservative and the Liberal. In general, the Conservatives represented the interests of the large landowners, and the Liberals those of the growing urban commercial and industrial middle class. The great landlords (and those who leased their estates, the *arendaşi*) favored free trade, as advocated by the Conservatives, because it would enable them to export their grain and animals more easily, while the middle class, represented by the Liberals, saw its interests best served by protective tariffs for fledgling industries. Yet the boundaries between the two classes were far from rigid. The bourgeoisie, especially those merchants and bankers who left their commercial and financial occupations and bought land, often adopted the outlook of the old conservatives, while those among the latter who had sold or lost their estates tended to join the ranks of the urban middle class as they invested in commerce or industry or assumed positions in the bureaucracy.

Politics was dominated by the upper classes, while the largest segments of the population were practically excluded from the political process and thus exerted little direct influence on the course of events. The peasants, for the most part, continued to be merely onlookers. Their voting strength was diluted by high income qualifications for the ballot, and despite several bold attempts, a strong peasant party failed to emerge before the First World War. The urban working class was also underrepresented, but politically it was somewhat better off than the peasantry. After a period of crisis, a viable Social Democratic Party was formed in 1910 and promised a sturdy defense of workers' economic and political interests. But a small constituency prevented the socialists from mounting a serious challenge to the major parties, and on the eve of the war, they had no deputies in parliament.

The king played a key role in determining the outcome of elections through his constitutional authority to appoint the incoming prime minister. By the final decades of the century procedures for changing governments had been perfected. The process began with the resignation of the sitting government, consultations between the king and leading politicians, and the selection of one among the latter to form a new government. The first task of the newly designated prime minister after he had chosen his cabinet was to organize elections for a new Chamber and Senate. That responsibility belonged chiefly to the minister of the interior, who mobilized the prefects of the counties (*judeţe*) and other officials to make certain that the opposition would be overwhelmed in the coming elections. Between 1881 and 1914, as the result of their zeal, no government designated by the king was ever disappointed at the polls. The "rotation" of parties was also the rule during this period. It became customary for the king to alternate the Liberals and the Conservatives in office as a means of resolving serious economic and political problems and of maintaining his own political power by balancing one party off against the other and requiring them to compete for his favor. Yet the political system offered substantial protection of the civil liberties of individual citizens, and constitutional guarantees of freedom of association and of assembly were respected, as was the widest possible freedom of the press.

The Liberals dominated political life for an unprecedented ten years after the War for Independence, from 1878 to 1888. The prime minister and the foremost politician of this era was Ion C. Brătianu (1821–91). Possessed of enormous political experience dating back to 1848, he had managed with great skill the complex problems arising out of the struggle for independence and the proclamation

10 Prince Ferdinand, King Carol I, Prince Carol, *c.* 1900

of the kingdom. He had thus made himself indispensable to both the king and his party. But he became increasingly authoritarian in his dual capacity as prime minister and party head. He had little to fear from the members of his own party or the opposition because he enjoyed the full confidence of King Carol. A congenial working relationship developed between them based on similar ideas about major issues of domestic and foreign policy. Brătianu accepted Carol's pro-German orientation in international relations and the reorganization of the army on the Prussian model, while Carol allowed his prime minister a relatively free hand in carrying out his domestic agenda as long as he respected the prerogatives of the Crown. Yet Brătianu's relationship with the King was never one of friendship. Carol judged his prime ministers solely on the basis of their usefulness.

The Brătianu government initiated major political and economic policies which moved the country closer to modern forms. The revision of the Constitution in 1884, which fostered middle-class democracy by enabling a few more citizens to vote, also hastened the reorganization of local government in favor of the ministries in Bucharest fostered and, in general, promoted the centralization of public administration. A protectionist trade policy and state support of industry laid the foundations of a diversified national economy.

Several Conservative governments followed the Liberals between 1888 and 1895. They focused particularly on economic development, generally in accordance with their customary agricultural interests. A noteworthy exception was the law on mines of 1895, sponsored by Petre Carp. His purpose was to develop the petroleum resources of the country as rapidly as possible by encouraging foreign investment. It was Carp's way of adapting the Romanian economy to the needs and opportunities presented by Western Europe without seriously altering social and political structures at home.

After 1895 until the First World War Liberal and Conservative governments followed one another in easy rotation. Among the notable accomplishments of the Liberals were the measures taken by the minister of education, Spiru Haret (1851–1912), to improve the situation of the peasantry through laws establishing local credit banks (*băncile populare*) in 1903 and allowing peasants to form village cooperatives (*obşti săteşti*) in 1904. His actions were a reflection of the deep involvement of rural schoolteachers in efforts at agrarian reform. On the Conservative side the legislation enacted by the government of Petre Carp between 1910 and 1912 took on a number of the country's major economic and social problems. In sponsoring laws to encourage industry and expand the government's role in the economy, especially in support of agriculture, Carp violated Conservative principles in order to enhance productivity and ensure social stability.

Third parties generally did not fare well under the prevailing system, dominated as it was by Liberals and Conservatives. Nonetheless, serious efforts to organize the peasants and the urban workers for political action took place in the final decade of the century.

The systematic political organization of the peasantry began with the efforts of Constantin Dobrescu-Argeş (1859–1903), a young teacher, to rouse the peasants to action. Supported by other teachers and well-to-do peasants in his native Argeş County and neighboring counties, he formed the Peasant Committee (Comitet Ţărănesc) in 1880, to promote economic development in the countryside and improve the working and living conditions of the peasants. In 1895, he established the Peasant Party (Partida Ţărănească), the first formal party in Romania devoted to peasant interests. It did not prosper, and, unsuccessful in the elections of 1899, it disbanded.

The most consistent champions of the peasantry in the decade before the First World War were rural schoolteachers. At the national teachers' congress in Bucharest in 1913, Ion Mihalache (1882–1963), an ardent advocate of peasant rights, was elected president of the National Association of Teachers. Critical of the agrarian policies of both the Liberals and Conservatives, he demanded reductions in the size of all large estates, the distribution of land to those who tilled it, and the extension of full political rights to the peasants as a class. To ensure the enactment of these reforms, he set about organizing a mass peasant party, but the outbreak of the First World War interrupted his work.

The urban working class entered organized political life with the founding of the Social Democratic Party of Workers of Romania (Partidul Social-Democrat al Muncitorilor din România) in 1893. Its emergence followed the growth of industry and the general evolution of economic and social conditions. But the party also owed much to the maturing of socialist thought and its application to Romania by a small number of committed intellectuals. In drawing up a program, the party's founders, adhering to Constantin Dobrogeanu-Gherea's adaptation of Marxist theory, accepted the crucial role of the proletariat in transforming Romanian society and urged that the industrialization of the country proceed as rapidly as possible. Their primary objective was to lay the "bourgeois-capitalist foundations" for the passage to socialism. They intended to hasten this process by raising the class-consciousness of the working masses and by democratizing political life. Yet their party remained small and its leadership divided. They themselves were middle-class intellectuals, not revolutionaries, and their program was in harmony with what younger, reform-minded Liberals stood for. When their party failed at the polls, they decided that their immediate objectives could best be served by supporting the Liberal Party. Thus, in 1899, most of them, the *generoşi* (generous), joined the Liberal Party in order to bring into being as quickly as possible a bourgeois-democratic political system and a capitalist economic order as a necessary stage in the building of socialism.

SOCIETY AND THE ECONOMY

The latter decades of the nineteenth century down to the outbreak of the First World War witnessed decisive advances in social and economic development. Population grew steadily and slowly became more urban, industrialization gained momentum, and the infrastructure of a modern economy began to fill out. Both the Liberal and Conservative parties encouraged private enterprise, but they also acknowledged the state as an entrepreneur and regulator with a crucial role to play in sustained economic growth. At the same time, many characteristics of an underdeveloped country persisted. Agriculture remained the foundation of the economy, and despite an increase in production and agrarian reform legislation, agriculture in 1914 remained essentially what it had been structurally about mid-century, and rural inhabitants generally did not share in the benefits of economic progress. Industrialization, though making impressive gains, was uneven, as key industries and a mutually beneficial relationship between them and agriculture were slow to develop. Romania's economic ties to Europe increased in complexity, but the relationship was not one of equals. Foreign markets for agricultural products, foreign suppliers of manufactured goods for both industry and the consumer market, and foreign capital became indispensable for Romania's economic health, thereby increasing her dependence on the great powers of Western Europe.

The population of Romania grew from 3,970,000 inhabitants in 1861 to 5,956,690 in 1899, when the last pre-war census was taken. The majority of people, approximately 82 percent in 1912, lived in the countryside, but the urban population was growing, largely due to migration from the countryside, particularly to those cities with the most dynamic economies – Bucharest, the leading industrial center with by far the largest urban population (276,178); the two great ports on the Danube, Galaţi (62,545) and Brăila (56,330); and Ploieşti (45,107), the center of the new oil industry.

Social structure at the turn of the century preserved the broad outlines evident in 1850, but significant changes, as the growth of cities suggests, were underway. Immediately striking was the formal disappearance of the old boier class. Alexandru Cuza's Statut of 1864 abolished all privileges of class and, by extension, eliminated the boier ranks, action confirmed by the Constitution of 1866. But this legislation was hardly revolutionary. It simply recognized a state of things that already existed, for the boier hierarchy had been steadily undermined by economic change and the rise of the new, enterprising middle class. Yet the large landowning class (*moşierime*) remained a powerful force in the countryside, and it retained a key place in the country's economy as a whole.

The peasantry not only formed the largest segment of the rural population, but also remained the most numerous class in Romanian society as a whole. It was far from homogeneous. At the bottom were those peasants who had no land at all and worked as hired hands, in 1913 about 14 percent of those active in agriculture. At the other end of the scale were well-off peasants, roughly 36,000 heads of family who possessed 10 to 50 hectares each, or roughly 18 percent of all peasant property, and who formed the core of the village middle class. In between stood the great majority of peasants, a large segment of whom, some 750,000, possessed less than 5 hectares, the minimum considered necessary to maintain a family of five, and who, consequently, lived a precarious existence.

Of great significance for the development of modern Romania was the rise of the modern middle class to economic and political prominence in the half-century before the First World War. Composed of merchants and industrialists, civil servants, and professionals, especially lawyers and teachers, it was primarily a Romanian bourgeoisie and thus largely replaced the foreign commercial and money-lending class of the eighteenth and early nineteenth century. Of particular importance was the creation of Banca Naţională a României (the National Bank of Romania) by the Brătianu government in 1880. It gave impetus to the development of the middle class, particularly its upper strata, by laying the foundation for the entire banking system, which Liberal financial circles used to gain a dominant position in the national economy. As banking, industry, and trade expanded, increasing numbers of white-collar workers and professional people joined the middle class. The civil service steadily contributed additional members as the central government and its branches in the counties assumed new responsibilities.

Wage laborers were also becoming a significant component of the urban population by the turn of the century. They were employed especially in food-processing and other consumer-oriented industries, coal-mining, oil production, and transportation, and by the outbreak of the First World War they numbered about 200,000, or 10 percent of the active population. This new urban working class had diverse origins. The majority came from the countryside, where overpopulation had become a critical economic and social problem. These newcomers found work in factories, transportation, and commerce, but almost always at the lowest level, as unskilled labor. They usually preserved their links to the village and continued to obtain·a part of their income from agriculture. Other workers came from the growing reservoir of artisans impoverished by the steady decline of the guild system, but whose skills were eagerly sought by industry.

From an ethnic and religious standpoint the population of Romania between the middle of the nineteenth century and 1914 was remarkably homogeneous. In 1899, out of a total population of 5,956,690, there were 5,489,296 Romanians, or 92.1 percent. By religion, the Orthodox constituted 91.5 percent, the overwhelming majority of whom were Romanian (there were small numbers of Greeks, Bulgarians, Russians, and Serbs). The only significant minority in Romania during the period were Jews. Their numbers grew continuously in the second half of the century, mainly because of immigration from Russia and the Habsburg Monarchy. In 1912, they numbered 240,000, or 3.3 percent of the population. Residing mainly in cities and towns, they constituted 14.6 percent of all urban dwellers. This concentration was especially striking in Moldavia, where Jews formed almost 32 percent of the urban population.

Agriculture continued to be the basis of the Romanian economy in the second half of the nineteenth century down to the First World War; as late as 1900 it accounted for two-thirds of the gross national product and supplied over three-quarters of the country's exports. Yet despite advances in industry and banking, the strengthening of the infrastructure, and an increase in agricultural production itself, no significant changes occurred in the organization of agriculture. The direct responsibility for production remained in the hands of peasants, who owned most of the animals and tools and followed traditional ways of working the land. Agrarian relations also changed but little. Despite several notable attempts at reform, the majority of peasants remained subject to the will of landlords or middlemen, the lease-holders (*arendaş*), and ultimately bore the chief burdens of taxation and economic crises.

The peasant became increasingly less able to control his own way of life, as agriculture took on a distinctly commercial character during this period and as the production of grain became ever more closely linked to the demands of the international market. The completion of the first railroad lines between 1869 and 1875 had decisively affected this trade, for they not only reduced the costs of transporting grain to the Danube ports, but also made possible its export overland directly to the industrial centers of Central Europe. No other branch of economic activity showed such rapid growth in so short a time as the export of grain. At the end of the century grain production accounted for nearly 85 percent of the total value of Romanian exports, and in the second decade of the twentieth century Romania ranked fourth in the world as an exporter of wheat and third as an exporter of corn. Not only was the great landowner inextricably linked to the international market, but, because of the peculiar organization of Romanian agriculture, the small peasant producer, too, was directly affected by fluctuations in world prices and demand.

Peasants, largely excluded from the political process, responded to the hard conditions they endured by the only means available to them – violence. Their massive uprising in 1907, which led to the death of nearly 1,000 peasants and the wholesale destruction of property, shook the conscience of the nation. Politicians on both the right and the left viewed the event as a national tragedy and demanded an end to what some condemned as a moral wrong and others saw as a barrier to economic progress.

Yet agrarian reform came slowly and piecemeal. In parliament, the Liberals were its most consistent champions, and in 1913 Ion I. C. (Ionel) Brătianu (1864–1927), president of the party and the son of Ion C. Brătianu, proposed a partial expropriation of private large estates in order to allot additional land to peasants. But Brătianu and his colleagues were mainly concerned with strengthening only a part of the peasantry, the successful smallholder, whom they considered a pillar of the existing economic and social order. The outbreak of the First World War halted consideration of agrarian reform.

The structure of industry underwent continuous, if uneven, changes during the period. The final disintegration of the old guild system occurred, as the undermining of the artisan craft industry ran its inexorable course in both the city and, even if more slowly, the countryside. The causes lay in the growth of large-scale processing and manufacturing at home and Romania's further integration into the Western European economic system, which opened the gates wide to foreign manufactured goods and capital. By 1914 Romanian industry as a whole had achieved notable progress, but serious gaps remained. Key elements of a modern industrial base, such as metallurgy and machine building, were still practically nonexistent, and industry remained closely linked to agriculture, as the processing of raw materials – foodstuffs, forestry products, and oil – predominated.

Foreign capital played a crucial role in the development of heavy industry and of the economy in general. It began to flow into Romania in substantial amounts after the War for Independence, and, besides industry, it was invested in banks, commerce, and insurance. In industry, by the First World War, foreign capital had become predominant in gas and electricity (95.5 percent), oil (94 percent), sugar (94 percent), and metallurgy (74 percent). Anglo-Dutch and Franco-Belgian capital together held about 57 percent of all the capital invested in industry, and foreign capital was a crucial presence in banking after 1880, as a national system of credit institutions became fully functional.

Industry benefited greatly from the patronage of the Liberal Party. Beginning in 1886, it put in place a consistent industrial policy based upon protective tariffs and direct state support for large and medium-sized enterprises. The long-term goal of these and similar measures was the creation of a modern capitalist industry patterned after that of Western Europe. But the Liberals insisted that control of the new national industry be in Romanian hands.

The transportation network was also expanded to accommodate the growing agricultural and industrial production. Railroad building began in 1865, and by 1914 some 3,500 kilometers of track were in operation. As in so many areas of economic development, the state assumed responsibility for the entire railroad system, which finally became a state monopoly in 1889. Railroads stimulated the economy by facilitating exports and imports. Between 1880 and 1914 the quantity of goods they carried tripled from 3 million to nearly 9 million tons a year. Railroads also contributed directly to the growth of industry, for they were the main consumers of domestic coal, accounting for almost 90 percent of annual production, and were the chief customers for locomotives, freight and passenger cars, and rails.

The structures thus in place by 1914 offered Romanian politicians, economists, and social theorists of the most diverse persuasions well-founded expectations of continued economic and social advances. The First World War was to subject them and their fellow countrymen to the supreme test of national endurance and cohesiveness, and, having passed it, the creation of Greater Romania in 1918 and 1919 reinforced their hopes of unprecedented growth and well-being.

ROMANTICISM AND REALITY

Literature offered yet another measure of modernization, of the degree to which Romanian society was becoming more European. In the latter half of the nineteenth century the literary language became more supple and expressive, as new genres, such as the novel, appeared, and new currents, notably realism and symbolism, gained ascendancy. Literary creativity, like political institutions and economic and financial activity, experienced synchronization with Western Europe, but Romanian writers by no means abandoned native sources of inspiration. Folk literature, especially poetry, was a constant leavening agent, but the steady progress of realism led both prose writers and poets to examine the village more critically than before and to turn to the city in search of new and more complex artistic challenges. Thus, paradoxically, the more closely Romanian writers entered into a communion with Europe the more deeply their art became rooted in the native experience.

A new type of national literature thus came into being paralleling the emergence of a new national state and a national economy. But as with models of political and economic development, opinions on what constituted the proper subject matter and form of literature were far from unanimous. Many writers and critics stood for traditional values. The Junimists, for example, led by Titu Maiorescu, advocated a literature based on native realities, but remained faithful to the principle of art for art's sake. By contrast, the Sămănătorists demanded an essentially social and didactic role for literature. They argued that prose and poetry could fulfill their proper functions only if they were national. They thus urged authors to draw inspiration from "native sources," by which they meant the peasant and the village, and they tended to exclude the city from consideration because its society was "mixed" and "un-Romanian." Not surprisingly, they recommended conventional forms and techniques in depicting the rural world.

Squarely on the side of modernism stood the literary critic and poet Ovid Densuşianu (1873–1938). He championed symbolism and was eager to shift the sources of poetic inspiration from the village to the city. As the theoretician of an urban verse, he intended to lead Romanian poetry out of the "melancholy and resignation" he found inherent in folklore toward the technology and dynamism of the modern world, which he associated with the city, the "center of intensive life."

Somewhere between the modernists and traditionalists stood Garabet Ibrăileanu (1871–1936), the co-founder with Constantin Stere of the monthly *Viaţa Românească* in 1906, a leading voice of enlightened social and cultural opinion. His approach to literature was that of the sociologist and philosopher of culture, as is evident in his most influential theoretical work *Spiritul critic în cultura românească* (The critical spirit in Romanian culture; 1909). Although he was a leading theorist of Populism, he denied that literature could be accommodated to ideology. Rejecting the Sămănătorist formula of an idealized rustic life, he demanded originality and realism in portraying the life of the peasant.

Down to the First World War four major literary currents manifested themselves: Romanticism, realism, symbolism, and the avant-garde. The creativity of poets and prose writers and the ways they approached the material and spiritual life of their time suggest how profoundly the mental climate and the sensibilities of educated Romanians were changing.

Romanticism in Romanian literature achieved its most perfect expression in the work of Mihai Eminescu (1850–89), who is universally acclaimed as Romania's greatest poet. He brought to Romanian poetry an exceptional appreciation of the native literary tradition and folklore, an exhaustive knowledge of the classics of Western literature and philosophy, and a command of language such as no Romanian poet before him had possessed. He belonged to the European Romantic movement. His poetry is suffused with Romantic images of nature, but the picture of it that he evokes is one of unusual freshness. The standard Romantic nature is indeed present – the lake or the endless expanse of the sea illuminated by the glow of the moon – but what Eminescu deeply felt was the forest, its cool depths, luxuriant vegetation, and bustle of animal life, an indigenous setting that harmonized with his passion for the folk ballad.

Eminescu shared with the Junimists an appreciation of German philosophy, especially Schopenhauer, and folk literature, and he also accepted their point of view on political and economic development. Like Titu Maiorescu, he opposed the liberal political system that had evolved after 1866, preferring instead the earlier "natural" or "organic" state. In article after article in *Timpul* (Time), the Conservative daily in Bucharest, he condemned the liberal state as a product of foreign capitalism and disavowed its parliamentary superstructure as unsuited to Romanian conditions, and he made Maiorescu's dictum about form and substance his own. He gave artistic expression to these ideas in his philosophical (and autobiographical) novel, *Geniu pustiu* (Forsaken genius; 1868–69). It is the confession of Toma Nour, a Byronic figure, who rejects contemporary Romanian society, which he classifies as a borrowed civilization, and yearns for a sweeping moral revolution.

It is as a great poet that Eminescu occupies his place in the Romanian national consciousness. In a sense, his poetry marked a crisis for Romanian sensibility, for when he turned into himself and

11 Mihai Eminescu as a young man

discovered the complexities of the inner life, his readers experienced
a depth of feeling that none of his predecessors had revealed. His
poem *Luceafărul* (1883), inspired by a Romanian folktale, was a
synthesis of all his lyrical gifts. The evening star was a symbol of
the conflict between man's aspiration to eternity and the ephemeral
nature of all worldly things.

    In the later decades of the nineteenth century, two writers – Ion
Creangă and Ion Luca Caragiale – anchored prose and drama
firmly to the realities of everyday life. Creangă treated the village
and the peasant as they were, not as ideology or the imagination
would have them be, and Caragiale added the city to the landscape
of Romanian prose and drama.

Ion Creangă (1839–89) approached the village and its inhabitants from the inside, unlike intellectuals who viewed the peasant from a cultural distance. He was too deeply a part of his own world to harbor illusions or indulge in sentimentality. His peasants are genuine, not the creations of traditionalist ideologues. The authenticity of his famous stories and of his *Amintiri din copilărie* (Memories of childhood; 1881–82) contrasted sharply with the often idealized and romantic characters and landscapes of other "rural writers." He was a true rural type without the romanticism of intellectuals like the Sămănătorists, who, nostalgically, sought a return to their origins or to enter a world they felt to be purer than the one in which they lived. There is none of this in Creangă. His occasional nostalgia, as in his memories of childhood, is personal, a journey back to his own early life, not to the world of another social class.

In the works of Ion Luca Caragiale (1852–1912) Romanian drama and narrative prose reached the same level of perfection as poetry had in the works of Eminescu. He shared with the Junimists their convictions about the misguided development of modern Romania. Like Maiorescu, he was struck by the incongruity between the showy surface of public life and institutions and the somber reality underneath. He never tired of depicting the contradictions between the Eastern substance of the "authentic" culture of the Romanians and the outward form of Western civilization which they were imitating. He found the most striking evidence of these contradictions in the city. In the same way that Creangă drew an aesthetic portrait of the village Caragiale introduced the spirit of the city into Romanian literature. His city is peopled by the petty bourgeoisie – functionaries and clerks, lawyers and teachers of modest standing, who had only recently acquired property and possessions. They formed a motley society, where the mores of an earlier time persisted. Caragiale seized upon the essential defects of this bourgeoisie in the making to interweave social observation with a comedy of character and situation and, occasionally, farce. His favorite targets were the inhabitants of Bucharest. Out of his depiction of their foibles in short stories and sketches, brought together under the title *Momente şi schiţe* (Moments and sketches), emerged a specific urban type. He was usually a petty functionary, and his invariable attributes were perpetual animation, cleverness, opposition to all and everything at the drop of a hat, a sugary vulgarity, and the relentless pursuit of small successes. But behind the façade of frivolity and coarseness Caragiale reveals a new society in process of formation, as in his plays, *O noapte furtunoasă* (A stormy night; 1879) and *Scrisoarea pierdută* (The lost letter; 1884).

The most dynamic and innovative current in poetry at the turn of the century was symbolism. It filtered into Romania from outside, and like Romanticism earlier, it was gradually assimilated to Romanian social reality and sensibilities. Alexandru Macedonski (1854–1920), whose poetry was sometimes soft and melancholy and other times jubilant and frenetic, was eager to introduce the new poetry. As he explained in his essay *Poesia viitorului* (The poetry of the future; 1892), true poetry was in essence the art of the word and thus its expressive power came from the quality of its sounds. Some of his thoughts were so new that at first they elicited only sarcasm from the majority of critics. Macedonski gave full expression to his new poetic sensibility in his volume *Excelsior* (1895), which was a milestone in the development of modern Romanian poetry.

Younger poets shared the symbolists' impatience with old artistic formulas, but to a far greater degree they were initiators of a radical modernism that aimed at nothing less than the destruction of existing poetic forms and language. Tristan Tzara (1896–1963) and Ion Vinea (1895–1964), eager promoters of symbolism in their "little magazine," *Simbolul* (The symbol; 1912), had already asserted leadership of the "avant-garde." Before Tzara achieved international fame as the founder of Dadaism he stood at the forefront of radicals who were bent on overthrowing the logical structures of poetry. In works he published before 1916, when he settled in Switzerland, he pushed the new techniques to the limit, creating a poetry of disjointed rhetoric and disassociated images.

These and other poets and novelists of the late nineteenth and early twentieth century were harbingers of things to come. Their innovations and masterpieces and, no less, their theoretical boldness inaugurated the modern European Romanian literature that was to reveal itself fully between the two World Wars.

THE ROMANIANS OF TRANSYLVANIA,
BUKOVINA, AND BESSARABIA

Many Romanians in the second half of the nineteenth century continued to live outside the borders of the United Principalities and the Romanian kingdom. As of 1900, there were approximately 2,785,000 in Hungary (the historical principality of Transylvania and the adjoining regions of the Banat, Crişana, and Maramureş), 230,000 in Bukovina, and 1,092,000 in Bessarabia. In some ways their course of development under Hungarian, Austrian, and Russian administration, respectively, was similar. They were unable to participate in political life as distinct ethnic communities, and their cultural life was under constant pressure from an unsympathetic government bureaucracy. Of the three communities, the Romanians of Transylvania put up the strongest defense of their national identity. They were conscious of their historical position in Transylvania and had behind them a long period of struggle. They also benefited from two vigorous national institutions – the Orthodox and Greek Catholic churches – and from increasingly close relations with politicians in the Romanian kingdom since the latter decades of the nineteenth century. The Romanians of Bukovina and Bessarabia were less fortunate. Cut off abruptly from their Moldavian homeland in 1774 and 1812, respectively, and subject almost at once to the centralizing ambitions of two absolutist empires, they suffered from the lack of strong native institutions and of a distinct political identity.

The leaders of the Romanians of Transylvania in the latter decades of the nineteenth century down to the First World War came from a small but growing middle class. They were mainly business and professional people, especially lawyers, who had gradually replaced the Orthodox and Greek Catholic clergies as national leaders as Romanian society itself became more secular. Their primary aim was political autonomy and later, after the turn of the century, self-determination. But they were also much concerned about economic questions. They were certain that unless they modernized their economy, the Romanians would be condemned to a condition of perpetual inferiority. They were just as certain that a viable economy could be organized only on an ethnic basis, and thus they sought to create a Romanian agriculture, a Romanian industry, and Romanian banks.

While recognizing the primacy of agriculture as an immediate fact of life, the majority of Romanian leaders were convinced that in the long run industrialization and urbanization were the keys to the progress of the Romanian nation. They perceived the root cause of Romanian economic backwardness to be the absence of industry in Romanian-inhabited areas and increasingly saw in industrialization the solution to the agrarian problem and the foundation of a strong national movement. For the time being they set modest goals. They decided to build on Romanian strengths and thus concentrated their resources on developing the artisan crafts. At the turn of the century, rejecting Sămănătorist ideas from Romania about the unfortunate social effects of capitalism and the city, they made the formation of a strong Romanian middle class, which they esteemed as the most dynamic class of modern society, and the Romanianization of Transylvanian cities their most urgent economic tasks.

Yet it was political struggle that mainly preoccupied them. They rejected the Compromise of 1867, which had brought Austria-Hungary into being as a partnership between the Austrian Germans and the Hungarians, primarily because it destroyed the separate political existence of Transylvania by joining it to Hungary. In this way, the Romanians ceased to be the majority population in the historical principality of Transylvania and became a minority in Greater Hungary. To direct their opposition to dualism and coordinate all their other political, economic, and cultural activities they established the Romanian National Party in 1881.

For a time the restoration of Transylvania's autonomy was their main goal, but by the 1890s their attitude had changed drastically. The legislation and administrative acts of successive Hungarian governments had gradually destroyed their hopes that cooperation between Hungarians and Romanians was any longer possible. A watershed in their relations came in 1879 when the Hungarian parliament passed a law which made the teaching of Hungarian obligatory in Romanian Orthodox and Greek Catholic church elementary schools. It was the first of a series of laws designed to bring the education of Romanians (and other nationalities) into harmony with the idea of Hungary as a Hungarian national state. It was followed in 1883 by a similar law affecting non-Hungarian-language middle schools and in 1891 by a law requiring the use of Hungarian in non-Hungarian-language kindergartens. The Hungarian parliament passed other laws designed to undermine the autonomy of the Romanian Orthodox and Greek Catholic churches, notably the law of 1893, which provided for the state payment of the salaries of teachers in Romanian church schools, and the law of 1899, which offered state supplements to the salaries of Romanian priests. The object of both was to extend the government's control over Romanian teachers and priests, whom it regarded as the chief fomenters of resistance to its assimilation policies. The Hungarian government also used its considerable administrative powers to curtail Romanian political activity, especially by dissolving the National Party in 1894. All these acts undermined expectations of an eventual Romanian–Hungarian understanding, and as a result, Romanian leaders sought solutions to national problems elsewhere.

A striking manifestation of a change in their political thinking was their abandonment of an autonomous Transylvania in favor of a new idea of nation, which Aurel C. Popovici (1863–1917), a young National Party activist, had elaborated in a series of writings published in the 1890s. He argued that the driving creative force in contemporary Europe was the idea of nationality, which he defined as the striving of every people to develop in accordance with its own distinctive character. He thought that once a nation had become conscious of itself, as the Romanians had, it took on all the attributes of a living organism and was thus endowed by nature with the inherent right of survival and freedom to develop. He was certain that neither government legislation nor political boundaries could prevent a people from achieving their highest aspirations. His theory found practical expression in the plan elaborated by leaders of the National Party for Romanian autonomy within the Habsburg Monarchy. Popovici himself expanded upon his theory by proposing the federalization of the Habsburg Monarchy in his influential book, *Die Vereinigten Staaten von Gross-Österreich* (1906).

Despite decades of suspicion and hostility, the National Party and the Hungarian government made efforts to reach an understanding during extended negotiations between 1910 and 1914. On the Hungarian side István Tisza, the head of the National Party of Work, and prime minister 1913–17, thought that the moment had come for a comprehensive settlement of the "Romanian question" (and the nationality problem in Hungary, in general). But his chief aim was to strengthen the Hungarian state, not to satisfy the minorities. He never wavered in his commitment to the idea of Hungary as a Hungarian national state and the maintenance of Hungarian political supremacy as the guarantee of the unity of the state.

The objectives of Romanian leaders were diametrically opposed to Tisza's ambitions. Their chief spokesman, Iuliu Maniu (1873–1953), aimed at national autonomy and urged the federalization of the Habsburg Monarchy as the best way to achieve it. But he went beyond questions of political organization to urge changes in the very political and social structure of Hungary. He thought, first of all, that the introduction of universal suffrage was essential. The right of all citizens to vote freely seemed to him the key to a solution of the nationality question in general because it would ensure each ethnic community's proportional representation in parliament and enable each to organize itself on an autonomous basis in those areas where it formed a majority of the population.

Not surprisingly, negotiations between Tisza and the National Party reached a final impasse in February 1914. They failed because both parties had become convinced that theirs was no ordinary political give-and-take but that national survival itself was at stake. Consequently, as Tisza and the Romanians pursued their own respective ideal of the national state, the middle ground between assimilation of the minorities and dissolution of historical Hungary gradually disappeared.

In Bukovina, which Austria had seized from Moldavia in 1774, the social structure and economic preoccupations of the Romanians were similar to those of the Romanians of Transylvania. Agriculture lay at the foundation of both. But Romanian artisan crafts, commerce, and banking showed comparatively little development, and the middle class and intellectuals were less cohesive than their counterparts in Transylvania. Political activity among the Romanians never achieved the same level of organization as in Transylvania. The Orthodox Church, which was raised to the rank of a Metropolitanate in 1873, made a significant contribution to

Romanian cultural life through its support of schools and its faculty of theology at the University of Cernăuți. But because of its multinational character (Romanian and Ruthenian), it could not serve the Romanian national cause as steadfastly as it did in Transylvania.

The defense of nationality was a major issue for Romanian leaders. By 1880 the Romanians were no longer the most numerous ethnic community, having been overtaken by the Ruthenians (240,000 to 190,000). Many accused the Austrian government of deliberately undermining the historical character of the province by encouraging the immigration of Ruthenians from Galicia and by favoring Germans in the civil service and Jews in the economy. But on the eve of the First World War there seem to have been few Romanian irredentists. Their absence must be attributed primarily to the relative efficiency and integrity of the bureaucracy, especially at elections, and to its recognition, however lukewarm and uneven, of the individuality and cultural aspirations of the various nationalities. Important also was the willingness of the latter, despite sharp differences among them, to compromise. This state of things contrasts sharply with the situation of the national minorities in Hungary during the same period.

Ever since the annexation of Bessarabia in 1812 Russia's intent had been to integrate that part of Moldavia between the Prut and Dniester rivers fully into the structures of the empire. As a consequence, the Romanian character of the province was steadily eroded. The population became increasingly mixed, especially in cities, as immigration by Russians, Ukrainians, and Jews from neighboring provinces grew. Whereas Moldavians had formed 86 percent of the population in 1817, by the end of the century, according to the Russian census of 1897, they represented no more than 56 percent. The majority of boiers, who could have provided leadership of the Moldavian community, were gradually assimilated to the Russian nobility. The Orthodox Church was subjected to relentless Russification and centralization as its activities and clergy came under the supervision of the Holy Synod of the Russian Orthodox Church in St. Petersburg. Romanian intellectual and cultural life stagnated as Russian became the language of instruction in state schools and Romanian ceased to be a subject of study and as publications in Romanian were reduced to a trickle and literary creativity practically ceased. Yet the native language and traditions survived at the village level, where the population was largely Moldavian, and in the parishes, where the clergy and faithful resisted or simply ignored instructions from St. Petersburg.

A small group of intellectuals, mainly university students, who had remained faithful to their native heritage, were roused to action when the tsarist system was shaken by revolution in 1905. Calling themselves national democrats, they demanded the recognition of the Moldavians as the predominant nationality and the granting of autonomy to Bessarabia in accordance with its "historical character." But they were too weak to sustain a movement for national rights against the conservative reaction that set in after 1906. Organized political activity ceased, and the national movement languished until 1917, because of the lack of money, institutional support, and a sufficient number of persons willing to make sacrifices for a cause that appeared all but hopeless.

INTERNATIONAL RELATIONS, 1881–1914

In the Romanian kingdom the War for Independence and the Congress of Berlin had impressed upon King Carol and politicians the hazards of conducting a foreign policy that lacked the patronage of one or more of the great powers. They were convinced that only adherence to an alliance system could further the country's international goals and ensure protection against hostile external forces. The creation of the Three Emperors' League (Germany, Russia, Austria-Hungary) in Berlin in 1881 much affected their calculations because it signaled an end to the relatively independent foreign policy they had been able to pursue since the reign of Alexandru Cuza. Now Austria-Hungary and Russia agreed to temper their rivalries in Southeastern Europe and to pursue policies in such a way as to avoid disturbing the status quo. Although Romanian officials did not know the exact provisions of the treaty, they realized that they could no longer take advantage of differences between the two neighboring, and unfriendly, empires and decided that the time for making binding commitments to one side or the other was thus at hand.

Carol and Prime Minister Brătianu examined various possibilities for the alliance they sought. They acknowledged France as the sentimental favorite of public opinion, but the disdainful attitude of the French government toward Romania at the Congress of Berlin and afterwards and French lack of interest in strengthening economic ties with Romania raised serious doubts about the level of support they could expect. An alliance with Russia was out of the question, since Romanian politicians, especially the Liberals, and the public generally thought of her as an enemy. It was the Triple Alliance of Germany, Austria-Hungary, and Italy that they found most appealing. The main attraction for them was, without question, Germany, whose economic vitality and military might they much admired.

Romania's adherence to the Triple Alliance took the form of a bilateral treaty with Austria-Hungary on October 30, 1883. The new allies agreed to come to the aid of the other if it was attacked by Russia, although the latter was not named, and they promised not to join any alliance directed against either of them. Germany adhered to the agreement on the same day by a separate act. Carol and Brătianu insisted that the arrangement be kept secret because they knew that it would raise a storm of protest among politicians and the public, who were for the most part pro-French. For good reason, then, the treaty was never submitted to parliament for discussion or ratification; the execution of its provisions depended mainly upon the King.

The alliance with the Central Powers formed the cornerstone of Romania's foreign policy for thirty years because Carol and the handful of Liberal and Conservative politicians who knew of the treaty judged the Central Powers to be the strongest military and economic force in Europe. But they followed closely any variations in the balance between competing alliance systems. They were especially sensitive to changes in the relationship between Germany and Austria-Hungary. With Germany they felt a close community of interests, and they were constantly troubled by the prospects of Austria-Hungary's taking over leadership of the Triple Alliance. Romanians also followed closely the evolution of the Franco-Russian alliance after 1891 and the rapprochement between Britain and France signaled by the Entente Cordiale of 1904.

As time passed numerous fissures opened in Romania's alliance with the Central Powers. The Romanian question in Hungary, in particular, became a matter of growing concern to all sides. The actions taken by the Hungarian government against Romanian politicians and the Orthodox and Greek Catholic churches and their schools in Transylvania in the 1890s even became the object of public disputes between Liberals and Conservatives in Bucharest, as each used the issue to gain political advantage over the other. Pleas from King Carol to Vienna and Berlin to exert pressure on the Hungarian government to make concessions to the Romanians were in vain, and Romanian public opinion grew increasingly hostile to Austria-Hungary.

The Balkan Wars provided the severest test of Romania's alliance with Austria-Hungary. The swift and decisive victory of Bulgaria and her allies over Turkey in the First Balkan War in 1912 caused deep misgivings in Bucharest because it threatened to upset the balance of power in the region. The Romanian government sought territorial compensation from Bulgaria, but received little support from Austria, whose own primary aim was to win Bulgaria over to the Triple Alliance as a counterweight to Serbia. When Bulgaria attacked its former allies, Serbia and Greece, in the summer of 1913 in a bitter dispute over the division of territory taken from Turkey, Romania declared war on Bulgaria in defiance of Austrian and German appeals for restraint. The Second Balkan War was brief and disastrous for Bulgaria, and by the Treaty of Bucharest of August 10, 1913, Bulgaria ceded southern Dobrudja to Romania. Romania thus emerged from the war with enhanced prestige as a guarantor of the balance of power in the Balkans and with a heightened sense of self-confidence. There can be little doubt that the Balkan crisis of 1912–13 completed the alienation of Romania from Austria-Hungary and the Triple Alliance.

A rapprochement between Romania and the Triple Entente (Great Britain, France, and Russia) was well underway by the spring of 1914. Relations between France and Romania warmed perceptibly, as French diplomats had given full support to Romania during the Second Balkan War. They coordinated their plans with Russia's assiduous courting of Romania under Foreign Minister Sergei Sazonov's direction. The visit of Tsar Nicholas II to Constanţa on June 14, 1914 marked the beginning of a new era in relations between the two countries. But Prime Minister

Ionel Brătianu refused to commit his country formally to the Triple Entente. He was indeed eager to continue the rapprochement with Russia, but he had no desire to increase tensions with Austria-Hungary and respected the military and economic power of Germany.

THE FIRST WORLD WAR

In the weeks following the assassination of Archduke Franz Ferdinand, the heir to the Austro-Hungarian throne, in Sarajevo on June 28, 1914 King Carol and Liberal and Conservative politicians watched the deteriorating international situation with increasing anxiety. They decided on a policy of neutrality at a meeting of the Crown Council on August 3. Presided over by the King and attended by members of the cabinet, former prime ministers, and the heads of major political parties, it weighed two choices. The first – the immediate entrance into the war on the side of the Central Powers – was championed by Carol, who expressed his certainty of a German victory and appealed to his listeners' sense of honor to uphold treaty commitments to Germany and Austria-Hungary. But he stood alone, except for Petre Carp, the Conservative leader, who dismissed the overwhelming public sentiment in favor of the Entente as irrelevant and expressed a lack of interest in the situation of the Romanians of Transylvania. But these were precisely the questions uppermost in the minds of everyone else. Confronted by the strong sentiment in favor of neutrality expressed by party leaders, who declared that they could not assume responsibility for a government which embarked upon war alongside the Central Powers, the King, emphasizing his role as a constitutional monarch, acquiesced in their decision.

When King Carol died on October 10, 1914, Brătianu took full charge of foreign policy. Although his sympathies lay with the Entente, neither he nor Carol's successor, his nephew, Ferdinand, had any intention of abandoning neutrality until the course of the war had become clear and they could be certain of achieving their national goals.

Brătianu carried on negotiations with the Entente intermittently during 1915 and the beginning of 1916. He made the stakes high for Romania's entrance into the war, and he was determined not to join the conflict prematurely. Foremost among his conditions was a written guarantee that Romania would receive Transylvania, Bukovina, and the Banat as a reward for services rendered. He was also acutely aware of his country's geographic isolation from the Western Allies and sought guarantees of a continuous flow of armaments and supplies, which could come only through Russia.

The Western Allies finally accepted Brătianu's conditions in July 1916. But even then, he did not make the decision for war lightly. Six more weeks of negotiations ensued before all the details of Romania's joining the Entente had been worked out. Russia, in particular, thought Brătianu's terms excessive, and the other Allies also were less interested in satisfying Romania's national aspirations than in using her army to open another battlefront against the Central Powers. France offered a formula that proved acceptable: Russia, which had taken the lead in negotiations with Brătianu, should grant, on paper, everything he demanded, even equality with the other Allies at the peace conference, but if at the end of the war all Romania's conditions could not be met, then the principal Allies would simply force Romania to accept less than what had been promised.

At last, on August 17, 1916 Brătianu and the diplomatic representatives of France, Britain, Russia, and Italy in Bucharest signed political and military conventions stipulating the conditions of Romania's entrance into the war. Of immediate importance were the provisions for an attack on Austria-Hungary to commence not later than August 28 and the recognition of the right of the Romanians of Austria-Hungary to self-determination and to union with the kingdom of Romania. The Romanian Crown Council formally approved the treaties and declared war on Austria-Hungary on August 27. On the following day, Germany declared war on Romania. Turkey followed suit on August 30 and Bulgaria on September 1.

Romanian military operations, which began on August 27–28 with a thrust into Transylvania, were at first successful, but the Romanian army was unable to sustain campaigns in both the north against German and Austro-Hungarian armies and in the south against a combined German and Bulgarian force. The decisive encounter took place in western Wallachia in November and early December 1916. Craiova fell on November 21 and Austrian and German forces drove

12 Ion I. C. Brătianu

eastward to the Argeş and Neajlov rivers, where between November 30 and December 3 they defeated the Romanian army and forced a general retreat. German troops entered Bucharest on December 6. The front finally stabilized in southern Moldavia along the Danube and Siret rivers on January 10, 1917.

Romania's losses in four months of war had been severe, as the army had suffered some 250,000 soldiers killed, wounded, and prisoners, or nearly one third the force mobilized in August 1916, and had lost considerable equipment: two-thirds of its rifles, half its machine guns, and a quarter of its cannon. Over half the country, home to its most important agricultural regions and industrial centers, was under enemy occupation.

One of Brătianu's first acts after the evacuation of the King and his government from Bucharest to Iaşi had been to form a government of national unity on December 24, 1916. Take Ionescu, a leading Conservative politician, and a number of other fellow Democratic Conservatives closed ranks with the Liberals, but the majority of Conservatives remained aloof. Fully aware of the low morale among the rank and file of the army and fearing widespread social unrest, Brătianu made agrarian and electoral reform the main domestic goals of the coalition government.

The Russian Revolution of March 1917 gave impetus to reform. The possible repercussions of events just across the border on Romanian soldiers and peasants caused genuine alarm in government circles. Many politicians feared that the revolutionary contagion would quickly spread to Moldavia. Under the pressure of these events the King issued a proclamation to his troops on April 5, 1917 promising them land and the right to vote as soon as the war had ended. His gesture was supported by both Liberals and Conservatives and seems to have had the desired effect on army morale.

War resumed in earnest on the Moldavian front in July 1917, when General Alexandru Averescu took the offensive near Mărăşti as part of a coordinated Allied effort on the Eastern and Western fronts to defeat the Central Powers. After several days of advances Averescu halted the operation, because of the worsening situation in Galicia and the breakdown of morale and discipline among Russian troops in Moldavia. Marshal August von Mackensen, commander of German and Austro-Hungarian forces, launched a powerful offensive of his own on August 6, whose goal was to deliver a knockout blow to Romanian and Russian armies and thereby force Romania from the war. The ferocious fighting reached a climax at Mărăşeşti on the 19th, when the Romanian army halted the enemy advance and brought the offensive to an end.

A new danger now arose. By the end of the summer of 1917 revolutionary events in Russia threatened to disrupt the battle front and undermine political and social stability in Moldavia. As more and more war-weary Russian soldiers were drawn to radical causes by promises of peace and social and economic justice, Brătianu and the King feared that such unrest might well envelop their own peasant soldiers. The Bolshevik Revolution in November deepened their sense of foreboding.

The volatile situation on the Moldavian front was further complicated by political events in Bessarabia, where the collapse of the tsarist regime had set Moldavians of all social classes in motion. Their representatives in an elected National Assembly (Sfat al Țării) proclaimed the establishment of a Moldavian Democratic Federated Republic on December 4, and to survive against Bolshevik forces the Assembly appealed to the Romanian government in Iași for aid. Brătianu responded with a division of troops, which drove the Bolsheviks out of Chișinău, the capital, on January 26, and, then, on March 27 the Moldavian majority in the Assembly voted for union with Romania.

The Romanian government could take little comfort in the impending acquisition of Bessarabia. On March 3, 1918 the new Bolshevik government in Petrograd signed the Peace of Brest-Litovsk with the Central Powers and left the war, thereby depriving Romania of Russian military support and cutting her supply lines to the West. Two months later, on May 7, the Romanian government, now headed by the pro-German Conservative Alexandru Marghiloman, signed the Treaty of Bucharest, which left Romania politically and economically dependent on the Central Powers.

Decisive events on far-off battlefields dramatically changed Romania's fortunes. On the Western front the Allies blunted the final German offensive in July 1918 and steadily advanced toward Germany, and in northern Italy they drove back Austro-Hungarian armies, all of which forced Austria-Hungary on November 3 and Germany on November 11 to agree to a cease-fire. The Marghiloman government fell, and on the 12th Ionel Brătianu returned as prime minister, determined to pursue his goal of a united Romanian national state and bring to a conclusion his efforts to enact agrarian and electoral reform. On November 10 King Ferdinand had already ordered his army to re-enter the war, and on December 1 he returned to Bucharest in triumph at the head of his troops.

Greater Romania came rapidly into being, but not without challenges. As the Austro-Hungarian Monarchy disintegrated the

Romanians in Bukovina on November 28 and in Transylvania on December 1 declared for union with the Romanian kingdom. Ten days later the National Assembly in Bessarabia announced its decision to do the same. At the Paris Peace Conference, which opened on January 18, 1919, Prime Minister Ionel Brătianu had as his primary goal to gain international recognition of his country's new boundaries by ensuring that it received all the territories the Allies had promised in the treaty of 1916 as well as Bessarabia. But the Allies' treatment of Romania at the conference came as a rude shock. The Big Four (Great Britain, France, the United States, and Italy), which together with Japan constituted the Supreme Council, reserved final decisions to themselves and declined to treat Romania as an equal in the task of peace-making.

Brătianu pressed Romania's case vigorously. For him, the most important territorial issue was Transylvania, and he was determined to push the new frontier with Hungary as far west as the Tisza River. In the process, he sent the Romanian army deep into Hungary, in defiance of the Supreme Council's demand that he halt its advance. The Romanian offensive led to the downfall of the Hungarian Soviet Republic headed by Béla Kun on August 1, 1919 and the occupation of Budapest three days later. Brătianu intended to install a government willing to make peace on terms favorable to Romania, but his intransigence over territory had turned the Western Allies against him.

In the meantime, Brătianu also became embroiled in a dispute with the Allies over minority rights. The key matter at issue was the civil status of Romanian Jews. The Allies inserted in the proposed treaty with Austria guarantees of equal rights of citizenship for Jews and a commitment to take other measures on their behalf in the future which they might deem necessary. All these matters were also to be set down in detail in a separate minorities treaty, which the Allies would draw up and Romania would be obliged to sign. Brătianu responded by promising the Allies on May 3 that Romania would ensure absolute equality and broad political liberties for all ethnic minorities, but he refused to compromise his country's sovereignty by allowing other states to dictate government policy. Matters reached an impasse, and Romania did not sign

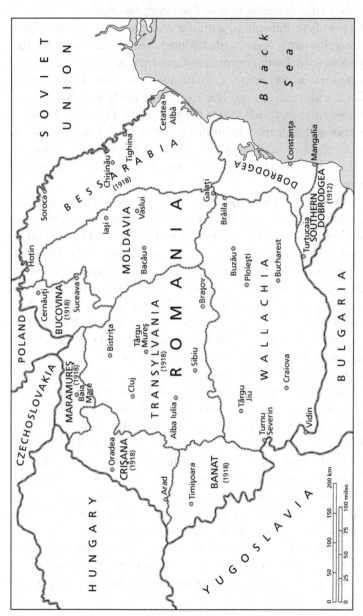

Map 7 Greater Romania between the World Wars

the Treaty of Saint-Germain with Austria on September 10, 1919. Two days later Brătianu, now in Bucharest, resigned.

Despite these difficulties, within a year the territorial questions affecting Romania were settled. Under heavy pressure from the Allies a new coalition government signed the Austrian and minorities treaties on December 9, 1919. Other territorial issues were resolved with relative ease. The Treaty of Neuilly with Bulgaria of November 27, 1919 left intact the frontier in Dobrudja between Romania and Bulgaria established in 1913. As for the Banat, the Supreme Council itself drew the boundary line between Romania and the new Yugoslavia, awarding about two-thirds of the region to Romania.

The Allies' recognition of Romania's acquisition of Bessarabia came more slowly because they made it dependent on the settlement of Romania's outstanding differences with Hungary. That condition was satisfied on June 4, 1920, when Romania signed the Treaty of Trianon, which awarded her all of Transylvania and part of eastern Hungary, including the cities of Oradea (Nagyvárad) and Arad. Then, on October 28, 1920 the Council of Ambassadors, which had taken the place of the full Peace Conference, recognized Romania's acquisition of Bessarabia, but left the details of the settlement to direct negotiations between Romania and Russia.

By the fall of 1920, then, all Romania's territorial acquisitions had received international sanction. They added 156,000 square kilometers (now 296,000 square kilometers) and 8,500,000 inhabitants (now 16,250,000) to the pre-war kingdom. But in the process of fulfilling long-cherished national aspirations Romania had acquired substantial minorities. In 1920, roughly 30 percent of the population was non-Romanian, as opposed to 8 percent before the war. At the same time the new provinces added greatly to Romania's productive capacity, as the industrial potential of the country in 1919 increased 235 percent over what it had been in 1916.

Daunting tasks lay ahead. The damage of war had first to be repaired, and then the new provinces and new citizens had to be integrated into existing structures and the institutions of a modern national state further refined.

5

Peace and war, 1919–1947

Broad trends of political, economic, and social development discernible a century earlier reached their culmination in the two decades between the World Wars, as modern Romania achieved its fullest expression as a nation-state. It was an era of enormous vitality and creativity, as the leading classes experimented with new ideas and forms from politics to business and from philosophy to poetry. But it was also an era of contentiousness and division, as they were obliged to reorder long-established institutions, re-examine venerable traditions, and confront the problems of an urbanizing, middle-class society on the rise common to Europe as a whole.

Economic and social life in certain respects followed familiar patterns. Agriculture remained the foundation of the Romanian economy, since it provided a livelihood for the majority of the population and supplied the bulk of exports, upon which the financial health of the country mainly depended. But at the same time industry was making substantial progress and was steadily increasing its share of the national income. The peasantry continued to form the majority of the population, and the urban working class grew as industry and commerce expanded. But it was the middle class that put its stamp on the interwar period. Although still relatively small, it came into its own in these two decades as the guiding force in both economic and political life.

The critical issue of the day in politics was the survival of parliamentary democracy in the face of severe challenges from the forces of authoritarianism. The prospects for democracy seemed auspicious in the 1920s, as the two leading parties – the National Liberal and the National Peasant – both committed themselves to parliamentary government. But in the following decade, uncertainties about economic progress and social stability called into question the viability and even the suitability to Romanian conditions of liberal democratic institutions. Movements and parties on the right responded to widespread fears and doubts by offering their own, authoritarian solutions.

Romania's role in international relations and her very security depended primarily upon the aims and maneuverings of the great powers. Successive Romanian governments aligned themselves with France and Great Britain because they were the chief guarantors of the peace settlement of Versailles and were, thus, the protectors of Greater Romania. But by the late 1930s, as the Western powers repeatedly demonstrated their unwillingness to stand up to the aggressive designs of Adolf Hitler after his accession to power in 1933, Romanian leaders were inclined to seek an accommodation with Germany.

All these matters of domestic and foreign policy found a place in the great national debate about national identity and development. At issue, as in the time of the Junimists, was whether Romania should follow the Western model and thus join the ranks of modern urbanized and industrialized European nations, or whether she should cleave to her peasant, agrarian, and Orthodox traditions and thus, as some argued, remain true to herself. Those who advocated a third way offered Romanians the assurance of preserving all that was best in their traditional way of life and yet suggested that they might also share in the general social and economic progress of Europe. As before the First World War, all these issues drew politicians and social thinkers of the most diverse ideological persuasions into an intellectual free-for-all, which, in its enthusiasm and desperation, captured the essence of the interwar period.

THE GREAT DEBATE

The intellectuals who debated the future course that their country should take fell into two broad groupings, Europeanists and traditionalists, as in the second half of the nineteenth century. The former treated Romania as a part of Europe and insisted that she had no other choice but to take the path of economic and social progress already trodden by the urbanized and industrialized West. The traditionalists, on the other hand, emphasized Romania's agrarian character and sought models of development based upon the country's own long-standing, unique social heritage. The affinities of both groups with pre-war currents of thought are striking, but not surprising, for they drew abundantly upon earlier agrarian and industrial visions of the future Romania. Yet their thought yielded nothing in originality to their intellectual forebears as they reinterpreted Romania's place in Europe in the light of their own experience and their expectations of the new century.

The Europeanists, though approaching development from diverse perspectives, nonetheless shared similar views about Romania's modern history and her place in Europe. Two figures stand out: the literary critic Eugen Lovinescu and the economist and sociologist Ştefan Zeletin. For the first time in scholarly literature they undertook a comprehensive investigation of the causes that lay behind the emergence of modern Romania. They both linked the process to the introduction of Western-style capitalism in the Romanian principalities and treated the revolution of 1848 and the Constitution of 1866 as landmarks in assuring its survival. But Lovinescu found the motive force of change in ideas, whereas Zeletin emphasized economic and social causes. They could, nonetheless, agree that "Westernization" was a necessary historical stage through which every country was destined to pass, and they had no doubt that outside European influences, rather than internal forces, had been the main catalyst for the emergence of modern Romania.

Eugen Lovinescu (1881–1943), the most influential literary critic of the time, traced the origins of modern Romania back to the first half of the nineteenth century, to the beginnings of massive intellectual and cultural contacts with Western Europe. In his three-volume *Istoria civilizaţiei române moderne* (The history of modern Romanian civilization; 1924–26) he treated the encounter as a struggle between Western and indigenous systems of ideas. The former triumphed, he argued, because the elites in the principalities of Moldavia and Wallachia judged Europe to be superior to the East. These elites thus undertook to close the enormous gap they perceived between themselves and the West by adopting the latter's institutions, ethics, and methods, in accordance with what Lovinescu called "synchronism." For him, this "law" was the key to understanding the relationship between agricultural, patriarchal Romania, on the one hand, and the industrial, urban West, on the other. Accordingly, the inferior imitated the superior, the underdeveloped peoples the more advanced, and the village the city. At first, the imitation was complete. It was superficial and unselective, but, then, as maturity set in, it was transformed into the adaptation of what was consciously judged to be necessary and superior, a stage, in Lovinescu's view, that Romania had reached in the 1920s.

Ştefan Zeletin (1882–1934), a materialist, insisted that Romania's fate was inextricably linked to the fortunes of Western capitalism. His most influential work, *Burghezia română: origina şi rolul ei istoric* (The Romanian bourgeoisie: its origin and historical role; 1925) offered an economic interpretation of Romania's "Westernization" complementing and balancing Lovinescu's analysis of the intellectual and cultural aspects of the process. He tried to show that modern Romania was the product of fundamental economic changes brought about by the introduction of Western European capital after the Treaty of Adrianople (1829), which had freed the Romanian principalities from the stifling effects of the long Ottoman domination of their commerce. He then showed how a native bourgeoisie emerged out of the processes of economic change, the class, he was certain, that would guide the country through all the successive stages of modernization.

Opposed to Europeanists were groups and individuals who sought models for Romania's future in the native past, real or imagined. "Traditionalists" accurately describes them, but they were by no means unanimous about what constituted the Romanian tradition. In general, they shared a belief in the predominantly rural character of Romanian historical development and staunchly opposed "inorganic" cultural and institutional imports from the West. They all drew from currents of ideas that had come to the fore in European intellectual life in the second half of the nineteenth century and the beginning of the twentieth. It is perhaps paradoxical that they should have been so indebted to Western European thought, for they tended to reject Western political and economic institutions.

Of all the traditionalist currents of the interwar period, none had greater influence on intellectual and cultural life than that nurtured by the founders of the literary review *Gândirea* (Thinking). The Gândirists, as they came to be known, were attracted to speculative thought, mystical and religious experiences, and the primitive spirituality of folklore, and they were anxious to communicate their own ideas in a wholly modern idiom.

Nichifor Crainic (1889–1972) represented one of the two main currents within the *Gândirea* circle. A staunch advocate of nativist values, he had been alarmed by what he perceived as the steady moral and spiritual decay of Romanian society since the nineteenth century. He sought to reverse the trend by leading a return to the "authentic values" of the Romanian spirit, that is, to the teachings of Eastern Orthodoxy. His emphasis on Orthodox spirituality helped to differentiate his brand of autochthonism from Sămănătorism and Poporanism, which had emphasized, respectively, cultural and economic means to a national regeneration.

The poet and philosopher Lucian Blaga (1895–1961) was the leading representative of the other main current within the *Gândirea* circle. He and his colleagues, the poets and novelists largely responsible for the review's enormous literary prestige, looked beyond Eastern Orthodoxy in their search for the deeper sources of the native tradition and the proper path of national development. While acknowledging the contribution Orthodoxy had made to Romanian spiritual and cultural life in the past, they extended their investigations to the popular psyche as revealed in folklore and mythology, to oriental religions, and to contemporary philosophical and sociological thought in Western Europe. Blaga took a broader, more European approach to national character and development than Crainic. The key to his understanding of these matters is to be found in his all-encompassing theory of style, which he elaborated in *Orizont şi stil* (Horizon and style; 1935). He applied his general theory to the Romanians in *Spaţiul mioritic* (Mioritic space; 1936), in which he insisted that Romanian spirituality, which primarily determined national character, had been preserved intact in the rural world. In the final analysis, his quest penetrated more deeply than just the discovery of national character. He sought in the ancestral world of the village the forgotten secrets of the age

13 Lucian Blaga

of innocence before the sin of knowledge had alienated man from nature and his true self.

Traditionalist ideas appeared in a variety of forms. The philosopher Nae Ionescu (1888–1940), the theorist of *trăirism*, a form of existentialism, was certain that Europe stood at the threshold of a new age of spirituality which would replace the moral and ethical emptiness of a world dominated by modern science and technology. He found the sources of Romanian spirituality in Orthodoxy, which, he insisted, had always separated the Romanians from Catholic and Protestant Europe, and, thus, had set them on a separate path of development.

Ionescu won an extraordinary following among the young generation of intellectuals who came to maturity in the late 1920s. Notable among them was the Criterion circle, whose members included Mircea Eliade (1907–86), who was to become a renowned historian of religion, and Emil Cioran (1911–95), the later philosopher of man's tragic destiny. Although they acknowledged the role Orthodoxy had had in shaping the destiny of the Romanians, they were eager to explore the different meanings of existence for themselves.

Alongside the Europeanists and the traditionalists proponents of other currents of ideas sought a third path of development that would reconcile Romania's agrarian heritage with the need to adapt from modern European experience all that would be useful to the peasant and congenial to economic and social progress. Of all these currents, the Peasantists (Ţărănişti) were the most consistent and effective advocates of a Romania in harmony with its "pre-eminently agricultural character." They stood close to the Populists and were, in a sense, their successors. They both favored an agrarian society grounded in native institutions and both were suspicious of bourgeois, industrial society and the city. Yet Peasantism was not just an extension of Populism, as it was deeply influenced by the advances in social and economic theory of the interwar period. Their most original contribution to Romanian social thought as elaborated by their leading theorist, Virgil Madgearu (1887–1940), was the doctrine of agrarian Romania as a third world situated between the capitalist individualism of the West and the socialist collectivism of the East. This doctrine, in turn, rested upon two fundamental assumptions: first, that the family holding was a distinct mode of production and constituted the very foundation of the national economy, and, second, that the "peasant state," a political entity administered by and responsible to the majority of the population, must replace the existing order.

As the political foundation of Peasantism Madgearu stood for a new type of state that would satisfy the needs and aspirations of the great mass of population and would be guided by the theory that Romania's social and economic progress was destined to remain different from that of the capitalist West. Implicit was his assumption that the peasantry formed a separate class, distinct both economically and psychologically from the bourgeoisie and the urban proletariat, and that, consequently, the state which represented the peasantry must also differ from bourgeois and socialist political systems. He called the new entity a peasant state. As for political forms, he unhesitatingly chose parliamentary democracy.

Yet Madgearu had serious doubts about the foundations of Greater Romania, based as they were largely on private enterprise and the market. As he contemplated the tasks of managing an increasingly complex economy, he came to regard the state as an indispensable coordinator. The world economic depression had convinced him that the era of economic liberalism in Europe had run its course. Although he did not share the assumptions of some of his Peasantist colleagues about the imminent demise of Western capitalism, he was no longer willing to leave the economic initiative solely in private hands. He proposed, instead, state planning and coordination, which he called *dirijism*. The early successes of the New Deal or, as he called it, the "Roosevelt Revolution," in reviving and restructuring the American economy after the Great Depression encouraged him to think that state intervention might have similar beneficial results in his own country. He thought that *dirijism* would operate best in a socialist setting, but he stopped short of advocating a socialist transformation of the Romanian economy, in part because of his commitment to private peasant holdings and his conception of peasant individualism. Nonetheless, he thought that Romania, because of her unique agrarian structure, might be able to adapt the principles of *dirijism* to her particular needs.

All the participants in the debate over national character and paths of development agreed at least on one point: that Romania had experienced rapid and significant change in the preceding century. Behind the rhetoric they also recognized, some reluctantly, that their country had become more like Western Europe. But they could not agree on whether the process of Europeanization had been good or bad and how deeply it had affected the structure of Romanian society. The internal economic and political crises and the unsettled state of international relations in the 1930s provided a stern test of their different visions of Romania's future.

POLITICS

The crucial issue in Romanian political life in the interwar period was the contest between democracy and authoritarianism. The prospects for the consolidation of a parliamentary system on the Western European model seemed bright in the 1920s. The enactment of universal manhood suffrage held out the hope that government by oligarchy would soon be over. The leaders of the Romanian National Party of Transylvania and the Peasant Party of the Old Kingdom, both of which had broad support, were committed to the full participation of all citizens in the political process and insisted on genuine consultations with the voters through fair elections. Both the Peasantists and the Europeanists were ardent advocates of parliamentary government. Among the general population, too, support for it was strong; when given the opportunity to express their preferences freely, as in the election of 1928, they voted overwhelmingly for those parties that stood for democracy.

Yet formidable obstacles stood in their way. First of all, there were the habits of a half-century. The apathy and inexperience of the peasants, caused mainly by their almost total exclusion from the political process, were never entirely overcome, and, as a result, the impact of universal suffrage was diminished. The old spirit in which politics had been carried on persisted, as politics for the sake of short-term advantages, instead of high principle, intensified. The Liberal Party, the strongest political organization of the 1920s, interfered but little with custom. In theory committed to the parliamentary system, it preferred to conduct elections in the time-honored fashion and to govern in a strong-willed manner through a small financial and industrial oligarchy. Then, too, many groups and individuals opposed everything that modern Europe represented – urbanism, industry, rationalism, and not least of all, democratic political institutions. The followers of Nichifor Crainic and Nae Ionescu, among others, fell into this category and fostered a climate favorable to extreme nationalist and authoritarian political movements.

The 1930s was the decade of crisis for Romanian democracy. The world depression exacerbated existing economic problems and sharpened social tensions and thus gave impetus to those forces hostile to the prevailing parliamentary system. The crisis enhanced the appeal of anti-Semitism among certain elements of society, who used it to rally support for their particular brand of nationalism. Foremost among organizations that made anti-Semitism the ideological core of their new Romania was the Iron Guard, which reached the height of its popularity in the mid 1930s. The accession of Carol II to the throne in 1930 also boded ill for democracy, as he made no secret of his disdain for parliamentary institutions and of his intention to become the undisputed source of power in the state. Nor can shifts in the European balance of power be ignored. The rise of Nazi Germany and the aggressive behavior of fascist Italy combined with the policy of appeasement adopted by the Western democracies encouraged both the declared opponents of democracy and the hesitant in Romania to conclude that the future belonged to the authoritarians. The leading democratic parties themselves seemed to have lost much of their élan of the preceding decade. They proved incapable of withstanding the assault from both within and outside the country and acquiesced in the establishment of Carol's dictatorship in 1938, an event which marked the end of the democratic experiment in Romania for half a century.

Two parties dominated political life in the interwar period – the Liberals and the National Peasants. The fortunes of the Liberal Party never seemed brighter, as it held power for long periods, especially between 1922 and 1926. The driving force within the party came from the so-called financial oligarchy, which was grouped around large banking and industrial families headed by the Brătianu family and its allies. The intertwining of banking, industry, and political power on such a grand scale was a consequence of the state's having assumed a crucial role in promoting economic development. Through this remarkable intermingling of business and financial interests and politicians the control of industry, banking, and government inevitably fell into the hands of the same people.

In the 1920s Liberal theoreticians, notably Ştefan Zeletin, and Liberal politicians, led by Ionel Brătianu, sought general acceptance of the idea that the Liberal Party, because of its dominant place in economic and political life, represented the whole nation. Liberal leaders themselves presented their party as being above classes, as promoting measures benefiting all elements of society. They buttressed these claims by pointing to their party's promotion of agrarian and electoral reform and its leading role in creating Greater Romania. Ionel Brătianu insisted that the Liberals took into account the needs and interests of all social groups and strove to harmonize them. Since theirs was the "party of the nation," he and his colleagues denounced parties based on class as foreign to the Romanian spirit. In their view, both the Peasant Party and the Socialist Party posed a clear danger to Greater Romania, for, by pursuing narrow class interests, so their argument ran, they undermined the very foundations of the national state.

The liberalism practiced by the Liberal Party differed in many ways from the Western European variety. In politics the Liberals used whatever means were available to ensure victory at the polls; they relied especially on the bureaucracy to further their cause and discourage the opposition. They ran the economy in a similar fashion. Without hesitation, they organized cartels, set tariffs, and distributed subsidies and other financial favors to achieve their main goals – industrialization and the creation of a modern infrastructure based on Western models. Such policies benefited the financial and industrial oligarchy, that is, themselves, but left other groups and classes disaffected.

The other major party of the interwar period, the National Peasant Party, was formed in 1926 when the Peasant Party of the Old Kingdom (Moldavia and Wallachia before 1918) united with the National Party of Transylvania. Although they shared certain fundamental ideals – democratic political institutions and civil liberties for all citizens – their respective economic and social programs were incompatible. The Peasant Party aimed at radical agrarian reform, while the National Party, though drawing substantial support from Romanian peasants in Transylvania, was essentially middle class in its outlook and more nationalist than peasant in its ideology. The union of the two parties, consequently, surprised contemporaries.

The leaders of the two parties overcame ideological and policy differences because they realized that separately they would never be strong enough to dislodge the Liberals from power. They promised to add explicit guarantees of civil liberties and political rights to the constitution, carry out a decentralization of the state administration, and expand the responsibilities of local government. They recognized the primacy of agriculture and proclaimed

14 National Peasant Party leaders (from left): Virgil Madgearu,
Iuliu Maniu, Ion Mihalache

their intention to strengthen the independent smallholder and promote the cooperative movement. But they also agreed to encourage
industry by giving equal treatment to foreign and domestic capital and by removing burdensome protective tariffs. Iuliu Maniu
(1873–1953) became president of the new National Peasant Party,
Ion Mihalache (1882–1963) vice-president, and Virgil Madgearu

secretary-general. Two years later the partnership achieved a notable victory over the Liberals in the elections of 1928, the freest in Romania until after 1989. Their success was in some measure due to the absence of the formidable strategist Ionel Brătianu, who had died the previous year.

Parties on the left, which drew support from the urban working class, had little direct influence on political life in the interwar period. The Social Democratic Party emerged from the war badly divided between moderates, who followed the Western socialist tradition, and radicals, who took as their model the Bolsheviks of Russia. These divisions came into the open at the general socialist party congress held in Bucharest on May 8–12, 1921. The radicals, who were in the majority, voted to accept affiliation with the Communist International on May 8, which is usually taken as the founding date of the Romanian Communist Party. Then, in 1922, the Communists formally adopted as their name the Communist Party of Romania, Section of the Communist International and approved statutes that mandated a secret organization.

For various reasons, the Romanian Communist Party did not prosper. The government declared it illegal on April 11, 1924, and, henceforth, until the end of the Second World War, it was obliged to carry on its activities underground or through front organizations. The illegal status of the party increased its dependence on the Soviet Communist Party, which through the Comintern arrogated to itself the right to choose party leaders and determine their policies. Party congresses installed non-Romanians as secretary-generals of the party, thereby reinforcing the widely held view in Romania that the party was a foreign organization which put the interests of the Soviet Union ahead of those of Romania. Soviet domination of the party was enhanced by the presence in Moscow in the 1930s of numerous Romanian Communists who formed the Romanian Communist "Bureau," in effect, simply a branch of the Soviet Communist Party.

Many of those socialists who had rejected affiliation with the Communist International and submission to the Soviet Communist Party eventually established a new Social Democratic Party in 1927, uniting all the regional parties into a single political organization headed by Constantin Titel Petrescu (1888–1957), the leading figure of interwar Romanian democratic socialism. It pledged to replace the existing financial and political oligarchy with a democratic system based on the principle of the civil equality of all citizens and the socialization of the means of production. Its leaders were at pains to differentiate themselves from the Communists by insisting that the reforms they demanded would be carried out through the processes of parliamentary democracy rather than by a revolutionary seizure of power. This program remained the basic document of Romanian Social Democracy until after the Second World War.

Political formations on the right were relatively insignificant in the 1920s. Various attempts to establish a Romanian fascist movement modeled on that of Mussolini's Italy failed to attract more than a handful of members. Nor did experiments with national socialism fare any better. Until the end of the decade their slogans about radical economic and social change had little appeal, mainly because the economy was relatively stable and the majority of the population was still confident that political democracy would solve pressing economic and social problems.

One issue, nonetheless, continued to nurture rightist movements – anti-Semitism. By no means a post-war phenomenon, it could in its modern form be traced back at least to the early decades of the nineteenth century as Jewish immigration into the principalities steadily grew. In the interwar period a leading advocate of action against Jews was Alexandru C. Cuza (1857–1947), professor of political economy at the University of Iaşi. In 1923, he formed the League of National-Christian Defense (Liga Apărării Naţional Creştine), which had as its primary goals the expulsion of the Jews from all areas of economic and cultural life and the education of young people in a Christian and nationalist spirit.

One of Cuza's most ardent followers, at least initially, was Corneliu Zelea Codreanu (1899–1938), who created his own, more extreme nationalist organization, the Legion of the Archangel Michael, in 1927. Three years later, he established a military wing of the Legion, which he called the Iron Guard, a name that was soon applied to the entire organization. Outwardly, the Guard resembled German and Italian fascism with its uniforms and salutes and its glorification of its leader – the Căpitan – but all this was merely form. The substance of Romanian fascism – the anti-Semitism, the Orthodox Christian (in a distorted form), and the cult of the peasant as the embodiment of natural, unspoiled man – came from native sources. Here, the traditionalist hostility to cosmopolitanism, rationalism, and industrialization found a crude expression. But lacking was an ideology. Guard leaders ignored calls for a Romanian corporate state on the grounds that the appearance of the new man must precede the adoption of programs. Otherwise, they argued, institutions would simply reinforce the existing "corrupt" society. While there was thus a strain of idealism in the Guard's doctrine, repeated acts of violence and intimidation against opponents revealed at the same time its thuggish nature. When the new head of the Liberal Party and prime minister Ion G. Duca outlawed the Guard in 1933 in order to eliminate the "forces of subversion," it retaliated by assassinating him. He was succeeded as prime minister by Gheorghe Tătărescu (1886–1957), the leader of the so-called Young Liberals, who were more tolerant of the extreme right than the mainstream Liberals.

Between the elections of 1931 and 1937 the Iron Guard became a mass movement, rising from 1 to 15.58 percent of the popular vote. Its strongest constituency was young and urban, but it cut across class boundaries, appealing at the same time to peasants and rural clergy, elements of the urban working class and the middle class, and the periphery of society. The leadership of the Guard at this time, its heyday, was formed by university-educated, middle-class intellectuals, but its nationalism appealed to all those who felt alienated by a political and social system which seemed to them to have been created outside and at the expense of "Romanian realities."

The Iron Guard appealed especially to members of the young generation of intellectuals. Its call for a national rebirth based on the simple, traditional virtues of the Romanian countryside offered salvation from a social and political order that seemed to them corrupt and adrift. They enthusiastically embraced the exhortations of their mentor Nae Ionescu, the spiritual father of the Iron Guard, to experience life, not reduce it to abstract formulas, and they proclaimed themselves the missionaries of a new spirituality. Their mission, as they defined it, was to bring about the spiritual reconstruction of Romania, just as the previous generation had achieved political unity. The Iron Guard seemed to many of them to be the embodiment of the youthful vitality needed to set the country on the way to returning to itself. But Emil Cioran wanted to accomplish just the opposite. In his dissection of modern Romania, *Schimbarea la faţă a României* (The transfiguration of Romania; 1936), he looked to the Iron Guard to carry out a "creatively barbarian" revolution to save the country from disintegration by substituting totalitarianism for democracy. He praised the Guard for their "irrational merging" of themselves into the nation and for their heroism, which "began in brutality and ended in sacrifice."

The elections of 1937 were a critical test of strength between democracy and its opponents. The Iron Guard through its party, Totul Pentru Ţară (Everything for the Homeland), gained 66 seats, becoming the third largest party in parliament behind the Liberals (152 seats) and the National Peasants (86 seats). But King Carol did not turn to any of these parties for a prime minister. Instead, he invited the poet Octavian Goga, the head of the small National Christian Party, to form a government. Carol welcomed this opportunity to further his own ambitions. By bringing to power a party that had gained less than 10 percent of the vote, he intended to show that elections could not determine the way things were done and that it was, after all, his will that counted. In any case, he had no wish to install a strong government, since he was certain that the time had come to establish a royal dictatorship. Indeed, he brought his personal rule into being quickly on February 10 and 11, 1938, simply by replacing the Goga government with an "advisory government" headed by the Patriarch of the Orthodox Church, Miron Cristea, and including seven former prime ministers and General Ion Antonescu as minister of national defense.

Carol moved swiftly to consolidate his power by sweeping away the parliamentary system. On February 20, he abolished the Constitution of 1923, replacing it with a new one based upon corporatist principles and concentrating power in the hands of the king. On March 30 he decreed the dissolution of all political parties and groups, but promised that after a period of "adaptation to the new circumstances" a law would be drawn up setting forth the conditions under which political "associations" could be formed. But a series of subsequent decree-laws imposed severe penalties on any opposition to the new order and showed that Carol had no intention of restoring the old party system. The leaders of the National Peasant Party,

15 King Carol II

Iuliu Maniu, and of the Liberal Party, Constantin Brătianu, the
brother of Ionel, informed Carol that their parties would carry on
as before March 30 and, if necessary, were prepared to challenge the
constitutionality of his acts. Carol took the warning to heart, and a
kind of armistice prevailed between them for the next two years.

Carol took drastic action against the Iron Guard, which he now
regarded as his chief enemy. He instructed Armand Călinescu, the
minister of the interior and the strongman in his new cabinet, to

destroy it by whatever means, legal or illegal, he thought necessary. Large numbers of Guard members, including Codreanu, and sympathizers were rounded up and interned in concentration camps. The brutality of these measures seems to have been motivated by Carol's perception of the Guard as a dangerous rival for power and an agent of Germany. The arrest of Guardists and the killing of Codreanu and thirteen other Guardists, "while trying to escape," occurred immediately after Carol's visit to Germany, during which Hitler had urged the freeing of the Guardists and the formation of a Codreanu cabinet.

Dramatic changes in the international situation vitiated Carol's efforts to maintain control over political forces at home. The fall of France in June 1940 finally undid all his calculations. It forced him further to the right. He decreed the establishment of Partidul Naţiunii (the Party of the Nation), a "totalitarian" party whose task would be to mobilize and direct the entire moral and material life of the nation. But it was of little consequence, as international events, rather than Carol's will, determined the political evolution of the country.

SOCIETY AND THE ECONOMY

Between the World Wars Romania presented striking contrasts of entrenched underdevelopment and bourgeoning, if uneven, industrialization and urbanization. On the one hand, the economic and social structure preserved in broad outline its pre-war configuration. Agriculture remained the foundation of the country's economy, and its organization had changed but little, despite an extensive land reform. The great majority of the population continued to live in the countryside and to draw its income primarily from agriculture. As before the First World War, Romania remained dependent on the West as a market for its agricultural products and raw materials and as a source of many kinds of manufactured goods and investment capital.

Yet signs of change were evident. Industry grew and became increasingly able to satisfy the needs of consumers, and imports of raw materials and semi-processed goods rose at a faster rate than manufactured items. The urban population grew as cities expanded their role in the organization and direction of the economy. Even agriculture gave evidence of change as the traditional reliance on grain production shifted slightly in favor of vegetable and industrial crops. In all branches of the economy the state played a key role. Although it respected private property and ownership of the means of production and granted private capital, both domestic and foreign, numerous advantages, it reserved to itself the responsibility for the planning and overseeing of what came to be called the "national economy."

In the 1920s, the economic fortunes of Romania were in the hands of the Liberals, and their ideas about fundamental issues of development were much influenced by the chief theorist of Romanian liberalism, Ştefan Zeletin. Like him, they assigned to the middle class, that is, to themselves, the leading role in transforming Romania into a modern European nation. Vintilă Brătianu, the minister of finance in the Liberal governments of 1922–28 and brother of Ionel Brătianu, served as the chief interpreter of Zeletin's theories. He pursued not only economic goals, but was intent upon consolidating the Romanian national state. He and his colleagues relied heavily on the intervention of the state to achieve their ambitious economic and social goals. Theirs was the so-called doctrine of neoliberalism, as formulated by Zeletin, who taught that the era of economic liberty, which had served useful purposes in the nineteenth century, had run its course and must now give way to systematic organization and direction and the pursuit of well-defined national goals.

The Liberals, as economic nationalists, were determined to share as little power and wealth as possible with foreigners. Although they recognized the need to maintain good relations with the industrialized states of Europe for the simple reason that they dominated international commerce and the financial markets, the Liberals wanted to avoid economic subordination to the West. They insisted that the infrastructure and the main industries be in Romanian, that is, their own, hands. Under the motto "By ourselves" (Prin noi înşine), they even toyed with the notion of financing their ambitious economic projects with native capital alone.

The National Peasants, who came to power for a few years in 1928, pursued economic goals in appearance markedly different from those of the Liberals. Their primary concern was, of course, agriculture, but they also recognized the importance of a modern infrastructure and sound finances. To carry out their ambitious plans they encouraged investments from abroad in accordance with a policy that came to be known as "Doors open to foreign capital" (Porţi deschise capitalului străin). They were motivated in part by the realization that native sources of capital were insufficient, but they were also loath to pass up an opportunity to strike a blow at the immense power of the Liberal financial and industrial oligarchy.

Agrarian reform, along with industrialization, was crucial in shaping economic development during the interwar period. The agrarian reforms, promised in 1917, were introduced between 1918 and 1921. They differed in detail from province to province, thus reflecting the specific economic and social conditions under which each province had evolved, but all these laws had as their main goal the distribution of land to the peasants and were motivated more by social than strictly economic concerns. In the new provinces acquired after the First World War, such as Transylvania with its large Hungarian and German populations, the agrarian reforms, from a Romanian nationalist point of view, had the additional benefit of weakening the landowning classes of the minorities and diminishing the social and cultural roles of their churches and schools, which drew much of their income from land. In the final analysis, Romanian politicians enacted land reform because all classes, even landowners, had come to recognize the futility, and the danger, of trying to maintain the old agrarian order. Liberals generally stood for agrarian reform in principle, but many wanted to be certain that agriculture would continue to serve the needs of industry. Agrarianists, on the other hand, saw the reform as a giant step toward the "peasantizing" of agriculture and the creation of a peasant state, a view which in time proved to be too sanguine. Undoubtedly, all these groups were also stirred to action in the immediate post-war years by the specter of social upheaval from below.

Whatever the motivations of politicians and social theorists may have been, the agrarian reform laws brought about a massive transfer of land from large landowners to smallholders. About 6 million hectares of land were expropriated for distribution to peasants, and some 1,400,000 peasants received land. The most striking and obvious result was thus a decrease in the number and extent of large properties in favor of medium and small holdings. But the change did not bring prosperity to agriculture, for many holdings were too small to be economically viable. Nor did the agrarian reform laws change existing structures significantly. The remaining landlords made greater use of machinery and hired hands in order to compensate for the loss of peasant labor. But in time a partial return to pre-reform conditions occurred, as increasing numbers of peasants were forced to rent land from landlords to supplement what they had received from the expropriated estates and thus fell back into a condition of economic dependency. Nonetheless, the blame for continued shortcomings in agriculture cannot be laid solely on the land reform. There were forces at work that had little to do with the legislation of 1918–21, notably a rapidly growing population in the countryside; the uninterrupted fragmentation of peasant holdings through inheritance and partial sales, which impeded innovation in farming; the vagaries of the international market, which affected even the small producer; the slow development of industry, which hindered the growth of a mutually beneficial relationship between city and countryside; and the Romanian government's own economic priorities. Nor did the reforms drastically affect the reliance of Romanian agriculture on grain production, even though a tendency on the part of some peasants to diversify their crops was evident. In 1939, grains occupied 83.5 percent of all arable land, compared to 84.7 percent in 1927.

Industry made a rapid recovery from the enormous destruction caused by the war. Its progress through the interwar period owed much to the Liberals and to the accession of the new provinces, especially Transylvania and the Banat. The dynamism of the 1920s is suggested by the spectacular development of the oil industry from 968,000 tons in 1918 to 5,800,000 tons in 1930, giving Romania sixth place among the world's producers, and the growth of steel production from 38,000 tons in 1925 to 144,000 tons in 1928.

Despite impressive progress in many branches of industry, the fundamental economic structure of the country did not change significantly. As of 1939, 78 percent of the active population continued to rely on agriculture for its main source of income, while only 10 percent were similarly engaged in industry. Romania was still dependent upon foreign imports to equip her factories and provide consumers with a wide range of goods.

Romanian society of the 1920s and 1930s differed in significant ways from that of the pre-war era. First of all, the population was larger and ethnically more diverse. The total population in 1939 was 18,052,896, a figure which represented a growth of about 2,500,000 over the estimated population in 1920. This growth was the result of a high birth rate, almost double that of western and northern Europe, and a modest decline in the death rate. Ethnically, the Romanians formed a substantial majority of the population. In 1930, they made up 71.9 percent of the total (12,981,324) while the largest minority, the Hungarians represented 7.2 percent (1,415,507), followed by the Germans, 4.1 percent (745,421), Jews, 4 percent (728,115), and Ukrainians, 3.2 percent (582,115). But these proportions varied significantly from region to region. For example, the Hungarians formed 29 percent of the population of Transylvania, Germans made up 24 percent of the inhabitants of the Banat and 8 percent in Transylvania, and Jews 10.8 percent of the population in Bukovina and 7 percent in Bessarabia. Minorities constituted an especially significant proportion of the urban population: Jews, for example, were 30 percent in Bukovina, 27 percent in Bessarabia, and 23 percent in Moldavia.

Economic and social change raised the level of debate about civil and political rights for women. Their status remained much as it had been before the First World War: they were subject to their fathers and, if married, to their husbands, and they could not vote or be candidates in parliamentary elections. Even though the Constitution of 1923 proclaimed equality between the sexes, and a number of prominent politicians supported legislation to turn principle into practice, the situation remained essentially unchanged throughout the interwar period. Women themselves, mainly from the upper and educated classes, continued to press their case for emancipation through new organizations, notably the National Council of Romanian Women (Consiliul Național al Femeilor Române), founded and led by Calypso Botez, one of the most important figures in the Romanian feminist movement. Although she and her colleagues did not achieve their goals, they increased public awareness of the issues involved and the justice of their cause. The electoral law promulgated by Carol II in 1939 during his experiment with authoritarian rule indeed granted women limited rights to vote in national elections, but it was illusory because he had abolished political parties and representative government. The dictatorship of Ion Antonescu and Romania's involvement in the Second World War postponed further consideration of women's civil and political equality.

In the interwar period as a whole Romanian society was becoming more urban. In 1930 urban dwellers accounted for about 20 percent of the total population, and in the following decade their numbers grew by over 14 percent, an increase due almost exclusively to migration from the countryside. Bucharest had a place apart in the urbanization process. As a complex administrative, economic, and cultural center it grew at a rate and exercised an influence in public affairs far greater than any other city. Its population increased from 382,000 in 1918 to approximately 870,000 in 1939, the most sustained growth in the city's history. It owed much of its dramatic expansion to its role as the capital of Greater Romania, which required new and larger administrative institutions and a more extensive bureaucracy. But the main reason was economic. Nowhere else in the country did industry expand so rapidly, and by 1938 the city's industrial production accounted for 17 percent of the country's total (28 percent if a twenty-mile radius around the city is counted). The financial and economic life of the entire country was decisively affected by its industry.

At the end of the 1920s the world economic depression interrupted Romania's promising economic development and ushered in a decade of social and political uncertainty. The depression struck Romania with particular force, mainly because of its predominantly agricultural economy. The lack of diversification diminished its capacity to respond to the crisis because, dependent on the export of grains, it was at the mercy of the international market. Not only falling agricultural prices in the West but new, high tariffs on Romanian agricultural products imposed by the industrialized states in order to protect their own farmers jeopardized Romania's economic and financial stability. The Romanian government could do little. Retaliation against the West's manufactured goods was out of the question because they were indispensable and, in any case, the government had to avoid antagonizing the West, which was its only source of loans and investments.

The depression had a profound and lasting influence on the economic thought of Romanian politicians of both the Liberal and National Peasant parties. The dangers of too great a dependence on the great industrial powers persuaded the leaders of both parties to adopt a policy of accelerated industrialization. Virgil Madgearu's reaction was typical. Previously opposed to large-scale industrialization, he now urged the creation of a strong industry as essential to economic and political independence. All parties saw the wisdom of greater state coordination of the economy. The Liberals, who were in power between 1934 and 1937 and continued to make industrialization the centerpiece of their domestic program, set the pattern of increased state intervention in and control of the economy. But they were not alone. It had become evident to politicians of other parties that the problems of industry and of the economy as a whole could be solved only by firm direction from above. Yet the Liberals failed to achieve their ambitions fully because they lacked a coherent agricultural policy; they carried out industrialization at the expense of agriculture, rather than by treating the two branches as complementary.

The royal dictatorship of Carol II between 1938 and 1940 pursued the same economic policies as the Liberals. State intervention became more pronounced as projects for industrialization were accelerated with particular emphasis on the needs of national defense. In agriculture the middling and well-to-do peasants were favored over those, more numerous, who had holdings of less than 5 hectares. The government made new credit available to the "worthy peasant" and undertook to rationalize and intensify agricultural production in accordance with a master five-year plan drawn up in March 1940. But all these initiatives became increasingly tentative as Romania was drawn into the general European political crisis of the late 1930s.

THE MINORITIES

The substantial increase in minority populations in Greater Romania confronted Romanian elites with complex issues that would require adjustments in their approaches to nation-building and raised fundamental questions about the nature of the Romanian democratic model. At the end of the First World War the Romanian government had committed itself to protect the rights of ethnic minorities by adhering to the Minorities Treaty drawn up by the Paris Peace Conference. But Romanian political elites were intent on consolidating the Greater Romania that had emerged from the war into a Romanian national state, and, consequently, they had little incentive to promote the religious and cultural autonomy of the minorities, let alone their political ambitions. The Constitution of 1923, promulgated in order to provide the proper structural framework for Greater Romania, largely ignored the new ethnic and cultural realities, for it declared Romania to be a unitary, indivisible national state, thereby rejecting any suggestion of its multi-national character. It did, indeed, ensure all citizens' equal rights, but it offered the minorities individual, not collective, rights and thus fell far short of responding to their aspirations.

The minorities, nonetheless, in practice enjoyed a certain degree of school and church autonomy. The law on secondary education of 1928, for example, provided for the establishment of minority "sections" in state schools in places where the minority population was predominant. In them the language of instruction would be the language of the minority, with the proviso that the teaching of the Romanian language, history, and geography would have to be done in Romanian. The education law of 1925 already allowed minorities to establish their own private schools and to choose the language of instruction, but it also obligated them to teach the Romanian language, history, and geography in Romanian. As for minority churches, the Constitution guaranteed them full freedom to carry on their activities as before. Yet it served notice that the Romanian Orthodox and Greek Catholic churches enjoyed a special status. Both churches were declared national churches, while the Orthodox was singled out as the dominant church. The Roman Catholic Church, ethnically mainly Hungarian, was also accorded a special place through the Concordat signed by the Romanian government and the Vatican in 1927. It allowed the church to elude some of the restrictions on relations with foreign entities imposed on other churches and in this way maintain its traditional links with Rome.

The minorities were able to establish their own organizations to represent their interests and carry on their activities with little interference from the government. The Hungarians of Transylvania were represented throughout the interwar period by the Hungarian Party (Magyar Párt), which was established in 1922. It generally followed a policy of intransigence toward the Romanian government and sought to create conditions of cultural and especially administrative autonomy in those regions where Hungarians formed a large majority of the inhabitants. To achieve its goals it participated in the parliamentary system and was represented in the legislature by some fifteen to twenty deputies and senators; it took advantage of the extensive freedom of the press in interwar Romania to present its case in a variety of publications; and it submitted memoranda and complaints about infringements of minority rights to the League of Nations. A number of party leaders drew moral and financial support from the government of Hungary, a situation that could only increase the suspicions of the Romanian government and public generally that the true objective of the Hungarian Party was the return of Transylvania to Hungary. But the Hungarian Party was by no means the sole representative of the Hungarian community. Groups and organizations of various kinds were formed which advocated other approaches to minority issues. The literary society around the monthly review *Erdélyi Helikon* (The Transylvanian helicon), founded in 1928, sought to create a sense of common purpose among Hungarians and Romanians. It elaborated the doctrine of Transzilvanizmus (Transylvanism), which emphasized that over the centuries a common historical experience had brought into being among all the inhabitants of Transylvania a "Transylvanian spirit," which set them apart from the other inhabitants of Romania. A more direct political challenge to the Hungarian Party came from MADOSZ (Magyar Dolgozók Szövetsége; Union of Hungarian Workers), which was formed in 1934. It advocated class struggle against the privileged and emphasized the inherent solidarity of the Hungarian and Romanian working classes.

The Germans of Greater Romania maintained their separate provincial organizations, but in 1921 they formed the Union of Germans in Romania (Verband der Deutschen in Rumänien) as a coordinating body to represent their interests before the government and public opinion. Its primary concerns had to do with cultural matters, mainly school and church autonomy as a means of preserving the community's ethnic identity. The party followed a policy of cooperation with the Romanian party in power, regardless of its ideological bent, as the most effective way of achieving their goals. Challenges to its predominance came in the 1930s, especially after the coming to power of Adolf Hitler in Germany in 1933. Local adherents of national socialism brought great pressure to bear on the Union of Germans in Romania and by 1936 had gained a predominant place within it.

The Jews after the First World War also sought to achieve some degree of unity, and in order to coordinate the activities of their various organizations they formed the Union of Jews of Romania (Uniunea Evreilor din România) in 1923. But provincial traditions remained strong and impeded the formation of a single Jewish political party. Indeed, the leaders of the Union urged affiliation with Romanian parties in order to avoid what they feared would be the political isolation of Jews, if they formed their own party. Many Jews were in fact active in the Romanian Liberal and National Peasant parties and in the Hungarian Party in Transylvania and the Communist Party. Still others created their own organizations. One of the most effective was the Zionist Union of Romania (Uniunea Sionistă a României), which was established in 1924 to collect funds to buy land in Palestine and prepare Jews for emigration. Yet the need for a party representing specifically Jewish interests grew more pressing as authoritarian and, especially, anti-Semitic organizations came increasingly to the fore in the 1930s. The Jewish Party of Romania (Partidul Evreiesc din România) was thus formed in 1931 and had some success in national elections in 1932, sending five deputies to parliament. In 1936 it gave way to a general coalition of Jewish organizations united in the Central Council of Jews of Romania (Consiliul Central al Evreilor din România) to defend the individual and collective rights of Jews as defined in the Constitution of 1923. The crisis of Romanian democracy and its inability to halt the steady growth of nationalist and extreme-right forces thwarted Jewish attempts at effective self-defense.

The Gypsies made modest economic and social progress in the interwar period. Numbering 262,000, according to the census of

1930, they were undergoing a certain degree of assimilation to the Romanian community. Evidence of the process is the abandonment of their language in favor of Romanian, as only 37 percent in 1930 declared Romany to be their mother tongue. Many were settling down on land acquired through the agrarian reforms after the First World War and were becoming farmers. But many others remained nomads and continued to practice their traditional crafts as they moved from place to place, all of which reinforced the popular image of Gypsies. The Gypsy elite, in the majority assimilated, recognized the need for organization in order to defend Gypsy interests, and in 1933 they founded the General Union of Roma, which promoted Gypsy schools and churches and a sense of identity based on the study of their history. Yet the overall position of the Gypsies as a marginal population did not change.

A salient aspect of the condition of minorities in Greater Romania was the ability of small groups to initiate projects to achieve specific goals and, in so doing, to create local autonomies of all kinds, especially cultural and economic. Young Hungarian intellectuals, organized as the Transylvanian Youth (Erdélyi Fiatalok), young Saxon intellectuals in Transylvania gathered around the monthly review of cultural and social thought, *Klingsor*, and the leaders of the Jewish credit cooperatives in Bessarabia had as their primary reason for being to protect the ethnic identity of their respective communities and, no less crucial, explore the precise nature of that identity. Although they represented specific cases and involved directly relatively small numbers of people, they nonetheless illustrated certain general trends in the relationship between the minorities and the new national state. They maintained contacts with the majority community, and they did not seek to isolate themselves from others, even though they were inevitably defensive about their status as minorities. Nor did the three groups hesitate to place themselves in a broad context – Hungarians in the Hungarian cultural world, Saxons in the greater German cultural world, and Jews with international Jewish organizations. Yet however much they saw themselves as parts of larger communities, their first concern was always their own respective community. They were thus intent on defining themselves and responding to the question of who they were as Hungarians, Saxons, or Jews and what their destiny could therefore be in Greater Romania. For the Transylvanian Youth the core of the community was the Hungarian village and its inhabitants; for the *Klingsor* circle that core was the educated Saxon; and for the Jews it was the Jewish middle class. They explored these fundamental questions with little significant interference from Bucharest.

SYNCHRONISM AND TRADITION

Romanian literature between the World Wars reflected changes in intellectual life and society that had been under way since the turn of the century. There was hardly a poet or a novelist who did not react in some way to the advance of capitalism, the undermining of the patriarchal village, urbanization, and social differentiation and wounded psyches in both the city and the countryside. Interwar Romanian writers also shared the élan and the anxieties of their contemporaries in Western Europe. They participated in the latest literary movements and experimented with the newest forms and modes of expression. Their daring and their commitment to their art fundamentally changed poetry and the novel and produced an astonishing variety of masterworks. These were signs not of imitation but of integration into Europe, and, no less, of sustained individual creativity.

The most important critical authority was Eugen Lovinescu. A staunch advocate of modernism, he sought to gain acceptance of an urban literature – the "new poetry" and the psychological novel – which he thought was a necessary consequence of the progress of civilization. He insisted that literature could not limit itself to national character and the sufferings of the humble, and he warned that to make Romanian literature eternally rural would be to doom it to stagnation. As Romania assumed social and economic structures similar to those of the West, it seemed incongruous to him that Romanian novelists should be preoccupied with the village, where people displayed only the immediate and primitive sense of love and greed. They must, he urged, deal with true moral dilemmas, which were possible only among the intellectuals and the well-to-do of the cities.

George Călinescu (1899–1965), who practiced his own special brand of literary criticism, took a different approach. He insisted that the critic must have a sense of historical continuity, a feeling for the evolution of Romanian literature over the long term in order to give perspective to his judgments about contemporary creativity. He thought of social development as a gradual, organic process, and he viewed literature as marking its stages. He thus concluded that Romanian literature would for some time have to concern itself with the "objective" world of rural settings and the peasant, and he was skeptical about attempts by authors to create an urban literature, in which the analytical and the psychological would necessarily predominate.

The most influential promoter of literature with a social conscience was the monthly review of social and cultural commentary, *Viaţa Românească*. Its directors, the literary critic Garabet Ibrăileanu and the sociologist Mihai Ralea, viewed the writer first of all as a member of society who could not but reflect the mental climate of his community and his own time. They opposed the aesthetic principles put forward by Lovinescu and his colleagues and condemned the removal of political, social, and moral considerations from the creative process as a sign of spiritual decadence. Instead, they gave encouragement to writers who displayed a sense of moral responsibility, and they were less sympathetic to modern urban society than to the countryside, an attitude that betrayed the persistence of Populist ideas. But theirs was not the idyllic landscape of the Sămănătorists. They advocated realism. In prose they favored epic reconstructions of society, and the poets they admired maintained contact with their surroundings and avoided obscurity.

The adherents of Gândirism clearly favored literature with a message, a spiritual one. Nichifor Crainic was primarily responsible for elaborating their aesthetic theory, which came to be known as literary Orthodoxism. His views on the nature of beauty and the function of art grew out of a religious interpretation of history. For him, the purpose of artistic, man-made beauty was the same as that of beauty in nature – to orient the human soul toward the divinity and to reveal, however imperfectly, glimpses of the absolute. He attributed the creative urge in man to a "nostalgia for paradise," an attempt to recapture the innocence of Eden. Yet despite his passion and eloquence, few writers were willing to accept such narrow doctrinal constraints on their creativity.

A fascinating variety of themes and modes of expression characterized Romanian poetry in the interwar period. It was at once traditional, religious, metaphysical, realist, and avant-garde. The village
and the rural landscape, as in the past, remained a fertile source of
inspiration, but now they were exposed as never before to daring
experiments in language and form. Poets might be traditional in
their themes but utterly modern in their treatment of the countryside and its inhabitants. The city now appeared more regularly than
before. Yet even poets who were stimulated by its hurried rhythms
and myriad images remained wary of its impact on the human psyche. Whether modernist or traditional, Romanian poetry had thus
largely closed the gap between itself and Western poetic currents.
Fully attuned to what was happening in Europe, it had achieved
synchronism. It also fulfilled another of Eugen Lovinescu's proph-
ecies: through the avant-garde it had become international and had
begun to make its own original contributions to European aesthetic
values. Such a diversity of ideas and expression makes easy categor-
ization impossible. The work of great poets – Tudor Arghezi, Lucian
Blaga, Ion Barbu, and Ion Pillat – suggests the need for caution.

At first glance, Tudor Arghezi (1880–1967) would seem to be
a modernist. He brought changes to the form and language of
Romanian poetry more fundamental than any it had experienced
since Eminescu. His style was marked by extreme concision,
innovative syntax, and extraordinary verbal inventiveness. He
left no source of language untapped, blending archaic and rural
terms, urban slang, and neologisms into a new, yet natural poetic
language, as he revealed in his first volume of poems, *Cuvinte pot-
rivite* (Suitable words; 1927). Like other poets of the day, he had
mixed feelings about the pace and direction of modern civilization.
Its technology, capable of easing men's lives and at the same time
threatening a new form of slavery, struck him as demonic.

Arghezi was a poet of many universes. He turned to the world of
the peasant out of a profound inner calling to speak on behalf of
those whose existences were despised by others but who had made
the earth productive. He depicted the work in the fields as humble
and brutalizing, and yet, at fleeting moments, blessed, and he por-
trayed the peasant as crude, but possessed of indomitable vitality
and innate common sense. He revealed his true adherences in yet

another poetic world, one that coalesced around mold, which in *Flori de mucigai* (Flowers of mold; 1931) he made the symbol of an underworld from which all illusions about man's ability to progress beyond his coarse nature had disappeared. The rebel in Arghezi manifested itself in his quest for the God who would not hesitate to reveal himself to man. God's absence never ceased to torment him. But his failure to know the Absolute did not resign him to the thought that it was, after all, only a "transcendent emptiness." Where other poets saw nothingness, he glimpsed eternity.

Lucian Blaga, so different from Arghezi in temperament and approaches to art, nonetheless shared many of his concerns. Immediately apparent are the metaphysical depth and lyrical vitality and inventiveness of his verse. His poetry cannot be separated from his philosophy, for both reflect the same pursuit of first principles and the same striving for knowledge and understanding of the world and of man's place in it. Yet his poetry was not simply a lyrical exposition of his philosophy. It was, as he always insisted, a response to his own deep sensibility and creative impulses.

Blaga was part of the modernist movement in European poetry and, as in his philosophy, he was decisively influenced by currents of ideas in Germany. He shared with the post-war European generation of intellectuals anxiety at the absence of a tangible universal order and of a divine intelligence that would reveal itself and give meaning to man's existence. Like them, he was repelled by the mechanization and standardization of modern life that deprived man of his soul and thus reduced him to utter insignificance in the world.

Perhaps the most striking evidence of Blaga's integration into the broad currents of European poetry was his obvious debt to Bergson's *élan vital* and Nietzsche's Dionysian vitalism and the pervasive influence of German Expressionism. Expressionism becomes the dominant mode in *În marea trecere* (In the great passage; 1924) and *La cumpăna apelor* (At the watershed; 1933), where he is obsessed by the cycle of birth, maturity, and extinction to which each individual is subject and by the apparent emptiness of existence. He transforms the rural landscape and folklore motifs, which occupy an increasingly important place in his poetry, into a hallucinatory, Expressionistic world. Here he contrasts the atmosphere of magic and the earthiness of village life with the mechanical and brassy exterior of modern urban society, and a vague sense of impending doom permeates all things. Although in later volumes his metaphysical anxiety was softened by more common human feelings and by the discovery of the village as a place of "psychic refuge" from modern civilization, his longing for the absolute and his tragic sense of existence were never stilled.

Many of the principal strands of interwar Romanian poetry came together in the works of Ion Barbu (1896–1961). A mathematician, he was the most consistent advocate and practitioner of "pure poetry" of all the Romanian poets of the time. If poetry was to achieve absolute purity, he insisted, words, which were the raw material of poetry, must be freed of all notional content and logical syntactical connections and, instead, assume the task of suggestion. The poems in the cycle *Joc second* (A secondary game; 1930) were in essence experiments with words. They describe the ineffable – dusk, sunrise, morning dew on paths – as the poet himself reveals a fascination with the "perfections" of geometry, which, for him, were signs that a divine order dominated the universe.

Ion Pillat (1891–1945) was one of the leading practitioners of "nativism," a vital and popular current in interwar poetry. Like others who subscribed to its tenets, he found inspiration in the Romanian rural landscape and depicted the world of the village as patriarchal and eternal. The city and its inhabitants had no place in such poetry. Pillat found his true poetic voice in the volume *Pe Argeş în sus* (Up the Argeş; 1923), one of the purest expressions of nativist poetry and one of the most beautiful books of poetry in the Romanian language. He sings of specific Romanian landscapes in a rustic and patriarchal setting. In a sense, he puts the traditionalist program into aesthetic practice, but there is nothing here of a social program, and he does not treat the countryside and its people as abstractions. Rather, he sings naturally and spontaneously of the places where he grew up and of the simple joys of the harvest and family life. Despite obvious affinities to traditionalism, he is a traditionalist in his own way. Rather than a social theorist and a Romantic, he is a classicist whose expression of rural settings and bucolic pleasures is soft and serene.

At the opposite pole of creative theory and practice from nativism stood the avant-garde poets, who were fully attuned to the urbanism and technology of the twentieth century and aimed at creating a literature that would capture both the exhilaration and the tragedy of contemporary man. Their audacity was matched only by the variety of their means of expression. Ion Vinea, the editor of *Contimporanul* (The contemporary), the leading avant-garde review, and his colleagues thought that they had discovered in the latest technology what the form and function of literature should be. Resorting to associations that defied normal logic and produced dissonances that destroyed the musicality of ordinary speech, they used a rapid, telegraphic technique that allowed them to depict all at once the diverse and contradictory existences that life in the modern city had imposed on man. Ilarie Voronca (1905–46) employed similar techniques in an attempt to adapt poetry to the non-stop, mechanical pace of modern life in *Invitaţie la bal* (Invitation to the ball; 1931), where he overwhelms the reader with rapid, simultaneous impressions of myriad things. A prolific theoretician of modernist poetry, he defined one of his favorite genres thus: "Pictopoezia nu e poezie. Pictopoezia nu e pictură. Pictopoezia e pictopoezie." (Pictorial poetry is not poetry. Pictorial poetry is not pictorial. Pictorial poetry is pictorial poetry.)

The novel dominated Romanian prose in the interwar period. It became urbanized, and it underwent significant aesthetic changes, becoming more "objective" and realistic than its nineteenth-century predecessors. In construction, too, it was different, as novelists assimilated all the main accomplishments of the European novel from Zola to Proust and even Joyce. Eager to experiment, they abandoned Balzac. Among the innovators were Liviu Rebreanu and Hortensia Papadat-Bengescu. Rebreanu (1885–1944) wrote the first great realist novels of Romanian literature. His art and, hence, his approach to the rural world were quite unlike earlier lyrical and historical epics. *Ion* (John; 1920) established his reputation as a major novelist. It also marked a turning point in the development of the Romanian novel, as Rebreanu delivered a stunning rejoinder to the traditional image of rural life. His was an objective epic of the contemporary village, not the idyll of a rural paradise or of the ahistorical village that had eluded the processes of evolution.

The main conflict in *Ion* is the struggle for land, and the hero is the archetype of the Romanian peasant, who must have land at all costs and resorts to whatever means are necessary to achieve his dream. Land becomes an obsession, which leads to Ion's dehumanization and final tragedy. In a sequel, *Răscoala* (The uprising; 1932), Rebreanu explored the collective psychology of an entire class driven by an inexorable yearning for even the smallest piece of land. With the great peasant revolt of 1907 as background he created a realistic fresco of rural life, where peasants formed the instinctual, irrational force of rebellion against an order of things they could neither control nor comprehend. Rebreanu thus introduced the formula of harsh realism into the Romanian novel. His prose is spare and straightforward, which fits his artistic intentions perfectly. His cold, grave style enhanced the sense of foreboding as he revealed the play of great impersonal social and biological forces over the destinies of men.

With Hortensia Papadat-Bengescu (1876–1955) the epoch of the traditional novel comes to a close. She not only urbanized the novel, but, with Rebreanu, she created a new type of novel, that of psychological analysis. Yet her work was different from Rebreanu's, for she was more concerned than he with the obscure zones of consciousness. In the cycle about the Halippa family, consisting of four novels, among them *Concert din muzică de Bach* (A concert of Bach's music; 1927), she caught perfectly the spirit of the Romanian bourgeoisie on its way to becoming a social elite. Her characters live in the city and do the things that members of the urban upper class ordinarily do, and the city is a normal place, not the strange and abhorrent growth pictured by the traditionalists. Rather, her characters spend their time trying to live and act in a refined manner and thereby impress others. Although they fail, they are not the caricatures of Caragiale's plays. The contrast between form and substance that is so striking in his works, which leads inevitably to the ridiculous, is absent here, for the interwar bourgeoisie possessed the skills appropriate to their new station. Yet, egoism and amorality often lay just beneath the good manners.

Thanks to the work of Papadat-Bengescu and to the promoters of the new novel among such younger writers as Anton Holban, Max Blecher, Mihail Sebastian, and Mircea Eliade, the Romanian novel of the 1930s kept pace with the changes in form and theme occurring elsewhere in Europe. It achieved synchronism with the West, and their authors were certain that they were Europeans.

The novels of Anton Holban (1902–37) resemble diaries, and his heroes, intellectuals, are preoccupied with knowing themselves through an analysis of love and jealousy, as in *O moarte care nu dovedeşte nimic* (A death that proves nothing; 1931) and *Ioana* (Joan; 1934). Max Blecher's (1909–38) novels, *Întâmplări în irealitatea imediată* (Events in the immediate unreality; 1936) and *Inimi cicatrizate* (Hearts scarred over; 1937), are the diaries of a patient ill from tuberculosis, whose personality disintegrates under self-examination. In transcribing this existential drama, Blecher presents a mosaic of minutely described fragments, which, taken together, hint at the ultimate sense of things. In *De două mii de ani* (For two thousand years; 1934), Mihail Sebastian (1907–45) transformed the novel into an essay on the place of the Jew in Romanian interwar society. He, too, uses the formula of the diary to record the memories, thoughts, and conversations of the narrator, an assimilated Jew, like Sebastian himself, who seeks to understand what sets him apart from his Romanian friends. Sebastian's "essay" was the most important Romanian experiment up to that time with the thesis novel, in which the lives of the characters are secondary to their main function as expositions of principles.

Mircea Eliade (1907–86), was a philosopher, literary critic, journalist, and, no less, a novelist during the intellectually turbulent decade of the 1930s. His early novels were in effect diaries. In two of them, which focused on his stay in India, where he had gone to study the history of religions, the main subject is erotic love. His experiences, which he pushed to the limit of existentialist doctrine, were the occasion for self-knowledge. In *Isabel şi apele diavolului* (Isabel and the waters of the devil; 1930) he was obsessed with the demonic side of his being, and in *Maitreyi* (1933), a personal confession, he describes the initiation of a young European into a mysterious cosmic and moral order and reveals the ultimate failure of the attempt to reconcile East and West. Eliade also explored the nature and aspirations of his own generation in more objective prose. The heroes of *Întoarcerea din rai* (The return from paradise; 1934) and *Huliganii* (The hooligans; 1935) are the disciples of Nae

Ionescu who formed the anxious generation, eager to realize their potential at any cost and terrified of failure. In *Huliganii*, Eliade took this idea to extremes. Here, the young seek to break every connection with the older generation and the moral values which sustained it. Eliade sees their acts as an affirmation of vitality and as the means by which exceptional individuals impose their will on the mass of the population. It is a view of life from inside the Romania of the 1930s.

Such works as Eliade's were the product of a curious blend of the autochthonous and the European. The urgings of the traditionalist, Orthodoxist Nae Ionescu to experience life, which inspired a generation of intellectuals, including Eliade, were in the end, to bring a renunciation of tradition and religion in favor of Western individualism and nihilism, as the hooligans demonstrated.

INTERNATIONAL RELATIONS

The primary aim of Romania's foreign policy throughout the interwar period was to defend the frontiers drawn at the end of the First World War. All political parties, except the Communists, were consistent supporters of the Versailles system, a stance which dictated the choice of allies and provided continuity with the foreign policy pursued immediately before the war. Romanian politicians regarded France and, to a lesser extent, Britain as the chief guarantors of the peace settlement and relied upon them to counter threats to the territorial status quo in Eastern Europe from the Soviet Union, Germany, and the lesser revisionist states, Hungary and Bulgaria. Romanian governments were, understandably, champions of collective security. They supported efforts to make the League of Nations a reliable defender of European peace and stability, and they promoted regional alliances, such as the Little Entente and the Balkan Entente, in order to discourage revisionism in Eastern Europe. On all these fundamental issues the Liberals, National Peasants, and Carol II were in general agreement. They all recognized that the frontiers of Greater Romania would be secure only so long as the political equilibrium established in 1919 was not disturbed, and, hence, they were eager to prevent Germany and the Soviet Union from gaining dominance in regional affairs.

In the end, all the efforts by Romanian governments in the 1920s and 1930s to ensure the inviolability of their country's new frontiers proved in vain. They could not soften the differences between themselves and their two chief revisionist neighbors – Hungary and the Soviet Union – as neither could be reconciled to the loss of territory at the end of the war. The problem of Transylvania stood in the way of any significant rapprochement between Hungary and Romania. Hungarian governments throughout the interwar period never ceased to hope for the return of a territory they regarded as an integral part of historical Hungary, and no Romanian government would contemplate the slightest concession that might diminish its sovereignty over the province.

The bone of contention between Romania and the Soviet Union was Bessarabia. Its incorporation into Romania in 1918 had precipitated a break in relations and was to remain the chief obstacle to their resumption until 1934. The lack of significant trade between the two countries offered no economic incentive for an agreement. But pressure from other quarters eventually led both sides to moderate their intransigence. The example of France in seeking a pact with the Soviet Union seems to have been decisive for the Romanians. Foreign Minister Nicolae Titulescu (1882–1941) pursued a similar accommodation. In Geneva on June 9, 1934 under the auspices of the Little Entente, he and Maxim Litvinov, the Soviet foreign minister, exchanged letters establishing regular diplomatic relations. But they made no mention of Bessarabia. Then, in July 1936, Titulescu and Litvinov initialed an agreement for mutual aid within the framework of the League of Nations and scheduled the formal signing for September. But on August 29 Titulescu, whose efforts at a rapprochement with the Soviet Union had made powerful enemies for him on the right and whose ambition and international successes had aroused the King's animosity, was abruptly removed from office in a cabinet reshuffle. The Soviet government took the dismissal of Titulescu as a sign that Romanian foreign policy had changed course and declared the understanding of July null and void. In the deteriorating international situation of the latter 1930s neither side made a serious attempt to revive the treaty.

The dismissal of Titulescu as foreign minister symbolized a subtle shift in Romania's foreign policy in favor of Germany. The overall objective remained the same – security – but now King Carol and others thought it necessary to broaden the base of support for their country's territorial integrity. Carol and the majority of politicians and intellectuals preferred the traditional alliance with France and Britain. The relationship with France was not merely political; it grew out of the Romanians' perception of a general community of interests between the two countries, of mutual comprehension and even affection, feelings that were entirely absent in contacts with Germany. But the failure of France and Britain to stand up to Hitler's assault on the Versailles system had caused even the staunchest of Western sympathizers to reconsider the system of alliances they had been building since the end of the war. The unsettled relationship with the Soviet Union increased their anxiety about shifts in the international balance of power. Both the supporters and the opponents of Carol had an almost irrational fear of the Soviet Union. For them, it was Romania's hereditary enemy, always present, always a threat to her existence. Germany in the mid 1930s did not seem as dangerous.

Until this time, Romania's relations with Germany had not gone beyond the usual diplomatic forms. The war, especially the rigors of the occupation, had caused a sharp break in the pre-1914 tradition of respect for German economic and military power and appreciation of her cultural achievements, and Romanian opinion in fact never fully recovered. The world economic depression led to somewhat closer economic relations, but Romanian leaders, including Carol, were wary of Germany's penetration of the country's economy.

The Czechoslovak crisis in the spring and summer of 1938 narrowed the choices available to Romanian leaders. The immediate issue for Carol and his ministers was whether to come to the aid of their ally in the Little Entente. In the end, they decided not to. They had reached the conclusion that the initiative in international relations had passed to Germany, and, hence, they feared that any action they might take on behalf of Czechoslovakia, in the absence of determined leadership from France, would jeopardize the territorial integrity of their own country. Neither Carol nor other Romanian leaders seriously considered joining forces with the Soviet Union. Instead, they continued to hope that France and

Britain would finally awaken to the dangers that German ambitions posed to their own security. But the Munich agreement of September 29, in which France and Britain acquiesced in the dismemberment of Czechoslovakia, convinced political opinion in Bucharest from Carol to Maniu that closer relations with Germany were now essential in order to protect the country's borders against Soviet and Hungarian revisionism.

A measure of Germany's growing influence in Romania was the economic treaty concluded between the two countries on March 23, 1939. Valid for five years, it provided for a close linking of their economies through coordinated planning and joint companies, whose main tasks would be to develop Romania's mineral resources – copper, chromium, manganese, and especially oil. The intensified German interest in Romanian oil was linked to preparations for war and the need to become independent of overseas supplies, which could be cut off by a British blockade. For the same reasons, Germany wished to make certain of a regular supply of Romanian agricultural products. But Romania also stood to benefit from the treaty. Besides help in developing her economy, she had found in Germany a provider of modern military equipment and a reliable purchaser of large quantities of grain at better prices than anyone else was prepared to pay.

The non-aggression pact of August 23, 1939 between Germany and the Soviet Union came as a shock to Romanian leaders, for they had based their foreign policy in part on the deep-seated hostility between Nazism and Communism. Now, they felt more insecure than ever before. Although they did not know the details of the secret protocol, by which Germany recognized the Soviet Union's special interest in Bessarabia, the very existence of the treaty had undone their strategy of balance between the two powers.

The outbreak of war in September 1939 and the ominous turn of events on the Western front in the spring of 1940 brought a drastic change in Romanian foreign policy. German victories in the Low Countries and northern France in May convinced Carol that the Allied cause was lost. On May 29 he decided that only one course of action remained – to rely on Germany to protect the country's territorial integrity. The defeat of France in June removed all doubt about the course to be taken.

Yet, the wooing of Germany could not prevent the loss of territory to Romania's neighbors. The Soviet Union moved first. On June 26, it demanded the cession of Bessarabia and northern Bukovina within twenty-four hours. Carol immediately sought German support, but none was forthcoming, as Hitler had already assured the Soviet government of his "disinterest" in the territories, in accordance with the Nazi–Soviet Pact. Carol and his advisers saw no acceptable alternative but to yield.

Carol spared no effort to ingratiate himself with Hitler in a desperate attempt to deflect the territorial demands of Hungary and Bulgaria. On July 4 Carol brought in a new, pro-German government which immediately declared its wish to adhere to the Rome–Berlin Axis and announced Romania's withdrawal from the League of Nations. While these events were taking place, Carol sought a German guarantee of Romania's existing frontiers and the sending of a military mission to Bucharest to establish close cooperation between the armies of the two countries. But on July 15 Hitler replied that he could consider these requests only after the border questions with Hungary and Bulgaria had been settled. Agreement with Bulgaria over the strip of southern Dobrudja that Romania had acquired in 1913 was quickly reached. The Treaty of Craiova of September 7 restored the frontier of 1913 between the two countries.

Far more significant were negotiations with Hungary over Transylvania, since the Romanian public regarded it as the cradle of the nation. But negotiations, which began on August 16, got nowhere and were soon broken off. Hitler took the initiative to impose a settlement as tension rose along the Romanian border with Hungary and summoned delegations from both countries to meet in Vienna to resolve their dispute. He had, in fact, already reserved to himself the final decision on Transylvania's new frontiers. Strategic and economic goals were uppermost in his mind. He thought it necessary both to satisfy Hungary and to avoid crippling Romania, whose value to the German war effort he never ceased to acknowledge. Yet, he apparently also saw the importance of keeping both countries dissatisfied as a means of ensuring their cooperation in the German new order in Europe. Thus, he thought that Hungary would support Germany in hopes of gaining more of Transylvania, and that Romania would do the same in order to get back what had been lost. Moreover, the new frontier in Transylvania offered substantial protection to the Romanian oil fields by bringing German motorized troops (with the cooperation of Hungary) within a few hours of them. In Vienna, the Romanian delegation was anxious to argue its case in detail, but, instead, it was presented with Hitler's solution and was given the choice of either accepting it or facing war with Hungary supported by the Axis. Yet, the German foreign minister, Joachim von Ribbentrop, also promised that in exchange for accepting Hitler's "arbitration," Romania would receive a German military guarantee of her new frontiers, an offer that Ribbentrop characterized as "exceptional," not only because it had not been made to any other country, but because it would represent the cornerstone of Germany's new policy in the East. The Romanians asked for time to consult with the King. In the early morning of August 30 at a meeting of the Crown Council in Bucharest to decide on a course of action Carol and the majority agreed that acceptance together with German guarantees was the only way of preventing the destruction of the country.

Later, on August 30, Hitler's decision was formally read. Only then did the Romanian delegation learn the full extent of their country's losses. Hungary was awarded a large salient carved out of northern Transylvania beginning with Oradea and Maramureş in the north and encompassing Cluj and the Szekler districts along the western slopes of the Carpathians extending south to the vicinity of Braşov. Romania was thus deprived of 42,243 square kilometers of territory and approximately 2,600,000 inhabitants, roughly 50 percent of them Romanians and 37 percent Hungarians and Szeklers. At another level the Vienna Diktat, as the agreement came to be known in Romania, signified the loss of Romania's independence in foreign affairs and the subordination of her economy to the German war effort.

As a result of the cessions of territory to the Soviet Union, Hungary, and Bulgaria, the Romania that had come into being at the end of the First World War lost a third of its territory (99,790 square kilometers) and a third of its population (6,161,317). Carol could not survive the national catastrophe.

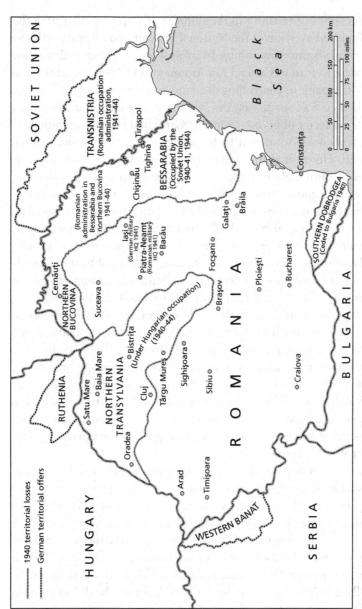

Map 8 Romania during the Second World War

THE SECOND WORLD WAR

The cessions of territory in the summer of 1940, together with the undisguised aversion of the National Peasant and Liberal parties to the royal dictatorship, obliged Carol, whose prestige had reached its nadir, to turn to General Ion Antonescu (1882–1946) as the one person capable of controlling the dangerous situation. The choice of Antonescu was not an easy one, for the dedicated career officer had made no secret of his contempt for Carol and his own ambition.

Carol chose Antonescu to form a government in order to save himself. He wanted to use Antonescu's connections with the Iron Guard to bring about a reconciliation between its leaders and the throne, his good relations with the National Peasants and Liberals to neutralize their opposition to the royal dictatorship, and his close contacts with members of the German legation in Bucharest to demonstrate Romania's firm attachment to Hitler's new order in Europe and ensure German support for its king and its political independence. But Carol made a grave miscalculation; he brought to power an enemy who was determined to remove him from the throne.

Although Antonescu welcomed support from diverse sources, notably Germany and the major political parties, he changed not at all his own idea of what the future Romania should be like. He was a nationalist who was intent on building a prosperous, strong ethnic state, a respected middle-sized power carrying out its international responsibilities at the regional level in harmony with the European state system. He was also an authoritarian who was convinced that he could achieve his goals only if he assumed absolute control of the country's destiny.

Antonescu had no intention of accepting political and economic vassalage to Germany. First of all, he was not pro-German. Like the majority of Romanian officers, he was pro-French and pro-English, and in December 1937 he had made his participation in the Goga government conditional upon the avoidance of close ties with Germany. He had even favored Romania's joining in a Western effort to prevent Hitler from destroying Czechoslovakia. When he finally decided to throw in his lot with Germany he did so because he saw no alternative if the country were to survive. His sentiments toward the West remained in place, but the international situation

16 Ion Antonescu

had changed drastically. Greatly affected by the defeat of France and the aggressive behavior of the Soviet Union against her small neighbors, and now convinced that Germany was going to win the war, he had already laid the foundations of his political alliance with Germany in conversations with German legation officials in

Bucharest in the summer of 1940. An arrangement with Antonescu was eminently satisfactory to the Germans. Although an apparent instrument of German policy lay readily at hand in the Iron Guard, many German officials doubted its effectiveness, because of its lack of capable leaders and a clear program. Antonescu, on the other hand, offered those guarantees of order and stability they judged essential for the furtherance of the German war effort.

As Antonescu pursued negotiations with various political leaders in early September with a view to forming an effective government, it became apparent that a solution to the political crisis was impossible as long as Carol remained on the throne. On the 5th Antonescu flatly demanded that he abdicate and leave the country. Carol hesitated, but finally yielded to an ultimatum from Antonescu to the effect that unless he abdicated immediately his own life would be in jeopardy and the country would dissolve in civil war and face occupation by a "foreign power." On September 6 Carol renounced the throne in favor of his 19-year-old son, Mihai, and left the country on the following day.

On the same day, upon his accession to the throne, Mihai issued a decree giving Antonescu full powers as the Leader of the Romanian State (Conducătorul Statului Român). Antonescu brought the political crisis to an end on September 15 by forming a coalition government with the Iron Guard. He himself assumed the presidency of the Council of Ministers and became minister of national defense, while the Iron Guard became the dominant political force in the new government. Horia Sima, Codreanu's successor as head of the Guard, was vice-president of the Council, and Guardists held five ministries, including Interior, Foreign Affairs, and Education and Cults. The Guard also controlled the press and propaganda services, the majority of the permanent secretaries and directors in the ministries and forty-five out of forty-six of the county prefectures. The announcement of the new cabinet was accompanied by the proclamation of Romania as a "National Legionary State" in which the only political movement allowed to function was the Iron Guard.

Antonescu set about at once replacing the old political order with one he later described as a "national totalitarian state." He made plain his utter disgust for political parties and the practices of Romanian democracy, which he considered inherently defective.

Underlying its failure, he thought, was its cultivation of liberty, which put the interests of individuals above those of collectivities and the state. He thus made no room for political parties in his new order. His earlier proposals to Iuliu Maniu and Constantin Brătianu, the head of the Liberal Party, for a government of national unity had been merely a device to enable him to draw upon the experience of National Peasant and Liberal parties, and even his sharing of power with the Iron Guard, in the light of subsequent events, was but a temporary expedient.

In foreign affairs, Antonescu's most pressing concern was to consolidate the alliance with Germany. The success of that endeavor required the fulfillment of the terms of the Vienna Diktat, which, though distasteful to him personally, he was determined to carry out fully. He also began to lay the foundations for Romania's new role in a German-dominated Europe by strengthening military and economic ties to Germany.

The speed with which Berlin responded to Antonescu's overtures suggests how important Romania had become in German strategic planning in Southeastern Europe. Because of the failure of the Italian invasion of Greece in October 1940, Hitler had decided that a German relief expedition would be necessary and that it would have to go through Romania and Bulgaria. But Romania's role in the East was not to be limited solely to that of a staging area and a supplier of raw materials. Worsening relations with the Soviet Union had persuaded Hitler to accelerate planning for the settlement of German–Soviet differences by military means. In the event of war, he intended to assign to Romania the key role of southern anchor of the German Eastern front. The first German troops arrived in Romania on October 10, 1940, in part in response to Antonescu's request for military assistance.

In order to ensure full Romanian cooperation Hitler invited Antonescu to Berlin on November 21–24. The official reason for the visit was to complete Romania's adherence to the German-Italian-Japanese Pact, which Antonescu, in fact, signed on the 23rd. Far more important, however, were the conversations between Hitler and Antonescu on the previous day, which decisively influenced the subsequent course of German–Romanian relations. Antonescu made a favorable impression on Hitler as someone he could trust, a conviction that lasted until Antonescu's downfall in August 1944. Antonescu, for his part insisted that the Vienna Diktat be revised. Hitler made no promises, stating simply that after the war the situation would be different from what it had been, but Antonescu took these words as a commitment to change the terms of the Diktat. From then on he had Transylvania constantly in mind, and he was certain that close cooperation with Germany was the only way to ensure the return of lost territory.

While Antonescu had thus achieved his main goal in foreign policy – a firm alliance with Germany – his cooperation with the Iron Guard at home failed to bring about the public order and economic progress he desired. The Guardists proved to be incompetent and unreliable partners, who, it was obvious, did not share Antonescu's vision of the new Romania.

The ambitions of Guard leaders were boundless. They challenged Antonescu's authority by attempting to gain control of the police and the army, institutions which had previously been impervious to Guard influence. They also created a separate force, the legionary police, to be used against their opponents. Its members were recruited from among the least desirable elements of society and had no professional training. With the army the Guard had little success. The officer corps had always been hostile to the legionary movement as an element of disorder and subordination to Germany. Only in the lower ranks did the Guard gain a few adherents.

Antonescu took drastic action to prevent the "legionary spirit" from gaining a foothold in the army. On December 5, 1940 he imposed severe penalties for "rebellion" and "insubordination," including death for instigators and leaders of such actions. These measures were undoubtedly a response to the atrocities committed by legionary death squads in the final week of November. Among the victims were Nicolae Iorga and Virgil Madgearu, who were taken from their homes and shot, and many former government ministers and other officials, who were among sixty-four prisoners killed in a Guardist rampage at Jilava prison, near Bucharest.

The conflict between Antonescu and the Guard had to do with fundamental differences about the form that the totalitarian state should take and how it should be administered. Horia Sima demanded that the country be governed in accordance with the "legionary spirit," by which he meant that power should be exercised solely by the Guard and that political activity by all other groups should be halted. On October 28 he accused Antonescu of violating the decree establishing the National Legionary State by permitting the National Peasant and Liberal parties to function, if only on paper. He also demanded an "economic revolution," by which he meant the application to Romania of German national socialist principles as a means of bringing every aspect of economic life under centralized control. But Antonescu had no intention of allowing the state or the economy to be run by legionaries. By late fall he had accumulated convincing evidence of their disloyalty and incompetence. Yet, his contest with the Guard went beyond matters of efficient administration and coherent economic policy. It was about power. Antonescu was determined to subordinate the legionary movement to his own vision of a disciplined, orderly Romania.

As the strained relations between Antonescu and Horia Sima moved inexorably toward open conflict, Antonescu consulted Hitler. At a meeting at the Berghof on January 14, 1941 he accused Iron Guard leaders of having brought the country to the brink of anarchy and proposed that he take over sole leadership of the National Legionary State. At first, Hitler was evasive. He explained how some years before he himself had faced a similar challenge from within his own party and had been obliged to liquidate such elements, and he suggested that Antonescu might have to do the same. Later, just before Antonescu's departure for home, Hitler assured him that he was the only man capable of guiding the destinies of Romania. This short conversation dispelled Antonescu's final doubts about Hitler's position in the struggle for power with the Guard. On the 22nd he sent the army against Guard strongholds in Bucharest, and by evening the issue had been decided. Sima and other Guard leaders vainly sought the intervention of German officials, but they advised surrender, promising only that they would seek permission from Antonescu for Guard leaders to go to Germany. They thought it wise to preserve the Guard in some form as a means of putting pressure on Antonescu if in the future he decided to act contrary to German interests. On the 23rd the legionary rank-and-file surrendered, but the chief of the German secret service in Romania arranged for Guard leaders to be spirited out of the country to Germany.

The regime that Antonescu now instituted cannot be classified as fascist. A more apt description would be military dictatorship. Unlike Hitler's Germany and Mussolini's Italy, it lacked an ideology and was not supported by a mass political party. Instead of a philosophical justification for its existence, Antonescu made order and security, which he thought essential for the progress of every society, the reason for being of his new order. He relied on neither the masses nor politicians. In their place he used the army and the security apparatus to provide direction and suppress dissent.

As Hitler's preparations for the attack on the Soviet Union proceeded in the spring of 1941, he and German army commanders foresaw only a limited role for the Romanian army because they had doubts about its capacity to carry out independent offensive actions. They were far more concerned about protecting the Romanian oil fields from a Soviet attack and entrusted their defense to the head of the German air force mission in Romania. They were certain that Romanian oil supplies would become critical once the war began because shipments from the Soviet Union, Germany's other major supplier, would obviously cease. On June 12 in Munich Hitler informed Antonescu of his plan to attack the Soviet Union. Antonescu's response was to promise his country's full military and economic participation.

On June 22, 1941, a few hours after the German invasion of the Soviet Union had begun, King Mihai and Antonescu proclaimed the beginning of a "holy war" to free Bessarabia and northern Bukovina from Soviet occupation. This war enjoyed widespread support among the Romanian people, who saw it as a means of removing the Russian threat to their country's existence once and for all. Political leaders and the public had full confidence in the military superiority of Germany and expected a short, victorious campaign. Antonescu committed the bulk of his army to the effort.

The general offensive on the Romanian front got underway only on July 2 because it had been much further east than the base from which the German South Army Group in Poland had begun operations. Within a month of the beginning of hostilities the primary Romanian military objectives – the liberation of Bessarabia and northern Bukovina – had been achieved. But Antonescu had already decided to send Romanian troops further east. He was certain that a German victory would come in the foreseeable future and he intended, as he wrote to Hitler on July 20, to fight alongside Germany until they had achieved their final goal of destroying the Soviet Union. When Hitler and Antonescu met at the headquarters of the South Army Group on August 6 they agreed that the Romanian army would occupy the area between the Dniester and the Dnieper rivers, that certain units would advance east of the Dnieper, and that the area between the Dniester and Bug rivers, which came to be called Transnistria, would come under Romanian civil administration. Antonescu insisted that the Romanian army take sole responsibility for capturing Odessa, but German forces eventually had to be brought in to complete the operation. The siege, which lasted from August 18 until the fall of the city on October 16, caused the Romanian army heavy casualties: 18,000 killed, 63,000 wounded, and 11,000 missing. In the aftermath of the siege Romanian army units destroyed what remained of the city's Jewish community.

At the end of 1941 Romania was also at war with the Western Allies. Great Britain, under pressure from the Soviet Union, declared war on Romania on December 7. After the United States entered the Second World War on that date, Germany obliged Romania to honor its commitment under the Tripartite Pact of November 1940 by declaring war on the United States on December 12. It was evident that Antonescu and the majority of Romanian politicians were reluctant partners in Germany's war against the Western Allies.

Large numbers of Romanian troops took part in the massive German offensive in southern Russia and the Caucasus in the summer of 1942. Some eight divisions were engaged in operations east of the Sea of Azov, but the bulk of Romanian forces took part in the drive to the Volga. They were assigned positions on the northern and southern flanks of the German spearhead. It was here that Soviet forces made a decisive breakthrough in their great winter offensive, which began on November 19. By the end of December they had completed the encirclement of the German Sixth Army at Stalingrad. Romanian units had fought well, but, lacking sufficient armor and artillery, they were ill-prepared to deal with the Soviet onslaught. The Romanian Third and Fourth armies sustained heavy losses, being reduced from 228,000 in November 1942 to 73,000 in January 1943.

One of the most serious domestic issues with which the Antonescu regime had to deal was "the Jewish question," as it had been called since the second half of the nineteenth century. Strong national feeling and tactical foreign-policy goals rather than doctrinaire anti-Semitism determined attempts to "solve" it. After the establishment of the National Legionary State Antonescu and the Iron Guard had proceeded to Romanianize the economy. The Guard used the occasion to give free rein to its violent brand of anti-Semitism. But for Antonescu, Romanianization was one of the means he intended to use to create a strong, self-reliant native middle class, which would form the political and social backbone of the country. Thus, he initiated the removal of Jews and foreigners from the country's economic structure and their replacement by ethnic Romanians. A series of decrees expropriated Jewish-owned rural and urban property (October 4, 1940), forests (November 17, 1940), and again urban property (March 28, 1941). Yet another decree (November 16, 1940) required private businesses and industries to replace all their Jewish employees with ethnic Romanians by December 31, 1941. Although official statistics showed that the number of Jews in these enterprises had been drastically reduced from 28,225 in 1940 to 6,506 by the spring of 1943, more credible secret reports indicated that many Jews remained in place (over 21,000 in 1943) because they were indispensable to the efficient operation of their respective enterprises.

Measures taken against Jews before the attack on the Soviet Union were primarily economic, except for the violent acts committed by legionaries against individuals. But after June 22, 1941 official policy assumed more ominous forms. The deportation of Jews began after the recovery of Bessarabia and northern Bukovina. Large numbers, perhaps as many as 130,000, had already fled these provinces for the Soviet Union as Romanian and German armies advanced. The killing of 4,000 Jews in Iaşi and during the deportation to Wallachia on June 28–30 by German and Romanian troops confirmed the wisdom of such flight. As soon as the Romanian army had secured Transnistria Romanian authorities began to deport the mass of Jews from Bessarabia and northern Bukovina as far to the east as possible. As many as 110,000 Jews were deported to Transnistria between 1941 and 1943, and, because of horrendous conditions, at least half perished. Another category of undesirables suffered a similar fate. Some 25,000 Gypsies were deported to Transnistria, of whom 11,000 died, many because of utter neglect of basic human needs.

The Antonescu regime did not participate in the mass deportation of Jews which Nazi officials were organizing as part of Hitler's "final solution" of the Jewish question in Europe. At first, it showed an interest in the project and agreed that beginning in September 1942 Jews fit for labor could be rounded up and sent to Lublin from specified counties in the Banat and Transylvania. But the deportations did not take place. Antonescu changed his policy toward Jews from destruction to the traditional separatist anti-Semitism. The main cause seems to have been the uncertain military situation on the Eastern front and his realization that after the war he would have to answer for his actions.

The disaster at Stalingrad was the crucial turning-point in Romania's participation in the Second World War. Convinced that Germany could not win the war, Antonescu bent all his efforts toward protecting Romania from the "great danger" to the east. That, after all, had been his primary motive in going to war against the Soviet Union. Despite increasing strains with Germany as Soviet forces moved relentlessly westward, his policy displayed a remarkable continuity. He maintained the alliance with Germany and supplied his ally with men and *matériel* as usual for the war effort, but, at the same time, he undertook to gain understanding for Romania's "difficult position" from the Western Allies. He encouraged Mihai Antonescu, deputy minister-president, to pursue contacts with them and to call their attention to the danger which the Soviet Union posed for all of Europe, not just the East.

By the spring of 1944 other political forces in Romania had joined the effort to extricate the country from war. The key figure was Iuliu Maniu, the leader of the democratic opposition to the Antonescu dictatorship. Between November 1942 and March 1943 he had sent a stream of messages to the British government through various channels, including Swiss and Turkish diplomats, in which he explained Romania's role in the war and her aspirations. He insisted that public opinion in Romania had opposed continuing the war against the Soviet Union beyond the Dniester and now sought only to ensure the territorial integrity of the country, including north Transylvania. It was evident in all Maniu's communications that he, like Mihai Antonescu and Romanian politicians generally, considered the Soviet Union the chief threat to the independence of Romania and saw in the West their only hope of avoiding a Soviet occupation.

The initial response from Britain was disheartening. In January 1943 the Foreign Office informed Maniu that the boundaries of post-war Romania would be drawn in accordance with general Allied objectives and the Soviet Union's security interests. The implication was clear that Romania could not hope to deal solely with the Western Allies, but would have to reach an accommodation with the Soviet Union.

Ion Antonescu continued to cooperate with Germany, despite the mounting evidence of military catastrophe, because he saw no viable alternative. Although he wished at all cost to avoid the subjugation of the country by the Soviet Union, he faced the more immediate threat of a German–legionary regime, which, he was certain, would complete the destruction of the country's political and economic superstructure and leave it at the mercy of "others." Such a danger was by no means imaginary, for on January 26, 1944 Hitler had ordered planning to begin for the occupation of Romania in the event of an anti-German coup. But the tension in Romanian–German relations was eased by a new economic agreement on February 9, and, especially, by Antonescu's renewed assurances of support at a meeting with Hitler on February 28.

Yet, efforts to withdraw from the war continued as contacts between Maniu and the West intensified. His representative, Barbu Ştirbey, of the nineteenth-century princely family, negotiated with the Allies in Cairo in early 1944. The Soviet Union also became involved as its armies reached the Prut and stood poised to strike deeply into Romania. To hasten a Romanian capitulation, Molotov announced on April 2 that the Soviet Union did not seek to acquire any Romanian territory or change the country's social order. On the 12th the Soviet representative in Cairo presented Ştirbey with his country's minimum conditions for an armistice, which had been worked out in consultation with the British and American governments. Communicated also to Ion Antonescu and Maniu by Romanian diplomats in Ankara, the Allies' terms demanded a complete break with Germany and a common struggle of Romanian and Allied armies against Germany; the re-establishment of the Russo-Romanian frontier as of June 22, 1941; the payment of reparations to the Soviet Union; the liberation of all Allied war prisoners; the unhindered movement of the Red Army on Romanian territory; and the nullification of the Vienna Diktat and Soviet support for the return of north Transylvania to Romania.

The reaction in Bucharest was mixed. Maniu responded on April 19 with counter-proposals. Obviously putting little faith in Soviet promises to respect Romanian sovereignty, he accepted the proposal for an armistice, but urged that no foreign (by which he meant Soviet) troops should be allowed to enter the country unless invited to do so. Anxious to avoid a Soviet occupation, he had already requested the Allied Middle East Command to send two airborne divisions to Romania, but the Allies demanded a clear acceptance or rejection of the armistice terms. After several further attempts to soften the Allied ultimatum had failed, Maniu on June 10 reluctantly accepted an armistice on the basis of the six points of April 12. But even now, rather than contact the Soviet government directly, he preferred to work through Cairo in order to make certain that Britain and the United States were full partners in any agreement.

Political groups in Romania opposed to the war and to the Antonescu dictatorship grew increasingly bold in the spring of 1944. The need for coordination led the National Peasant, Liberal, Social Democratic, and Communist parties to create the National Democratic Bloc (Blocul Naţional Democratic) in early June. Its objectives were the immediate conclusion of an armistice with the Allies, withdrawal from the Axis and all-out support for the Allied war effort, and the overthrow of the Antonescu dictatorship and its replacement by a democratic regime.

In the meantime, decisions affecting the political development of Romania had already been made. In mid May 1944 the British and Soviet governments agreed to divide Southeastern Europe into

17 King Mihai

military operational zones. The British, who had taken the initiative, proposed that Greece be in theirs and Romania in the Soviet zone. They then asked the American government if it could accept the plan. But before an answer was received, Churchill on June 8 proposed that Bulgaria be added to the Soviet zone and Yugoslavia to the British. On June 12, Roosevelt, with some reluctance, approved the arrangement. None of the parties intended it as a final delineation of spheres of influence, but the subsequent course of events nonetheless consigned Romania to the Soviet zone.

Matters came to a head with the massive Soviet offensive on the Romanian front, which began on August 20. The Red Army broke through defenses in a number of places. On the 22nd Antonescu visited field headquarters and recognized the gravity of the situation. If Soviet troops pierced the Focşani–Galaţi defense line between the Carpathians and the Danube, then he was certain that Romania's fate would be sealed "for all time."

The rapid pace of events, particularly the collapse on the Moldavian front in the middle of August, had surprised the democratic opposition. As late as August 20 it had set no date for the overthrow of Antonescu. The Soviet offensive made a decision imperative. Maniu and Brătianu in close cooperation with King Mihai, who were the principal organizers of the coup, decided to put their plan into effect on August 23. The King invited Antonescu to the palace, and when he refused to accept an immediate armistice he ordered his arrest and appointed General Constantin Sănătescu, one of the army commanders who had helped to plan the overthrow of Antonescu, as prime minister. Sănătescu immediately appointed a cabinet, including Maniu, Constantin Brătianu, Constantin Titel Petrescu, head of the Social Democratic Party, and Lucreţiu Pătrăşcanu, of the Communist Party, as ministers without portfolio who were to provide the new government with political direction as representatives of the National Democratic Bloc. That evening, the King broadcast a proclamation to the nation announcing a break of diplomatic relations with Germany and an armistice with the Allies. He declared that Romania had joined the Allies against the Axis and would mobilize all its forces to liberate north Transylvania. Sănătescu instructed the Romanian emissaries in Cairo to accept an armistice on the basis of the Allied terms of April 12.

German diplomatic and military representatives in Romania were caught off guard by the dramatic turn of events, and by August 31 German forces were in retreat throughout the country. On the same day, the Red Army entered Bucharest. A new era in Romanian history had begun.

THE SEIZURE OF POWER, 1944–1947

As the Red Army poured into the country, the most pressing task of the Sănătescu government was to stabilize its relations with the Allies, particularly the Soviet Union. It strove to conclude a formal armistice agreement as quickly as possible. The Soviet government was receptive to the idea because it wanted to secure its lines of communication with the front in Transylvania and Hungary to the north and the Balkans to the south and needed to bring Romanian manpower and supplies fully into play.

The draft of an armistice, drawn up by Soviet officials, was communicated to the American and British governments on August 31. It was evident to them that the Soviet Union regarded Romania as a conquered country. They objected particularly to the provision that the Soviet High Command in Romania would alone supervise the fulfillment of the terms of the armistice. Under American and British urging Molotov modified his position slightly. He agreed to the creation of an Allied Control Commission for Romania, which would include American and British representatives, but he made it clear that the Soviet High Command would reserve to itself all important decisions.

A Romanian delegation, headed by Lucreţiu Pătrăşcanu, traveled to Moscow and signed the armistice on September 13. In the main, it simply expanded upon the conditions set forth in Cairo. It required the Romanian government to join in the Allied war effort with at least twelve fully equipped infantry divisions, to allow the free movement of Allied forces on its territory, and to provide money and supplies to support Allied military operations against Germany and Hungary. Romania also had to assume the burden of paying reparations amounting to 300 million dollars to the Soviet Union for losses during military operations on its territory and to return all goods removed from its territory. The one bright spot for Romania was the abrogation of the Vienna Diktat, although the final disposition of north Transylvania was reserved to the general peace conference after the war.

The Romanian delegation left Moscow feeling that their country had, all things considered, been treated lightly. But at home, the leaders of the democratic political parties were deeply worried about how Soviet occupation authorities would interpret and carry out the terms of the armistice. Their concerns were shared by Averill Harriman, the American ambassador in Moscow, who had taken part in the armistice negotiations and had conferred with members of the Romanian delegation. He had no doubt that the armistice had given the Soviet Union complete political and economic control of Romania, at least until the conclusion of the final peace treaty.

Despite cooperation on the battlefield, the Sănătescu government and Soviet occupation authorities were continuously at odds with one another. The massive presence of Soviet military and civilian personnel was proving decisive in determining the direction of Romanian political life. Striking evidence of Soviet predominance was the impotence of the Allied Control Commission. The Soviet chairman regarded the Control Commission as an instrument for carrying out Soviet policy and treated his Western colleagues merely as observers. But the American and British governments chose not to challenge such behavior as long as the war against Germany was still in progress.

For Romanian domestic politics the fall of 1944 was a period of mobilization by the major parties. All had suffered a disruption of their normal activities under the dictatorships of Carol and Antonescu, and now, after six years, they turned their efforts toward reestablishing national and local organizations. In the process, the National Democratic Bloc disintegrated under the strain of competing political ideologies and ambitions.

Of the four parties composing the bloc, the Communist Party was the weakest. During the war, its membership had been reduced to perhaps 1,000 and the majority of its leaders before the August 23 coup had been in jail. In the waning days of the Antonescu dictatorship a number of them escaped or were released. They were joined by other Romanian Communists who had spent many years in Moscow and now arrived in Bucharest in the wake of the Red Army. As the local Communists and the so-called "Muscovites" strove to revive the party they benefited enormously from the presence of the Soviet occupation authorities. Within a week of the overthrow of Antonescu the Central Committee of the Romanian Communist Party had declared its intention to transform the National Democratic Bloc into a mass organization and called upon workers to organize their own political committees under the leadership of the Bloc.

The National Peasant and Liberal parties, which came to be known as the "historical parties," were also at work reviving their organizations. The Peasantists remained faithful to their pre-war economic and sociological theses. The Liberals were in some disarray. Many of the party's organizations in the provinces were rent by factionalism as their leaders at the center failed to present a dynamic plan of action. Constantin Brătianu, nonetheless, pledged that the party would remain faithful to its traditional principles and would defend the civil and political rights of all citizens.

By contrast, the Communists and their allies, intent on coming to power as quickly as possible, created the National Democratic Front on October 12. They left the Sănătescu government on the 16th and urged the formation of a new government under Petru Groza, the head of the Ploughmen's Front, a peasant party allied with the Communists. The National Democratic Front's aggressiveness and particularly its support by the Soviet Union led to the resignation of the Sănătescu government on December 6.

A new government, little changed from its predecessor, was headed by General Nicolae Rădescu, Chief of Staff of the Army, who had been arrested by Antonescu in 1941–42 because he had opposed sending Romanian troops beyond the Dniester after the recovery of Bessarabia. By this time the political initiative had shifted to the Communists, whose actions severely reduced the government's effectiveness. In the middle of January 1945 Communist leaders Gheorghe Gheorghiu-Dej and Ana Pauker traveled to Moscow for talks with Soviet party leaders. This meeting proved fateful for Romania, for Gheorghiu-Dej and company received assurances of full support for their drive to seize power. After the delegation returned home, the National Democratic Front – in fact, the Communists – initiated a systematic campaign to replace the Rădescu government with one of their own.

As the struggle for power gained momentum Soviet authorities intervened directly and decisively. Matters came to a head on February 28 when Andrei Vyshinsky, the deputy foreign minister dispatched from Moscow to coordinate the Communists' drive for power, demanded that King Mihai replace the Rădescu government immediately by a Front government headed by Petru Groza. When the King replied that he would have to await the outcome of consultations with party leaders, Vyshinsky gave him two hours to dismiss Rădescu and name his successor. Otherwise, he warned, he could not be responsible for the maintenance of Romania as an independent state. Lacking any promise of significant Western help, the King could no longer resist Soviet pressure and announced the formation of a government headed by Groza on March 6.

Soviet authorities thus ignored the decisions reached by representatives of the United States, Great Britain, and the Soviet Union who had met at Yalta to discuss the future of Europe now that the outcome of the war was no longer in doubt. The Declaration on Liberated Europe, which the three powers had signed on February 12, 1945, just weeks before the appointment of Groza as prime minister, played no part in determining Soviet policy toward Romania. The notion of broadly representative and democratic governments established through free elections and responsive to the will of their citizens, which the Declaration called for, ran counter to Soviet theory and practice, and if applied in this particular case would undoubtedly have prevented the installation of a friendly and docile government in Bucharest. The antipathy which the majority of Romanians felt toward the Soviet Union and their desire to maintain traditional ties to the West made the prospects of a freely elected pro-Soviet regime coming to power extremely remote. Romanian Communist leaders, aware of their party's unpopularity and weakness had no wish to leave the choice of government to the electorate. This was also the thinking of Soviet leaders. They moved so decisively and so early to secure their position in Romania because of its strategic importance as the gateway to the Balkans and to Central Europe.

The Western Allies, confronted by the Soviet challenge to both the armistice agreement with Romania and the Declaration on Liberated Europe did little but make protests, which had no effect on the course of events. Since the war was still going on and broader issues of the general European settlement had yet to be arranged and the final assault on Japan mounted, the American and British governments felt obliged to restrain their criticism of Soviet behavior.

The government headed by Petru Groza was clearly a minority government. Imposed by the Soviet Union, it did not represent the will of the majority of Romanians. No members of the two largest parties – the National Peasants and the Liberals – sat in the cabinet, where Communists held the key posts. Although Gheorghe Tătărescu, the dissident Liberal, was foreign minister, and Anton Alexandrescu, the dissident National Peasant, was minister of cooperatives, they represented only small factions of their respective parties.

To compensate for its lack of support in the country the new government took measures to fortify itself and cripple the opposition. Most important were sweeping changes in local government introduced by the Ministry of the Interior in May 1945. Communist prefects were appointed and Communist-dominated councils with extensive powers were created in every county. Intended as executors of central government decisions, the councils were empowered to consider "all important questions of the day" – economic reconstruction, administrative reform, public order, and the "democratization of the state apparatus" – and had the responsibility for mobilizing support for these policies among the local population. Similar bodies were installed in cities and villages. The Groza government also sponsored local "vigilance committees," which took over the duties of the regular police and gendarmerie and, like the political councils, served as instruments of its policies. In the countryside the government encouraged newly formed peasant committees to expropriate and distribute land from large properties, and in urban centers it spurred workers' committees to wrest control of factories and other businesses from their owners, even though such organizations had no legal authority to act. All these administrative bodies and ad hoc committees had as their ultimate objective the undermining of existing political and economic structures in order to smooth the way for the advent of the new Communist order.

The National Peasants and the Brătianu Liberals were the main opposition to the Groza government and the Communists. Maniu had established himself as the leader of all those who sought to create a genuine parliamentary democracy on the Western model and to protect the country from Soviet domination. But he himself was not hopeful about the future. In June 1945 he had concluded that Romania was no longer a sovereign state because the government consisted almost entirely of persons willing to do the bidding of the Soviet Union and because proposed economic agreements between the two countries would ensure the Soviet Union's control of Romania's industries and would, in effect, "communize" the entire economic structure of the country. Nonetheless, he was willing to risk a confrontation with Groza and the Communists by urging the King to dismiss the government as unrepresentative and, hence, in violation of the armistice and other Allied agreements. But he made any such initiative dependent on American and British support, which, in the end, he failed to receive. American officials made it clear to him that their government's policy was based on the armistice and the Declaration on Liberated Europe and that it would intervene in Romanian affairs only to the extent necessary to ensure the carrying out of these two agreements. But, in effect, they had no intention of jeopardizing the course of the war in Europe and in the Pacific, where they wanted Soviet aid against Japan, by mounting a serious challenge to Soviet policy in Eastern Europe.

The defeat of Germany in May brought an end to Romania's four-year ordeal of war. Its contributions to the campaigns in Hungary and Czechoslovakia had been substantial. Some eleven Romanian army divisions had taken part in the so-called Budapest Operation in central and northern Hungary between the end of October 1944 and the middle of January 1945, sustaining 11,000 killed and wounded. From December 1944 to May 1945 nearly 250,000 Romanian troops had been at the center of the drive through Slovakia and Moravia into Bohemia, advancing to within 80 kilometers of Prague before being ordered to halt on May 12. These forces, too, suffered heavy losses: 70,000 killed and wounded.

The Communist drive for power did not abate. In the summer and fall of 1945 the Communist Party grew stronger as the political struggle intensified. Communist leaders turned their attention to creating a disciplined party, and on October 16, 1945 they held the first national party conference. The delegates elected a Central Committee and a Politburo, composed of Gheorghiu-Dej as secretary-general and Ana Pauker and Teohari Georgescu, the minister of the interior, as secretaries. These three and several colleagues were, in effect, to rule Romania until 1952. Pauker seems to have played the leading role at the conference. Lucreţiu Pătrăşcanu, the minister of justice, who enjoyed wide support among party intellectuals, was, surprisingly, not elected to high party office. Although he was committed to the Communist program and during the next two years raised no objections to the methods which the party used to eliminate the opposition and solidify its control of the country, he seems to have been suspect to his colleagues and particularly to their Soviet mentors, perhaps because he was an intellectual and because he was inclined to lead rather than follow. As events in Romania ran their course the West and the Soviet Union agreed on the political reorganization of Romania at a conference in Moscow on December 16–26, 1945. In return for the inclusion of one National Peasant and one Liberal minister in the government, and for the promise of early free elections, the United States and Great Britain agreed to recognize the new government. A month later a National Peasant and a Liberal, not of the front rank, took their places in the cabinet as ministers without portfolio. Groza agreed to hold elections without delay, and on February 4, 1946 the United States and Britain recognized his government.

This settlement was a bitter defeat for the Romanian historical parties and the West. The new cabinet was by no means representative of the will of the majority of Romanians. Recognition of it before the holding of elections was a tactical error, since the United States and Britain gave up the one means they had of pressuring the Groza government to keep its promises.

Since taking office the Groza government had been busy eliminating the remnants of the wartime dictatorship. It thus prosecuted persons accused of war crimes and responsibility for the "national disaster" that had overtaken the country. But a law of April 21, 1945 defined such persons broadly and established new judicial bodies, people's tribunals, where the usual legal procedures were dispensed with in order to achieve the desired results. High officials in the Antonescu government and functionaries of all kinds were special objects of the campaign. Their arrests had the additional advantage of weakening the opposition, for decisions about who was or was not a "war criminal" fell to the Groza government itself. The most spectacular of the war crimes trials was that of Ion Antonescu, which began on May 4, 1946. The outcome was never in doubt, for both the judges and the defense lawyers, who had been appointed by the government, knew what was expected of them. On May 17 the court found Antonescu guilty and sentenced him to death. He was shot at Jilava prison on June 1.

In the middle of October 1946 the government finally set November 19 as the date for the elections, but, in fact, the campaign had been underway since the summer. Both the Communist-dominated Bloc of Democratic Parties and the National Peasants, who led the opposition, considered the elections the decisive battle in the struggle for power. The Communist Party had placed the Communist-run Ministry of Interior in charge of organizing the elections. A formidable administrative apparatus was thus mobilized to promote the candidates of the Bloc and prevent the opposition from mounting an effective campaign. Gheorghiu-Dej made no secret of Communist Party intentions. At the height of the campaign he informed members of the American mission in Bucharest that the election was a battle in which the enemy, the historical parties, had to be defeated, and he freely admitted that the government was taking advantage of every "weakness" of the opposition in order to win.

The balloting on November 19 took place in an atmosphere of extreme tension. The government was expected to announce the results on the following day, as was usual, but for reasons which it could not satisfactorily explain there was a delay of forty-eight hours. Only on the 22nd did it publish the figures. These showed an overwhelming victory for the Bloc, with some 70 percent of the votes and 349 seats in the new Assembly to 32 seats for the National Peasants and 33 for the other non-Bloc parties. But evidence uncovered since 1989 has revealed that just the opposite took place on election day, that the National Peasants were on their way to a landslide victory. It appears that when Communist leaders realized the extent of their impending defeat they had the reporting of returns suspended and sent instructions to all county prefects to "revise" the figures in order to show a victory for the Bloc. Ana Pauker and other Communists had consulted Moscow and received instructions to "win" the elections, that is, to falsify the results.

Although the United States and Britain denounced the elections as unrepresentative of the will of the Romanian people and held the Groza government responsible for reneging on its promises about free elections, neither was prepared to go further in support of those whom they had earlier encouraged to oppose Soviet and Communist pressure. The elections represented the end of attempts by the three wartime allies to resolve the Romanian question together. Henceforth, Western influence on the course of events in Romania for all intents and purposes ceased.

The negotiations for a final peace treaty with Romania, which had begun in Paris in August 1946, were brought to a conclusion early in the next year. The document, which was signed on February 10, 1947, incorporated decisions already made in the armistice of 1944 covering boundaries and war reparations. Noteworthy was the confirmation of the return of north Transylvania to Romania. The Soviet Union agreed to withdraw its army from Romania within three months after the treaty came into force, except for those units that were necessary to maintain communications with the Soviet occupation army in Austria (large Soviet ground and air forces, in fact, stayed in Romania until 1958). In article 3, the Romanian government bound itself to protect the fundamental rights of all citizens, including freedom of speech, of the press, of association, and of assembly, but, as events were to show, it had no intention of abiding by such pledges.

The new government, which had taken office on December 1, 1946, with Groza again as prime minister, was dominated by Communists. It faced daunting tasks. One of the most pressing was recovery from the war, as agriculture and industry and the entire economic infrastructure had suffered massive damage and disruption. An additional economic burden was the overwhelming presence of the Soviet Union. Reparation payments, which included foodstuffs and raw materials of all kinds and Soviet confiscations of industrial equipment, drained the country of critically needed resources. The Soviet government was also intent on monopolizing Romanian production and foreign trade through a series of long-term economic treaties. The most far-reaching of these had already been signed on May 8, 1945. It authorized the establishment of joint Soviet–Romanian companies, which in theory were partnerships of equals, but in practice became instruments of Soviet exploitation of the Romanian economy.

During the first half of 1947 the Communist Party moved to tighten its control of every branch of the economy. Central planning and controls became the order of the day, and all the measures it took were merely preparatory to the nationalization of industry and the collectivization of agriculture. On April 5 a new Ministry of Industry and Commerce assumed broad powers to collect and distribute all industrial and agricultural goods, to allocate raw materials to industry, to regulate investment in private and state-run enterprises, and to control credit. The unrelenting transformation of the Romanian economy in accordance with the Soviet model was accompanied by measures to integrate it fully into the Soviet bloc. One fateful consequence of the massive Soviet penetration of the Romanian economy was the severing of traditional ties to the West, an economic isolation far more complete than that prevailing under Ottoman suzerainty in the eighteenth or earlier centuries.

In political life the Communists were determined to eliminate what remained of the opposition. They judged the time ripe for a frontal assault on the National Peasant Party. Maniu and other leaders were brought to trial before a military court on October 29, 1947. Its purpose was to complete the Communist seizure of power, but it was also another skirmish in the uneven contest between East and West over Romania, as the Soviet Union sought to destroy once and for all the influence of the Western democracies by removing its foremost representatives in Romania from public life.

The main accusation against Maniu and his colleagues was treason, specifically, that they had conspired with secret service agents at the American and British legations in Bucharest to overthrow the Groza government. In accounting for his actions, Maniu pointed out that he had been engaged in a struggle to restore free elections, political liberties, and fundamental human rights, and declared that he was determined to use every means available to achieve these ends. He admitted that he had had frequent contacts with American and British representatives, but he insisted that the discussion of domestic and international questions was one of the duties of every statesman. The dignity which he displayed throughout the unfair proceedings added to his reputation for probity and courage. But the verdict was never in doubt. On November 11 the court sentenced Maniu to life imprisonment and the other defendants to terms of from five years to life in prison. Maniu died in prison in 1953.

The Communists also turned their attention to other political groups still outside their control. They brought the Independent Socialist Party and its leader Constantin Titel Petrescu under sustained attack in the fall of 1947. The Independent Socialists had become anathema to the Communists not only because they were committed to parliamentary democracy but also because they provided a rallying point for those on the left who opposed fusion with the Communist Party. Titel Petrescu's party was broken up by intimidation and the arrest of its activists, and he himself was arrested in May 1948 and imprisoned without trial.

The reckoning also finally came for Gheorghe Tătărescu and his Liberal faction, the only significant political group in the government not yet controlled by the Communist Party. As long as the Communists had thought it necessary to keep up the appearances of a coalition government and as long as Tătărescu proved useful in dealing with the Western powers as foreign minister, they kept him on, but the incompatibility between them had been evident for some time. They finally forced him to resign as foreign minister on November 6, and he was immediately replaced by Ana Pauker. He was arrested in 1950 and imprisoned until 1955.

As the Communists moved inexorably toward a monopoly of political power, the monarchy had become an anomaly. Fearful that this last vestige of the old order might yet serve as a center of opposition to the new order, the Communist Party took the final, logical step in assuring its domination of the country when it forced King Mihai to abdicate on December 30, 1947. The abdication and the proclamation of the Romanian People's Republic on the same day were the culmination of the Communists' three-year campaign to seize power. These actions signified the incorporation of the country into the Soviet sphere. They also served notice that the era of Romanian history that had begun with the loosening of ties to the East and the opening to the West, made manifest in parliamentary government, the multi-party system, the capitalist, entrepreneurial spirit, and unrestrained debate about identity and destiny, had come to an end.

6

Romanian Communism, 1948–1989

The four decades of Communist rule stand out as a distinct era in Romanian history. In certain ways they represent a break in the general course of modern Romania's development, modeled as it was after Western Europe's political and economic institutions and inspired by its intellectual and cultural values. Those who set Romania on a different course after the Second World War – the Soviet Communist Party and its Romanian Communist clients – imposed other models and other values, which drew their substance from experiences at odds with the Western European tradition. In some sense, the new Romanian elite continued the work of modernization, but the means they used and the ultimate goals they pursued separated the Romania of the later twentieth century from the Romania that had come before. Even though they occasionally made concessions to the population, they disdained genuine consultations with the citizenry and never relinquished their authority. Their consistency in applying the Stalinist model for four decades was remarkable. But it was their very inflexibility that, in the end, proved fatal to their project.

THE NEW ELITE

The proclamation of the People's Republic of Romania by the Communist elite at the end of 1947 brought to a culmination the more than three years of their unrelenting drive for power begun in the fall of 1944. This new elite was a diverse group. The majority were of working-class origins, of modest formal education, and ethnically Romanian. Most of them had joined the party as young men and had spent their careers as activists in Romania and often in prison. But others had bourgeois family backgrounds and were intellectuals and belonged to ethnic minorities, notably Jews and Hungarians. Some had spent much of their party lives in Moscow, where they contracted strong links to Soviet central party organs and the international Communist movement. The differences between the groups and between individuals were to be constant sources of tension within the elite during its first decade in power. But dependence on the Soviet Union and the sacrifice of national distinctiveness were not, at first, overt causes of friction. For all of them the Soviet Union of Joseph Stalin could not but be the object of emulation.

From among the new elite, the one who prevailed over his rivals and established himself for more than a decade as the acknowledged leader of the party was Gheorghe Gheorghiu-Dej (1901–65). He came from a poor family and had limited formal schooling and in the 1920s was employed at the Grivița railroad works in Bucharest. It was there that he joined the Communist Party. A zealous activist, he was one of the organizers of the railroad workers strike in 1933, an act that led to his arrest and imprisonment. Prison served as his university. Here he came into contact with a variety of individuals and sharpened his innate intelligence and satisfied a stubborn curiosity about men and their thoughts and actions. In the confusion of the last days of the Antonescu dictatorship he escaped from jail and joined other Communists who were gathering in Bucharest under Soviet patronage. In the coming struggle for power to come between the Communists and their Soviet mentors, on one side, and the National Peasants and the Liberals, on the other, Gheorghiu-Dej proved to be a skillful tactician. He was both clever and cautious and, when necessary, brutal, and most of all he understood the importance of keeping Stalin's trust.

Gheorghiu-Dej's chief rival was Ana Pauker (1893–1960). She was the daughter of a rabbi and was sent to Switzerland to study medicine, but she was attracted to socialism and joined the hardline Romanian Social Democratic faction led by Cristian Rakovski, who would become a leading figure of the Communist International

GHEORGHE GHEORGHIU-DEJ

18 Gheorghe Gheorghiu-Dej

(Comintern). She joined the Communist Party in 1921 and because of her activities she was arrested several times. Jailed in 1935, she benefited from an exchange of prisoners with the Soviet Union in 1940 and spent the war years in Moscow, where she gained the confidence of the Communist elite. She returned to Romania in September 1944 to represent the interests of the international Communist movement, that is, the Soviet Communist Party. For a time the beneficiary of Stalin's favor, she seemed destined for leadership of the Romanian party. But she was an unusual case in Romanian political life: her Jewishness and her gender stood out as deviations from tradition and aroused hostility even within the Communist Party. Although her chief antagonist in Bucharest was Gheorghiu-Dej, the power of decision lay in Moscow with Stalin.

Lucreţiu Pătrăşcanu (1900–54), too, did not fit easily into the mainstream of Romanian Communism in the immediate post-war years. He was, to be sure, a committed Communist. In 1919 he had joined the radical faction of the Social Democratic Party, which formed the nucleus of the Romanian Communist Party that came into being in 1921. But he was also an intellectual with a law agree from the University of Leipzig who thought for himself, and he was a Romanian who preferred that the communizing of his country be done by Romanians. His activism in the 1920s and 1930s, which included the defense of Communists at political trials and several brief imprisonments, could not overcome the widespread anti-intellectualism of the Romanian Communist movement. His background and fidelity to an orthodox Marxism left him out of the main currents of the Communists' drive for power, even though he served as minister of justice in the Groza government until 1948 and fully supported the perversion of the justice system to suit Communist Party ambitions.

Many of Gheorghiu-Dej's close collaborators were workers he met in prison and with whom he developed a relationship of comrades-in-arms. They were as a whole of modest intellectual accomplishments. Far different were two figures who became Gheorghiu-Dej's friends and confidants and supported his later daring enterprises such as the striving for autonomy within the Soviet bloc. Emil Bodnăraş (1904–76) was an army officer who joined the Communist Party in 1934 and spent the war years in the Soviet Union. He was an intellectual who combined wide reading with a pragmatic political sense and held high positions in the party and government. Of a similar, middle-class background was Ion Gheorghe Maurer (1902–2000), a man of broad views and a lawyer who joined the Communist Party in 1935 and defended Communists brought to trial for sedition. Among other important posts, he was president of the Council of Ministers, 1961–74. Both he and Bodnăraş expanded Gheorghiu-

Dej's intellectual horizons and knowledge of the world. Behind them and the central party leadership were specialists, key figures in elaborating and carrying out the economic transformation of the country. They were Gheorghiu-Dej's "work team." The two most prominent, both Communist Party members from the 1930s, were Gheorghe Gaston Marin, head of the State Planning Commission, 1954–65, and Alexandru Bîrlădeanu, who was in charge of coordinating the activities of all economic ministries, 1955–66.

The new elite had as its primary goal the modernization of Romania, but the model they aspired to and the methods they used were far different from the process that had brought prewar Romania into being. Rather than the Western Europe of earlier Romanian modernizers, Romanian Communists took as their model Stalin's Soviet Union. They also proposed to carry out their bold plans Soviet style by using a monopoly of power that would enable them to dispense with the inconveniences of bourgeois entrepreneurs and liberal politicians.

For the Communist elite, then, modernization meant the radical transformation of the Romania that had evolved in the century and a half down to the Second World War. The means they applied were both constructive and destructive. While they were creating new institutions, new elites, and a single social class, they were engaged in destroying the old order root and branch. In practical terms modernization meant for them industrialization, to be carried out through the massive nationalization of the means of production and centralized planning and direction in every branch of the economy. By mobilizing all available labor and material resources to further the development of heavy industry, they were certain that they could quickly overcome centuries of backwardness and bring forth a whole new order of society – Communism. In some sense, their vision was Romantic, even utopian.

There was a darker side to Communist modernization. It was invasive and often brutal, as the new elite sought to penetrate every sphere of social activity and bring individual lives under its direction. In the course of eliminating old elites and their institutions the Communists created a system of controls of hitherto unimagined proportions and authority. The immediate end they pursued was the monopoly of political power, which alone, they were convinced, could ensure the emergence of a new social order and a new mental climate. Their chief instruments were the Communist Party and its ideology, and they gave constant attention to the training of cadres, that is, devoted activists, from among whom the managers of party and state business would be chosen. They were, therefore, careful to enlist candidates with the proper social background and ideological preparation.

The Communist elite could have few illusions about the formidable obstacles that lay in their path, and they showed little hesitation in using every means available to remove them. Between 1948 and 1951 they put in place an apparatus of security and repression unprecedented in Romanian history. Soviet institutions provided the blueprints, and Soviet officials served as mentors. At first, Romanian Communist leaders and Soviet occupation authorities had maintained existing security institutions with, of course, loyalists to the Communist cause in charge, but in 1948 they judged the time had come to introduce a new style. In that year they established the General Directorate of Security of the People (Direcţia Generală a Securităţii Poporului), which became known simply as Securitatea (the Security) and had as its all-encompassing task the protection of the Communist regime against both internal and foreign enemies. The next year the Miliţie (Militia) came into being to replace the existing police forces and assume the primary responsibility for maintaining public order. Along with the Securitate it kept the population under constant surveillance, especially through its power to issue residence permits for cities. Then, in 1951, the Security Troops Command (Comandamentul Trupelor de Securitate) was organized. By the mid 1950s it was equipped with armored cars, artillery, and planes and had as its primary task the suppression of opposition to the regime.

These three units served as the armed force of the party and carried out its orders with impunity. As examples, they removed tens of thousands of peasants from their villages to break resistance to the new order, in general, and collectivization of agriculture, in particular, and they arrested tens of thousands more people from all social categories who were suspected of opposition. They acted on direct instructions from the Ministry of the Interior and other government agencies and in accordance with the provisions of the penal code that defined crimes in such sweeping and vague language – "conspiracy against the social order" and "undermining the national economy" – that the security forces could act without restraint. In any case, arrests were rarely followed by judicial proceedings, as the detainees went directly to prison. There was no appeal against such arbitrariness.

The security forces were also in charge of the extensive prison network, which was composed of over a hundred institutions of various kinds spread throughout the country. This Romanian gulag followed closely the Soviet model and became infamous for its inhuman treatment of prisoners. Among prisons where conditions were most appalling were Piteşti, where prisoners were taught to torture one another; Sighet, where members of the interwar political and intellectual elite died from systematic neglect; and the Danube–Black Sea canal, where work camps served the same purposes as other prisons under conditions of forced labor.

For nearly a decade after their seizure of power the new elite was dependent on the Soviet Union. It is not an exaggeration to describe the relationship as one of vassal and suzerain. It is tempting to liken it to the status of the Romanian principalities under Ottoman domination in the second half of the sixteenth century, but Soviet predominance was far more overpowering and pervasive. The elite's dependency was due in great measure to its origins and to the manner in which it had come to power. In the interwar period, as we have seen, the Romanian Communist Party lacked significant support among the population, and it took power after the Second World War not through an indigenous revolution but by the will of outsiders. The Communist model that the elite was to follow had been imposed, a fact that was not lost on the great majority of the population. One of the most persistent obstacles Romanian Communists thus had to overcome in mobilizing people for their modernization project was their lack of legitimacy.

Soviet "advisers" were everywhere – in the party apparatus, government bureaus, and the main branches of the economy. In the early years of dependency, especially, significant acts by Romanian officials required Soviet approval, and even at the highest level of the party Gheorghiu-Dej, Pauker, and others were ever conscious of being under close scrutiny by Moscow and its agents on the scene. At the Ministry of the Interior, which had responsibility for security and the suppression of opposition to the new order, Soviet officials took the lead in setting up its various branches and training their personnel. Not surprisingly, the Securitate was a faithful copy of the Soviet security apparatus. The Soviet legacy in these matters endured long after the last Soviet advisers left Romania in November 1964. In the economy, too, the Soviet presence was initially overwhelming. Joint Soviet–Romanian companies, the Sovroms, encompassed the most important industrial and commercial enterprises and were intended to subordinate Romania economically to the interests of the Soviet Union. Even the first five-year plan in 1949 was in great part the work of Soviet advisers.

The elite's ability to conduct relations with foreign countries independent of the will of Moscow was severely limited. Soviet officials attached to the Ministry of Foreign Affairs were numerous and had as their primary responsibility to make certain that Soviet interests were well served. That goal was the motive behind the series of formal links that bound Romania to the Soviet Union. Romania, of course, belonged to the Communist Information Bureau (Cominform), which Stalin had formed in October 1947 to take the place of the Comintern, dissolved by him in 1943, as a new instrument of Soviet political control over the members of the bloc. Stalin also proposed economic coordination within the bloc through the Council for Mutual Economic Assistance (CMEA or Comecon), which he established in 1949. Several years were to pass before its full effects on the economic independence of Romania and the other bloc countries became clear. A similar formal regulation of military affairs occurred only after the death of Stalin in 1953, mainly because he saw no need for a treaty, since the Sovietization of the bloc armies was proceeding according to plan. But in 1955 Stalin's successor, Nikita Khrushchev, decided that a suitable response to NATO, especially after West Germany had joined it, was necessary. The Warsaw Treaty Organization (WTO), which he sponsored, placed the whole of Romania's armed forces within its structure and yielded the power of decision to Moscow.

Soviet leaders continuously measured the loyalty of Romanian Communists in all these enterprises, and Gheorghiu-Dej took care to conform to the shifting political currents in Moscow. His behavior during the crisis between Yugoslavia and the Soviet Union reveals his dexterity. When Tito and Stalin split in 1948, Gheorghiu-Dej was prompt and unequivocal in showing his attachment to Stalin. His attack on Tito and the Yugoslav Communist Party leadership as spies and murderers, delivered at the November 1949 meeting of the Cominform, was, in fact, written by the Commission on Foreign Affairs of the Central Committee of the Soviet Communist Party. Later, when conciliation became Soviet policy, Gheorghiu-Dej warmly welcomed a Yugoslav delegation to Bucharest in 1956. Survival rather than ideology dictated his reactions on both occasions.

While adjusting to instructions from Moscow and taking the first steps toward the building of socialism, the Communist elite had to settle conflicts of interest among themselves. In the years just after the seizure of power two main factions emerged, one led by Gheorghiu-Dej and the other by Ana Pauker. The former is often referred to as the "indigenists," that is, working-class, ethnic Romanians who served the cause at home during the difficult 1930s and early 1940s, while the latter became known as the "Muscovites," that is, intellectuals and non-Romanians who spent the 1930s and early 1940s in the Soviet Union. But such distinctions break down upon close examination of often shifting alliances. Both sides were loyal to Moscow, and success went to those who could gain the favor of Stalin. Party strife had little to do with opposing ideologies, and even disputes over policy – how quickly and forcefully to proceed with the collectivization of agriculture, for example – were tactical moves in what was essentially a struggle between forceful personalities for power.

In the intra-party contest for supremacy Gheorghiu-Dej emerged the victor, mainly because he had convinced Stalin of his loyalty, but also because he possessed both consummate skills as a political infighter and a keen sense of when to strike and when to lie low. Examples abound. He had Pătrăşcanu removed from his party and state positions in 1948 because he feared him as a rival and distrusted him as an intellectual. But not even the most savage torture could force Pătrăşcanu to confess to accusations of disloyalty and espionage made against him. Mainly for this reason no public show trial was held. Rather, Gheorghiu-Dej had him executed in secret in 1954, lest Khrushchev find the less rigid Pătrăşcanu more in step with his de-Stalinization efforts than he, Gheorghiu-Dej, who was well known for his Stalinist ideals. Ana Pauker fared better than Pătrăşcanu in the power struggle with Gheorghiu-Dej. She indeed lost her posts in the party and government in 1952, but was spared prison and even received a decent position in a publishing house. Gheorghiu-Dej, then, by 1952 had gained control of the party apparatus and could enjoy the luxury of blaming defeated comrades for economic failures and abuses of power.

Gheorghiu-Dej's cunning and caution were soon tested again in the wake of Stalin's death. The de-Stalinization campaign initiated by Khrushchev, who became First Secretary of the Soviet Communist Party in 1953, alarmed Gheorghiu-Dej, who had found in Stalinism a congenial guide. Hastening, as always, to adapt to changing currents emanating from Moscow, he acquiesced in denunciations of the cult of personality by instituting a kind of collective leadership in Bucharest. In 1954 he made Gheorghe Apostol, a close, working-class confidant, head of the party, while he himself took the prime ministership, but no one doubted who was really in charge of the party, and the nominal division of labor lasted hardly a year.

The year 1956 was one of crisis for the Romanian Communist Party and of danger for Gheorghiu-Dej personally. Khrushchev's so-called secret report to the Twentieth Congress of the Soviet Communist Party in February, in which he condemned Stalin's crimes, raised serious questions about violations of "Leninist principles of legality" by the Romanian party's leadership. Then came the troubles in Poland in October and the replacement of the old party leadership with a reform-minded team in the Khrushchev mold. The Hungarian Revolution of October and November aroused a limited response in Romania. In university centers – notably, Timişoara, Cluj, and Bucharest – small groups, mainly composed of students, manifested solidarity with the resistance forces in Budapest. But workers and peasants did not actively support them, a failure that allowed the security forces to deal with the matter swiftly and with relative ease. Yet, Gheorghiu-Dej and company were alarmed by the violence in Hungary because of its possible long-term influence among the Hungarians in Romania and its destabilizing effects in the bloc as a whole. They interpreted the reaction of Hungarians in Transylvania as a manifestation of nationalist sentiments and concluded that education in Hungarian and in Hungarian schools was a serious policy error because it encouraged separation. They fully supported Khrushchev's suppression of the revolution.

Gheorghiu-Dej showed no hesitation in public in approving Khrushchev's condemnation of Stalin, but the whole de-Stalinization project, he thought, had undermined the credibility and power of Communist parties and had led directly to the crises in Poland and Hungary. He reluctantly decided that a de-Stalinization of sorts in Romania could not be avoided, but he was determined that it be a carefully controlled operation. To deflect accusations of Stalinism against himself he insisted that he had already dealt with the problem by removing Ana Pauker and her associates some years earlier: they were the culprits; he was the reformer. Although such a version of events gained little credibility in Moscow, it was enough to win him crucial support. A further proof of his loyalty to the center was his enthusiastic endorsement of Soviet actions in Poland and Hungary, since he shared Khrushchev's resolve to maintain the Communist Party's monopoly of power.

Gheorghiu-Dej's interpretation of the events in the Soviet bloc since the death of Stalin proved decisive for the evolution of the Romanian Communist Party. As he pressed forward with modernization as originally conceived in the late 1940s, and as he reflected on the relationship of his party to the Soviet party the contours of what came to be known as national Communism (some would say national Stalinism) slowly took shape. In domestic politics, his ideal was the monolithic party supreme, with himself exercising unchallenged authority over both the party and society. Accordingly, in 1957, when two members of the party's Political Bureau, its highest organ, and advocates of de-Stalinization, challenged his right to lead the party, he had them removed from all their posts, action that rendered his dominance of the party complete. In bloc politics, he dared a certain independence, as he raised the possibility of a partial disengagement from the Soviet Union. His intention was to keep control of the building of socialism in Romanian hands and, no less important, prevent his own replacement by someone more congenial to the Kremlin. It presaged a new era in Romanian–Soviet relations.

MODERNIZATION, 1948–1960

The supreme goal to which the Communist elite had committed itself was the sweeping transformation of Romanian politics, economy, society, culture, and worldview. Gheorghiu-Dej and his circle were thus engaged in a revolution in the true sense of the word. Their ideal, as always, was the Soviet Union as it had evolved under Stalin. They and their successors never abandoned it during the four decades they were in power. Nor did they ever relinquish their own absolute authority to set the goals and marshal the resources to carry out their vast enterprise.

At the center of their modernization project was, as we have noted, a massive restructuring and expansion of industry. Their reasoning was, in part, ideological – to hasten the transition to socialism and, in the end, attain a Communist society. But, in the meantime, after Gheorghiu-Dej and company had won the struggle for power in the early 1950s they intended to bring Romania fully up to a European standard of material prosperity. Their focus on Romania called to mind the bourgeois era and could hardly have been expressed openly during the Stalin years, since "proletarian internationalism," that is, subordination to Soviet interests, was the order of the day. Yet, by the later 1950s a form of national Communism, economic as well as political, had gradually emerged. Only then could the advanced economies of the West be openly objects of emulation and become valued, though limited, partners.

The Communists approached modernization on a broad front. It touched every aspect of citizens' lives and was expressly designed to do so. It affected how they earned their living, whether in industry, agriculture, or the infrastructure; how they were educated and trained; what kinds of social services they received; what responsibilities toward the larger community they were expected to bear; and what they thought and hoped for.

The elite was eager to mobilize the whole population for their undertaking. To do so they put in place a series of mass organizations encompassing every social category, a system, they were certain, that would enable them to exploit human and material resources to the fullest and, equally crucial, allow them to maintain tight control over the whole process. Under such an order of things citizens had the right, or, rather, the duty, to participate in the building of the new socialist nation, but the elite reserved to itself and its chosen collaborators all the important decisions concerning planning and direction. To bring everyone into the process they preferred persuasion, but if that approach failed, they did not hesitate to apply force to achieve the desired results.

In some sense, the Communists had to deal with problems left over from the interwar period. Then, as we have seen, industrialization was well underway as Liberal theorists and politicians judged industry and its associated infrastructure to be essential for the construction of a modern European nation. Like the National Peasants, the Communists recognized the vital importance of agriculture to the national economy, but, like the Liberals, they assigned it a secondary role behind industry. The Communists, like the interwar parties, also confronted serious social problems such as unemployment and poverty, the place of minorities in a national state, education, and the role of the churches in public life. A certain continuity of issues is thus discernible from the interwar to the post-war decades. But the political elites of the two eras differed fundamentally in their approaches to solutions. The Liberals and the National Peasants remained true to the democratic parliamentary traditions they had inherited from their nineteenth-century forebears. The process was sometimes inefficient and fell short of the ideal, but those who were thus engaged took heart, at least in the 1920s, that they were following European patterns and were thus contributing to the building of a modern nation. But the Communists adhered to another tradition. Perhaps "authoritarian" describes it best, but, in any case, it was the antithesis of European liberalism. It justified the exercise of power by a small, self-perpetuating elite that dispensed with consultations with the citizenry through honest elections and representative institutions. Instead, this tradition allowed the elite to use whatever means it judged necessary to achieve their ends.

Economic restructuring came first in the Communists' campaign to transform bourgeois, capitalist Romania into classless, socialist Romania. They assumed full powers to develop all branches of the economy as they saw fit. Central planning and direction were their watchwords as they rapidly dismantled the private entrepreneurship and market economy that had been the hallmarks of modern

Romania for over a century. The Communists substituted a bureau-cracy presided over at the center by the State Planning Commission and greatly expanded the Council of Ministers to enable it to super-vise every significant aspect of economic activity. To manage their vast undertaking and measure its progress they adopted the device of the five-year plan from Soviet practice. Intent on hastening the transition of a largely agrarian and rural country into one that was predominantly industrial and urban, they committed almost all available resources to forced industrialization and the total collect-ivization of agriculture. Society, culture, and even the mental cli-mate would, they were certain, be transformed in the process.

The Soviet Union was a muscular presence in the Romanian econ-omy during the first decade of the People's Republic. It provided Romanian party leaders with the general patterns to be followed in all the main branches of production, and it assigned experts and technicians to guide the process at every level. The Soviet party claimed to be giving this aid in the spirit of proletarian solidarity, and the Romanians were effusive in expressing their gratitude. This was the public face of the matter. In reality, the Soviet Union was mainly intent on asserting its control of the Romanian economy and on exploiting its resources and productive capacity to its own advantage.

As the relationship evolved after the death of Stalin the Soviet party under Nikita Khrushchev focused attention on integrating the Romanian economy into that of the East European bloc as a whole. On the Romanian side Gheorghiu-Dej and his associates, mainly among themselves at first, expressed anger at the cavalier way Soviet leaders were making decisions about the future of their country and about themselves. Thus, well before Romanian Communists made their sentiments about "independence" public, they were aiming to be masters in their own house, not just against the old Romanian elites but also in relations with their new mentors.

The Soviets initially used the device of joint Soviet–Romanian companies – the Sovroms – to achieve their economic objectives. They had begun their drive to dominate the Romanian economy immediately after they imposed the Groza government on King Mihai in March 1945. Thus, in May and June 1945 the joint com-panies began to be organized in fields of special Soviet interest:

Sovromtransport (transportation) and Sovrompetrol (oil), while in banking, Sovrombanc seemed destined to dominate all other Romanian banks. By 1952 a large number of joint companies were in operation, among them: Sovromgaz (natural gas), Sovromlemn (forestry products), Sovromchim (chemicals), Sovromtractor (tractors), Sovromcarbune (coal), Sovrommetal (metallurgy), and Sovromconstrucţii (construction). Gheorghiu-Dej and his colleagues opposed these designs on their country's economy, but had to react cautiously. To prevent Soviet control of the fishing industry Gheorghiu-Dej reorganized the state company into Rompescaria and was able to deflect insistent Soviet demands that it, too, become a joint venture. The Romanians also resented the way the Sovroms had been formed. Although the two partners were supposed to invest equal sums in the joint companies, the Soviets used funds obtained from confiscated Western enterprises as their share, while the Romanian side had to put up its own capital in full. Then, too, the Sovroms were not generally profitable and came to be seen by the Romanians as simply instruments of Soviet exploitation of their resources. The Romanians' persistence paid off. At first, as early as the spring of 1953, the Romanians won agreement in Moscow to place eight Sovroms under Romanian management, and, then, after Stalin's death, they succeeded in gradually eliminating all joint companies. But by then Soviet leaders had decided on other ways of managing the bloc's economies.

Romanian Communists embarked upon industrialization with a zeal that must have surprised even their Soviet patrons. They eschewed gradualism and, instead, launched a frontal assault on underdevelopment that they were certain would bring the socialist order quickly within reach. Their campaign was an obvious emulation of the Soviet drive to industrialize in the 1930s and was carried out with a similar disregard for human and material costs. They placed the same emphasis as the Soviets on the building of factories and other facilities and gave the same priority to producer goods such as machinery, all intended to create the solid foundation they judged essential for the emergence of a strong, many-sided economy. Investments, accordingly, were channeled into expanding productive capacity and increasing the quantities of key raw materials available for industry. The results in many sectors were impressive. Between 1950 and 1960 the production of oil doubled, that of coal almost doubled, and of methane gas, electrical energy, and steel tripled, while machines for the iron and steel and chemical industries and trucks and tractors were produced in unprecedented quantities.

All these successes came at a severe cost to the population as a whole. The relentless drive to build heavy industry in conditions of limited resources meant that the party elite had to withhold investments and expertise from other branches of the economy. The contrast between the attention lavished on industry and the relative neglect of agriculture is striking. Under the circumstances a modest growth of agricultural production is hardly surprising. But light industry, the production of consumer goods, and the general needs of the population were also sorely neglected in this first phase of industrialization. The overall result was a steady decline in the standard of living. The elite could not be oblivious to the consequences of forced industrialization, and for a time between 1953 and 1955 it slowed the pace of growth. Then, by 1956 it was ready to push ahead with greater coercive force than ever, but events in Poland and Hungary in that year caused another temporary slowing of momentum. Those shocks to the prevailing order in the East helped to persuade the party leadership to reach at least a partial accommodation with an aggrieved citizenry by improving living conditions.

Romanian Communist leaders were also preoccupied with reorganizing agriculture as part of their overall plan to bring the economy fully under their control. Even though they devoted their main effort to industrialization, they could not but recognize the crucial importance of agriculture for the success of their ambitious modernization project. The collectivization of agriculture figured in their plans from the beginning, but in the fall of 1944 and in 1945 and even 1946, as long as their domination of the country was still contested, they concealed their designs on peasant property from the peasants. But once in power they felt no constraints in transforming the countryside to fit their model. As in so many aspects of the building of socialism in the decade after the war, the Soviet Union provided them with a pattern, this time its collectivization campaign of the 1920s and 1930s. Thus, Romanian Communists not only aimed at economic change, but were determined to bring about a fundamental reordering of the social structure, the way of life, and even the mental and spiritual climate of the countryside. They thus brought revolution to the village by replacing tradition with new values, by suppressing the individualism of the peasant proprietor in favor of collectivism, and, over the long term, by turning agricultural holdings into factories and peasants into factory workers. Their zeal may be attributed, in part, to the need they felt to impress upon their mentors in Moscow that they were following the correct path to socialism, but they were also practical and realized that they must ensure adequate and cheap supplies of food for the thousands of workers streaming into the new industrial centers. The party's approach to collectivization is illustrative of the methods it used to solve other complex economic and social problems.

Roughly three phases of the collectivization process, which lasted from 1949 to 1962, are discernible. All three were marked by greater or lesser degrees of intimidation and violence and, often, by positive incentives to induce peasants to join collective farms. The party was in charge from beginning to end, as it decided on the pace of the campaign and the methods to be applied. Yet the progress of collectivization was far from uniform over the whole country, a variation that raises questions about the omnipotence of the party leadership. Success or temporary failure in a given district or village often depended upon the competence and inclinations of local party and government officials and activists. They often ignored directives from the center, as they had to contend with local circumstances or pursued personal ambitions.

During the first phase, 1949–53, the party advocated persuasion as the most desirable means of drawing peasants into collective farms (gospodăriile agricole colective; GAC) and offered various benefits, among them reductions in taxes and in delivery quotas for certain crops, to those who would join. But as few peasants were willing to give up their fields and animals, the party and its agents used other methods. A variation of the GACs was tried – the cooperatives (întovărăşirile agricole), in which work was done in common while peasants retained ownership of land, livestock, and tools, but they attracted few members. The party also engaged in intensive political education, but it, too, fell short of expectations.

Force, which at first party leaders had been reluctant to use because they were aware of how attached the peasants were to their land and traditions and how disruptive of production violence in the countryside could be, now became the instrument of choice. Threats and violence took various forms: well-off peasants, the so-called *chiabur*s, or kulaks, were arrested and their property seized, and, together with other leaders of the village, they were imprisoned or forced into internal exile far from home. A variation on this tactic was the party's encouragement of class warfare in the village. It sought to weaken resistance to collectivization by turning the poor and middling peasant against better-off neighbors, whom it condemned as the enemies of progress and prosperity. The *chiabur* did indeed disappear in time, but his demise was hardly a victory for other peasants, as they, too, in a sense, disappeared into the system of collective property and labor.

A slowdown characterized the second phase of collectivization between 1953 and 1956. The reasons for the change of rhythm were varied. Events in Moscow had strong repercussions in Bucharest, as was usual during this period. The death of Stalin in March 1953 and the advent of Georgi Malenkov and his advocacy of a new course, which emphasized greater attention to the quality of life and consumer needs, suggested to Gheorghiu-Dej and his circle the need for a similar change of direction. The new Soviet leaders made plain to Gheorghiu-Dej during his visits to Moscow during this time their unhappiness with Romania's overall economic performance. But the Romanians were already painfully aware of shortcomings in agricultural production and of the consequences of their own neglect of the population's material well-being. They were thus ready, at least for the moment, to consider a more moderate approach to solving problems in the countryside.

The period of relaxation indeed proved to be only temporary. Party leaders never considered abandoning collectivization, and in 1957 they resumed the process at the pace characteristic of the Stalin years. Undoubtedly, theoretical ambitions – the fulfillment of Marxist-Leninist teachings – figured in their decision. But they were also determined to reassert their full control over the rhythm of social and economic change and to make certain that agriculture played the crucial role assigned to it as the auxiliary of industrialization.

Gheorghiu-Dej had been obliged to admit, at least in private, that agriculture had lagged behind other sectors of the economy. Now he was anxious to eliminate once and for all opposition to collectivization by peasants and the indecision and incompetence of local officials and activists by bringing all matters related to agriculture fully under the direction of central authorities. The resort to force and intimidation led to uprisings in numerous villages, which, in turn, caused even more drastic responses from the authorities. In any case, the will of the party prevailed, and in 1962 Gheorghiu-Dej could announce the successful conclusion of the collectivization drive. Yet, not all agricultural land had been collectivized. The main exceptions were in the mountainous regions, which were unsuitable for large-scale, mechanized farming and where individual holdings survived.

KULTURKAMPF

As with industrialization and the collectivization of agriculture the Communist elite also treated "cultural struggle" as a means to an end – the building of socialism and the attainment of ideal Communism. But whereas economic goals were precisely determined and could be measured in terms of goods produced and quotas met, accomplishments in the diverse fields of culture defied easy calculation mainly because individual psychologies and creative impulses were at the heart of things. Party leaders, reluctantly, acknowledged the differences between the factory and the academy, but were certain that they could mobilize the workers of both to achieve their ends. Yet, to create the new society and the new socialist citizen they assigned to culture a specific, yet elusive, goal: the transformation of mentalities, a task that would require continuous commerce with intellectuals. The relationship was always tense, as the elite could never overcome its suspicion of intellectuals as somehow by their very nature ill-disposed to follow rules and bend to commands.

The elite conducted its cultural offensive in the same way it approached economic change: it imposed planning and direction from the center. Its chief agent was the Propaganda and Agitation Section of the Central Committee of the party, which had immense powers to achieve the desired results on the "cultural front." A great diversity of institutions came within its sphere, among them the Ministry of Education, the Romanian Academy, radio and cinema, publishing and printing, unions of writers and scientists, the press and news agencies, sports organizations, and, of course, the apparatus of censorship. Various members of the party's Political Executive Committee oversaw the Section's activities and approved its personnel. Their guide was the Soviet experience, and thus the way was opened to the emulation of Soviet literary and artistic achievements and the promotion of Russian language and culture, on the one hand, and the denigration of Western values, on the other.

The party elite reserved a special place for intellectuals in its modernization project. They were to be the intermediaries between the party and the citizenry by becoming popularizers of the new ideology of growth and progress and, hence, the creators of new values and new myths. They would thus assume a new style of life and serve a mass culture. They were, in effect, to be an engaged intellectual elite marching alongside party activists in the vanguard of those committed to the building of socialism. Their task was no less than the transformation of mentalities, of the Romanians' worldview and the molding of their consciousness of having entered a new era. It was to be a mission hardly less heroic than the economic transformation that had engaged millions of workers and peasants.

But the intellectual elite that the party had inherited from the interwar period would not do. By education and background it was Western at a time when, the party taught, the only source of light and inspiration could be the East. Intellectuals, any intellectuals and certainly those of the old regime, were for the party by definition unpredictable. Lucreţiu Pătrăşcanu, an intellectual, writing in 1945, was especially severe in his judgments. With the interwar period in mind, he accused the traditional intellectual elite of lacking principles and being given to "cheap opportunism," and he had a warning for such people: they must either align themselves with the forces of progress and the future or be "trampled by history."

The party had, in any case, given up on the old elite. Some members of it could still be salvaged, if they were willing to accept the party's blueprint for socialist Romania. Their talent and prestige could thus help sell the party's vision of the future to the broad public, but these intellectuals could never be entrusted with forming the new generation. Many of them, especially in the humanities and social sciences, were thus shunted aside and unable to pursue their careers. Some, who persisted in "standing in the way of progress," were treated more severely.

Members of the old intellectual elite, in their turn, treated the party with, at the very least, suspicion, as it espoused values that were incompatible with what they took to be the foundations of intellectual life – freedom of thought and expression. Educated in the spirit of Europe as it had evolved since the eighteenth century, whether they were Europeanists or traditionalists, they could not accommodate themselves to the intellectual and cultural values represented by the Soviet Union. Yet, they did not challenge the new regime directly; their reaction was one of powerless resignation. As Sovietization proceeded many of the most respected figures of the old elite acquiesced in the regime's repudiation of European values and the national cultural heritage.

The old generation of intellectuals approached the Communist regime in different ways. There were the committed Communists, relatively few in number, like Petre Constantinescu-Iaşi (1892–1977), who had a doctorate in Byzantine art and was a founding member of the Communist Party and held numerous official and academic posts after 1944. Constantin Parhon (1874–1969) belonged to a second category of intellectual – the leftist Social Democrat who joined the Communist Party. A renowned endocrinologist, he was appointed first president of the Grand National Assembly in 1948. The novelist Mihail Sadoveanu was representative of a larger category of intellectuals who joined the Communist Party after 1944 and served its causes in high positions, but did so without conviction. Many of his fellow intellectuals who had held official posts in the dictatorships of Carol II and Ion Antonescu or had compromised themselves by supporting nationalist and conservative causes expiated their sins by longer or shorter periods in prison.

While the Communist Party was at work dismantling the old intellectual elite it strove by all available means to bring the new into being as rapidly as possible. It tried various inducements to attract intellectuals. One was coercion. It might take the form of intensive ideological indoctrination, which was intended to persuade but also to intimidate. For those who fell into line the party offered rewards: suitable employment, financial support for writers and artists, the certainty of publication of approved works, and access to the medical services and retail stores of the party. Behind all these enticements lay the overwhelming power of the regime to impose its will and the somber examples of what happened to those who chose a contrary path.

The relationship between the party and intellectuals throughout the 1950s was uneasy and unstable. The most difficult time for intellectuals was undoubtedly 1948–53, when the party's drive for ideological conformity and its campaign against "cosmopolitanism," that is, Western intellectual and cultural values, was at its height. The harsh censorship discouraged authors in all fields of the humanities and social sciences, and, as a result, literary and scholarly production declined in both quality and variety. A relaxation of sorts occurred between 1953 and 1956, when, under the impress of de-Stalinization in the Soviet Union and elsewhere in the bloc, the Romanian party acknowledged the ill effects of heavy-handed intervention in cultural and intellectual activities and made modest concessions to writers and scholars. It even considered measures to end the cultural isolation that it had imposed during the period of high Stalinism. But the leadership could not free itself from its ingrained distrust of the interwar intellectuals as forever susceptible to "bourgeois ideology" and Western influences. The party was thus ever vigilant in dealing with intellectuals, especially those of the younger generation who showed a disconcerting independence of mind. In 1958 and 1959 it struck harshly at intellectuals in all age groups who failed to meet its severe test of loyalty and obedience. Small discussion groups that operated outside the approved cultural network, such as the one led by the philosopher Constantin Noica, which concerned itself with Eastern religious thought, were disbanded and its members imprisoned. For other acts of suspected non-conformity thousands of writers, professors, and students were arrested or disciplined in other ways.

To create a new intellectual class capable of providing the technological and managerial and, no less crucial, the ideological leadership of socialist Romania the party devoted substantial resources to education at every level. In so doing, it imitated the Soviet Union, a choice that required the abandonment of the traditional Romanian educational system which had come into being during the preceding century. Legislation, beginning in 1948, put in place a highly centralized network of institutions from the primary school to the university, all committed to achieving the fundamental goals set by the Communist Party of hastening economic modernization and creating the "new man" of the socialist era.

The party, through the state apparatus, took full charge of the education and training of the population and mounted an effort of truly massive proportions. After 1948 all forms of private education were eliminated and the state became the sole financial support of education. Its annual budget grew steadily to pay for an ambitious program that aimed at extending elementary education to everyone, thereby ending illiteracy and contributing to the increase of the skilled workforce; created numerous specialized secondary schools and greatly expanded higher education; and increased teaching staffs at all levels. The party's support for education was by no means limited to traditional institutions. It established so-called party schools to train party and government officials, and people's universities, usually within large industrial enterprises, to offer courses in technology to increase labor productivity, and it introduced evening classes for adults in cities and villages throughout the country.

The purpose of this mighty effort was not solely the spread of useful knowledge. It was also ideological, as the party carried on its work of indoctrination at all levels – in schools and universities, research institutes, factories, collective farms, and government and party offices. Children and young people received special attention, as they were the party's chief hope for creating the new men and women and the new mentality of socialist Romania. In pursuit of this goal party leaders were ever conscious of class origins. As it laid the foundations of a new intellectual elite it chose carefully the students to be admitted to universities and professional schools, giving preference to those from working-class and poor peasant families and limiting the number of or denying admission outright to those from "bourgeois" and other undesirable backgrounds. The party also brought young people of all ages into mass organizations such as the Pioneers, the Union of Working (later,

Communist) Youth, and student associations, all of which had as their main task to mobilize support for the party's modernization project.

The party elite made clear its preoccupation with ideology and mentalities by imposing its monopoly over the study and interpretation of Romanian history. Its involvement in the history profession never slackened, but the tasks it assigned to history steadily evolved as changes in domestic policy and the shifting political currents within the Soviet bloc dictated.

At first, the party limited the practice of history to the Soviet model. It thus required historians to demonstrate the correctness of the Marxist-Leninist (and for a time, Stalinist) interpretation of historical development and thereby focus on economic forces and the class struggle. The party elite conceived of history, in the first instance, as a reflection of the interests of the present, and, not surprisingly, it insisted that the Romanians' past, from Dacian and Roman times to the post-Second World War era, be reconfigured. Among the major changes introduced were new interpretations of the role of the Slavs in the ethnic and cultural development of the Romanians and revisions in descriptions of the relationship of the principalities and the Romanian kingdom to tsarist Russia and the Soviet Union. A downgrading of the Romanians' association with the West was an inevitable consequence of the new worldview. In any case, the party elite at this stage discouraged open, public debates about fundamental issues of historical development or even about what had actually happened at a given moment; there could be only one historical truth, even if it was constantly being altered to suit the party's needs of the moment. The party's version of historical truth was embodied, at least for a time, in the reshaping of the Romanian identity carried out by Mihail Roller (1908–58) and his associates in the sole official textbook permitted: *Istoria României* (then, *Istoria R. P. R.*), of which five editions were published between 1947 and 1956. It fitted in perfectly with the climate of opinion during the Stalin years and carried out a reinterpretation of Romanian history in keeping with the Romanian Communist Party's subservience to Moscow at the time.

The party was unwilling to leave the emergence of the "new history" to chance. Eager to mold the historical profession to suit its purposes, it kept historians, a category of intellectuals especially suspect, under close scrutiny. It did so by bringing them under the supervision of recently reorganized centers such as the Institutes of History of the Romanian Academy in Bucharest, Cluj, and Iaşi. Here historians were joined together in teams to carry out research on topics of particular relevance to the party's program. The planning and carrying out of projects bore striking resemblances to five-year plans in industry and agriculture. Historians of the older generation and many younger colleagues who could not adjust to the new methods of research and found the new criteria of historical truth repugnant were marginalized.

Yet, within a few years, by 1955, a new atmosphere was discernible in the study of history. The re-evaluation of Stalin's legacy in the Soviet Union after 1953 and the slight distancing from Soviet mentorship by the Romanian party elite required new sources of legitimacy for Gheorghiu-Dej and company. They were ever conscious of the taint of illegitimacy that was attached to them because they had not come to power by revolutionary means of their own, but had been imposed by a foreign power. They now discovered the uses to which patriotism, or national feeling, could be put to break down the suspicion and fear that separated them from the populace and thereby earn for themselves a measure of genuine popularity. They assigned to historians the task of restoring the national heritage and showing how the Communist regime of Gheorghiu-Dej fitted into the general course of Romanian history and how it was in essence the natural culmination of earlier strivings of "progressive forces" to promote a true people's democracy and secure social justice.

The decisive battle over the national history was played out between 1955 and 1958 by Communist ideologues led by Mihail Roller and Leonte Răutu (1910–93), the head for many years of the all-powerful Section of Propaganda and Agitation of the Central Committee of the Communist Party, on the one side, and the professional historians led by Andrei Oţetea, the newly appointed Director of the Institute of History in Bucharest, on the other. Roller's followers continued to view the course of Romanian history from the same perspective as that contained in the textbook of 1947, whereas the professionals sought to return to the more balanced approach characteristic of interwar historiography. The confrontation became a contest between advocates of proletarian internationalism with their pro-Soviet stance on key events in the Romanian past and those who adhered to the national tradition. On the nature of Romania's participation in the First World War, for example, the Rollerists, as they came to be known, claimed that Romanian leaders were motivated by "imperialist" ambitions to seize territory (tsarist and Soviet Bessarabia was always on their minds), while the professionals insisted that Romania's actions had been just because the primary aim had been to free Romanians from foreign rule by drawing them into Greater Romania.

The course of political events favored the professionals. As the party elite continued to loosen its ties to the Soviet Union in the late 1950s and relied increasingly on patriotic support from the population, it allowed the national trend in historiography to continue. In public the elite's position was often ambiguous. But by the time Roller died in 1958 the tide had turned in the professionals' favor, even though diehards like Răutu could still mount a campaign of intimidation against scholars later that year. It was short-lived. The celebration of the centenary of the union of the principalities of Moldavia and Wallachia by university students and the public in 1959 and the appearance of the first volume of the new *Istoria României* (The history of Romania) in late 1960 were milestones in the re-emergence of the national spirit that was to accompany the building of socialism up to its end in 1989.

The party elite treated literature as they did history (and industry and agriculture). Thus, they undertook to restructure the discipline, collectivize its workers, and impose new goals to pursue and new ways of achieving them. They made it clear from the beginning that the main purpose of literature was to contribute to the creation of the new society and the new man. They impressed upon novelists and poets and literary critics that they were to serve the needs of contemporary society by being militant and by placing themselves in the vanguard of the modernization project.

The party elite thus expected authors to produce works of a particular kind. The political and social message they contained had to be clear and had to explain and justify the party's program, and the heroes and villains, and good and evil, had to be sharply delineated.

Under the circumstances, much of the prose and poetry written in the early 1950s followed the approved formulas. One of the more striking examples of literature in the service of the party's agenda was the poetry of Alexandru Toma (1875–1954), a versifier of modest abilities who was, nonetheless, hailed as the national poet of the time for works about the Russian Revolution and the Communist movement. In all the creative endeavors of the period the literature of the Soviet Union was held up as the appropriate source of inspiration. The literary reviews were full of praise for the achievements of Soviet writers, whereas the new trends in Western literature were given scant, if any, attention.

Many writers of the older generation could not fit into the new order and fell silent. Lucian Blaga was one. His philosophy and poetry of the spirit, of the village and its traditions, and of wonder at God's capriciousness were ill-suited to the party's modernization project, and thus until his death he wrote only for his desk drawer. Some writers suffered persecution and were jailed. Others continued to write, but accepted compromises imposed by the party. Mihail Sadoveanu (1880–1961), the consummate story-teller of modern Romanian literature, whose novels and short stories formed a vast panorama of Romanian rural society, offered his services to the party elite. They, in turn, aware of their own unpopularity, welcomed his adherence with the expectation that it would win them the sympathy of the population. He dutifully produced a novel written to socialist realist specifications, *Mitrea Cocor* (1949), and, in return, was able to publish another novel more in his own style, *Nicoara Potcoavă* (1952). Up to his death he received all manner of high cultural and civic honors. Other authors underwent a rehabilitation as the party elite came to realize that it gained nothing by ignoring great writers. Tudor Arghezi is a prime example. Condemned in 1948 in the party daily, *Scânteia* (The spark), as a poet who had "sunk into the muck of bourgeois decadence," he was able to publish again in 1955. His first volume was *1907*, about the peasant uprising, and thereafter he was accorded numerous honors, even though his voluminous writings made few concessions to the new order. Even the dead could be made to conform. Eminescu and Caragiale, among others, were reinterpreted in the light of prevailing truths.

Despite the enormous pressures to adjust to the party's literary tastes, a number of novelists and poets tested the rigidity of socialist-realist principles and produced first-class work. In prose, *Cronica de familie* (The chronicle of a family; 3 vols.; 1956), by Petru Dumitriu (1924–2002), stands out. One of the best novels of the Communist era, it follows the fortunes of an aristocratic Romanian family from the middle of the nineteenth century to the middle of the twentieth with both the realist teachings of Balzac and the psychological complexities of Proust clearly in evidence. *Moromeţii* (1955), by Marin Preda (1922–80), is a remarkable portrait of a peasant family of the Wallachian plain between the spring and fall of a single year. One of the most powerful novels in Romanian literature, it defied the literary prescriptions of the time and revealed the real tragedy of the peasantry during the Communist regime. Among poets, A. E. Baconsky (1925–77) broke with the socialist-realist formula of the early 1950s to write beautiful lyric poetry whose predominant mood was melancholy and dreaming, as in *Fluxul memoriei* (The tide of memory; 1957).

The battle for the soul of literature was joined in the later 1950s between party cultural engineers, on one side, and, on the other, a small number of writers and editors of literary reviews, who chose, at some risk, to challenge the prevailing orthodoxy. At the first congress of the Union of Writers held in Bucharest in 1956 they rejected ideological and social criteria as the sole measures of value in creativity. A group of writers from *Steaua* (The star), the monthly literary review in Cluj, added their voices to the criticism of "pseudo-literary" authors who promoted "dogmatism" as the foundation of true art. Even several writers favored by the regime, including Titus Popovici, the author of the novel *Setea* (Thirst; 1958), about the rural world in transition after 1944, urged a "decentralization," that is, less control by party officials, of literary life. Already the editors of *Gazeta Literară* (The literary gazette), the weekly review of the Union of Writers, which had begun publication in 1954 with the charge of providing Marxist-Leninist guidance for authors, had changed sides and had declared aesthetics to be the sole criterion in evaluating a work of literature.

The party responded to criticism by tightening the procedures for publishing books and articles and by dismissing and in other

ways disciplining editors and writers who openly defied party directives. At *Steaua* A. E. Baconsky was removed as editor because he
persisted in his "error" of demanding that the writer be accorded
artistic autonomy, that is, the right to create in accordance with his
own aesthetic sense. In Bucharest the monthly *Viaţa Românească*
(Romanian life), under a new editor who shared the party's view of
literature, campaigned against writers who stood for "modernism"
in poetry, such as Baconsky, or who would not renounce their interwar ideas about the nature of art, such as the literary critic and novelist George Călinescu and the literary critic Tudor Vianu. Among
those who suffered arrest were the poet Ştefan August Doinaş and
the novelist Henriette Yvonne Stahl. Especially offensive in the eyes
of party literary supervisors was the utter disregard by writers of
the party's monopoly in cultural matters, which they expressed by
organizing their own "secret" discussion groups. Although such
heavy-handed involvement in literary matters extended into 1959,
attacks on non-conformist writers and editors were on the wane. A
kind of cultural calm, accompanied by the rehabilitation of many
writers, including Lucian Blaga, was setting in as the party elite
pressed forward with a re-evaluation of the national heritage.

Another field of intellectual and spiritual encounter between
tradition and Communist modernization, as in history and literature, was religion. The party elite, in elaborating their policy toward
the various churches in Romania, adhered in principle to atheist
doctrines as propounded by the Soviet Communist Party. In the
early years after seizing power they devised policies whose purpose
was to eliminate all influence by organized religion from society
and transform Romania into a purely secular state. The promotion
of atheism figured in many party initiatives, especially in education
and cultural life. The elite was hostile to religion, if for no other reason than they judged it an ideological rival with deep roots among
the population as a whole, especially in the countryside. It was thus
a formidable obstacle to their modernization project. The contest
that arose between the party and the Christian churches was a crucial test of the elite's ability to put in place the spiritual foundations
of their new society.

The legal framework within which the several churches were permitted to function in the new order were set down in the Constitution

of April 1948, which guaranteed freedom of conscience to all citizens and allowed all religious groups to organize themselves and operate freely. But these promises did not represent complete freedom of religion. Since the matter was declared to be of public concern, the guarantees churches received could be valid only if they conducted their activities in accordance with the requirements of good order and prevailing legal conventions, stipulations that were subject to the changing interpretations of party officials. The Law on Religious Denominations of August 4, 1948 laid down the specific conditions under which churches could function. In practice this law and others to come strictly limited the freedoms described in the constitution by bringing the churches under the supervision of the Ministry of Religions and later under the Department of Cults, which answered directly to the Central Committee of the Communist Party. The Council of Ministers on March 5, 1958 expanded the Department of Cults' control over the churches by recognizing its right to approve their auxiliary organizations and their personnel. From the very beginning the Department intervened regularly in all the affairs of the churches, except doctrine and ritual. Since its admonitions were often reinforced by similar notices from the Securitate, the Department served as one of the state organs of repression. The party thus used the Department to make certain that clergy and faithful contributed fully to the modernization project or, at the very least, did not obstruct its progress.

The laws and regulations governing the relations between church and state may, in a sense, have provided for a separation of the two by prescribing the autonomy of religious communities from the state and of the state from religious communities. But, in fact, there was no separation of church and state in the usual meaning of the term. The state, that is, the party, never ceased to treat the Romanian Orthodox Church and the thirteen other churches officially recognized in the constitution as more than instruments for carrying out its policies. Rather than a separation, what emerged between the Orthodox Church (and the other churches) and the state was a kind of coexistence, a *modus vivendi* which enabled each to pursue its particular aims with the support, most of the time half-hearted, of the other. As a result, the state had the benefit of the church's influence among its faithful in consolidating its political power and developing its economic and social programs, while the church was able to pursue its spiritual and cultural mission, at least within the confines of its own buildings, with the material support of a regime that officially disavowed religion.

In one sense, the relationship between church and state may be characterized as a separation, if the term refers to the virtual elimination of any church initiative in public affairs. The party reduced to nil the church's role in the formulation of public policies and programs. Party leaders repeatedly declared that the "era of Byzantinism" was over, and thus they drastically reduced the church's ability to undertake independent social action. They closed church-operated elementary and secondary schools and charitable institutions, eliminated religious instruction from the school system, and, in general, discouraged religious influences among young people and all public manifestations of religious faith. Consequently, worship and the study of religion were restricted to the home and to buildings and institutions specifically intended for these purposes such as churches and seminaries.

The party's contacts with the Romanian Orthodox Church were of fundamental importance in determining the general course of church–state relations during the Communist period, since the Orthodox Church was by far the largest in the country (Orthodox: 72.6%; Greek Catholic: 7.9%; Roman Catholic: 6.8%; Reformed: 3.9%; Lutheran: 3.2%, according to the census of 1930) and had been intimately linked to the fortunes of the Romanian people since the founding of Moldavia and Wallachia in the fourteenth century. The party elite had to take account of these facts, if only grudgingly, as it decided on its policy toward the church. It is therefore significant that while the party and its propaganda organs railed against religion, they never attacked the Orthodox Church as such. Nonetheless, the elite spared no effort to bring the church under its control and use its clergy to gain favor among the faithful and thereby hasten the building of socialism.

The success of the often precarious balance between the party and the church and the very survival of the church may have been due in great measure to the determination of Patriarch Justinian Marina (1901–77; patriarch, 1948–77) and the majority of his clergy to protect the church by working within a legal framework which they had no power to change. Justinian's personality and ideas largely determined the direction of church policy, which may best be summed up by the title of a series of volumes he published between 1948 and 1971 entitled *Apostolat social* (Social mission). Its dominant theme was the responsibility of the clergy and faithful to adapt to the circumstances of the time in which they found themselves and to contribute to the building of a new society. Justinian was convinced that such a course was fully in accordance with the traditions of the Orthodox Church. In advocating the church's assumption of a contemporary social mission, then, he was eager to prove that it was possible to reconcile Communism and Christianity, a People's Republic with a People's Church, but he made no claim of compatibility between Marxism and Christianity, only between Orthodoxy and Communism as their relationship evolved day-to-day in Romania. He sought harmony between church and party for the benefit of Orthodoxy and country.

The Patriarch was frequently reminded that harmony was an elusive goal. Shortly after his accession he undertook a sweeping reform of monastic life which aimed at reinforcing the regimen of prayer, study, and work and reinvigorating the spirit of service to others. His efforts soon began to yield the desired results as the monasteries became increasingly important spiritual and intellectual centers. This renascence could not but attract the close scrutiny of the regime. It decided that the monasteries had become focal points of reaction and disloyalty, and in 1958 it undertook a campaign against them which led to the closing of monastic schools, a reduction in the number of monks and nuns, and a drastic limitation on the number of novices. In the following year the authorities forced the Holy Synod to accept a new ordinance governing monastic affairs in keeping with party objectives. This episode reveals both the power of the state in religious matters and its limitations, and illustrates the resilience and perhaps even the bargaining power of the church. The monasteries were not abolished, and after a period of open conflict church–state relations gradually improved by 1961.

The fate of the Romanian Greek Catholic Church was far different from that of the Orthodox Church, as the party was determined to abolish the former because of its ties to the Vatican and its generally Western orientation. The number of Greek Catholics, most of whom lived in Transylvania, was, as we have noted, much smaller than that of the Orthodox, but in Transylvania they were more numerous than the Orthodox (31.1 percent to 27.7 percent, according to the census of 1930). The treatment of the Greek Catholic Church in Ukraine before the Second World War by Soviet authorities offered Romanian Communists a precedent for their actions and ensured approval in Moscow. The tactic they used drew from Romanian historical experience – the Church Union with Rome in Transylvania in 1701. Thus, with the cooperation of the Orthodox Church hierarchy the party sponsored a "re-Union" of the Greek Catholic with the Orthodox Church at a Church Congress in Alba Iulia in 1948. A number of Greek Catholic priests agreed to rejoin the Orthodox Church, but the six bishops adamantly refused. As a result, they were arrested and imprisoned, and Greek Catholic churches and other property were given to the Orthodox Church. The Orthodox hierarchy, including Patriarch Justinian, approved the actions at Alba Iulia as a means of repairing what they regarded as the spiritual division of the Romanian nation caused by the Church Union. But the re-Union was not complete. Despite the official disappearance of their church, many Greek Catholic priests and believers maintained their faith in subtle ways.

The party proceeded in an equally aggressive way against the Roman Catholic Church in Romania, mainly, it seems, because it was part of an international, Western organization hostile to Communism and would not submit to the kind of control imposed on the Romanian Orthodox Church. The ethnic composition of the church made the matter even more complex, since the majority of its members were not Romanian but Hungarian. Gheorghiu-Dej made the party's intentions clear at its congress in February 1948, when he denounced the Vatican as a member of the "imperialist camp." Subsequent measures followed the Soviet model in dealing with the Roman Catholic Church. The Romanian party abrogated the Concordat of 1927, seized the church's educational institutions and other property, expelled representatives of the Vatican in 1950, and put a number of clergy on trial in 1951 for spying for the "imperialist powers." Perhaps the most striking case of all involved the head of the church in Transylvania, Bishop Áron Márton (1896–1980) of Alba Iulia. Bishop since 1938, he was arrested and imprisoned in 1949, because of his resistance to the Communist Party's actions against the church. Released in 1955, he sought to take charge once again of church affairs, but he was put under house arrest in Alba Iulia until 1967. Nonetheless, he continued to oversee church affairs until his death. Relations between the Romanian state and the Roman Catholic Church in Romania and the Vatican remained strained throughout the 1950s.

Other non-Romanian churches were also subordinated to the new order and thus lost their schools and most of their property, except for church buildings, and ceased to have a significant role in public affairs. The Hungarian Reformed and Unitarian churches, the Saxon Evangelical Church, and a number of the so-called neo-Protestant sects, such as the Baptists and Pentecostals, were able to carry on their strictly religious activities, but always under the close supervision of the party through the Department of Cults.

Another front in the "cultural struggle" encompassed the minorities. The four most important minorities when the Communists came to power in 1947 were the Hungarians, Germans, Jews, and Gypsies. In certain respects they shared a common fate during the next four decades. From the beginning they were subordinated to the party and its aims and were thus expected to take their places among the builders of socialism. They also underwent the same processes of economic, social, and cultural transformation as the Romanian majority. Then, in the 1960s and later, as the doctrine of national Communism gained currency, their existence as distinct ethnicities came under still further pressure. They learned from these experiences that the party would tolerate no independent initiatives on their part and no competition from organizations of their own. Over time two minorities – the Germans and the Jews – became convinced that they had no future in a Communist Romania and departed in large numbers, while the two others – the Hungarians and the Gypsies – persevered.

The Hungarians of Transylvania presented Romanian Communist leaders with their most formidable minority problem. The Hungarians and Szeklers were the largest of the minorities (1,588,000 in 1956), whose deep historical roots in Transylvania caused them to revere it as their homeland. The party elite never seriously considered granting them administrative or cultural autonomy. Its way of proceeding was to retain power in its own hands and, at most, allow the Hungarians the forms of representation in approved organizations and thus without the substance. The Hungarian Autonomous Region (Regiunea Autonomă Maghiară; RAM) is a striking illustration of its policy. Encompassing the districts in eastern Transylvania with large Szekler majorities, it was formed in 1952 under pressure from the Soviet party and, apparently, at the behest of Stalin himself, as a means of coping with the Hungarian nationality problem in Soviet fashion. According to the Romanian Constitution of 1952, RAM was to have a special statute and its own administration elected by the inhabitants, all to be approved by the country's chief legislative body, the Grand National Assembly. But the Assembly never acted because the party had no desire to give formal recognition to Hungarian autonomy. RAM thus had no real autonomy; it was governed like all the other regions, from Bucharest, and was finally dissolved in 1968.

All the actions taken by the Communist Party under Gheorghiu-Dej and his successor Nicolae Ceauşescu continuously restricted the activities of those Hungarian economic and cultural institutions that had survived the struggle for power in 1944–47. The nationalization of businesses and banks and the collectivization of agriculture destroyed the middle class and other leading elements of Hungarian society and undermined the economic foundations of Hungarian churches and schools and cultural associations. The Communist Party struck a heavy blow at education in Hungarian through the law of 1948 nationalizing all schools, which dissolved the extensive school networks operated by the Hungarian churches (581 Reformed schools, 468 Roman Catholic, 34 Unitarian). Then, in the later 1950s, the party initiated a policy that would in time absorb Hungarian students into Romanian schools. It seems to have been inspired to some extent by the party's doubts about the loyalty of the Hungarians in the light of their sympathy for the revolution in Hungary in 1956. The most dramatic event of this campaign was undoubtedly the unification of the Hungarian Bolyai University with the Romanian Babeş University in Cluj in 1959, which was followed by a reduction in the amount of instruction in Hungarian. The disappearance of Bolyai University symbolized a fundamental change in the guiding principles of the Romanian Communist regime. The elite was already laying the foundations of national Communism, and from the 1960s on it spoke increasingly about the "socialist nation," a concept that provided the ideological justification for cultural (and economic and social) homogenization. It became more and more evident that the socialist nation the elite had in mind was ethnic and Romanian.

The Saxons of Transylvania emerged from the Second World War and the transition period of 1944–47 much weakened. Because many had supported or acquiesced in the National Socialist leadership of the community during the war and some 50,000 had fought in the German army on the Soviet front, the whole community was treated harshly by the Romanian Communist Party and Soviet occupation authorities. Romanian Communist leaders in 1945 even considered the expulsion of the Saxons (and the Swabians of the Banat) to Germany. But by 1948 the party had decided to recognize the German minority as a "co-inhabiting nationality" and thus entitled to enjoy rights of citizenship in the People's Republic and take part in the socialist transformation of the country.

The Saxons in general underwent the same experiences as the Hungarians. The nationalization of industry, banks, and businesses of all kinds between 1948 and 1952 deprived the Saxon urban middle class of their means of existence and effectively removed them from leadership of the community. In the countryside the collectivization of agriculture destroyed the foundations of Saxon village life, a consequence that obliged many Saxons to seek a livelihood in the cities. As with the Hungarians, drastic economic change undermined the financial condition of the Saxon Evangelical Church and deprived it of the means necessary to carry on its charitable and social activities. Saxon culture came under increasing pressure. The changes in education in 1948 abolished the extensive network of Saxon schools, and in subsequent years the use of German in state schools was steadily reduced. Although the party provided the Saxons with various organizations, their primary purpose was to mobilize support for its programs, and, hence, they did not truly represent Saxon interests. The national

Communist ideology adopted by the party in the late 1950s and 1960s gave Saxons little hope that the course of events could be altered.

The overall effect of what had happened since 1944 was to persuade the majority of Saxons that they could not survive as a distinct ethnic community. Their loss of hope expressed itself in emigration to West Germany, especially after the establishment of diplomatic relations between the two countries in 1967. By a secret agreement between them West Germany agreed to pay Romania a certain sum, usually between 4,000 and 10,000 Deutschmarks, for each Saxon who was allowed to emigrate. The terms were adjusted periodically. In 1978, for example, Romania agreed to allow 11,000 Saxons a year to go to West Germany in return for the usual payment for each individual and an addition 700 million Deutschmarks in credits. After the collapse of the Communist regime in December 1989 a massive departure of Saxons occurred, which reduced the remaining Saxon population to perhaps 120,000 in 1993. In this way the Saxons ceased to be a significant social and cultural force in Transylvania after six centuries.

For the Jews of Romania the first few years after the Second World War were a time of reconstruction. Their numbers (372,000 in 1946) had been reduced by half (756,000 in 1930) by the horrors of the war, but they set to work to rebuild communities, restore businesses, and reinvigorate education and cultural life, and they did so with their own organizations. But as the Romanian Communist Party relentlessly extended its control over the country it demanded that Jewish institutions be made subordinate to it, as was happening in the Hungarian, Saxon, and, no less, Romanian communities. It refused to tolerate any independent initiatives from other bodies, and thus in 1948 it replaced the Federation of Jewish Communities (Federaţia Comunităţilor Evreieşti), which genuinely represented Jewish interests, with the Jewish Democratic Committee (Comitetul Democratic Evreiesc), which was composed of Jewish Communists who would follow the lead of the Communist Party. The party carried out a similar operation in the Jewish religious organization. It forced the replacement of the Chief Rabbi, Alexandru Şafran, who refused to endorse Communist Party actions and lend his name to its propaganda efforts, with a more pliable figure who would fit

in with the new order. The only Jewish organization left functioning was the Zionist Organization of Romania (Organizaţia Sionistă
din România), but in 1948 the Communist Party undertook a violent campaign against it. It came in the wake of a declaration by
the Central Committee in 1948 on the national question, which
denounced Zionism as a plot by the nationalist Jewish bourgeoisie
to isolate Jewish workers from workers of other ethnic communities. In March 1949 the Council of Ministers dissolved all Zionist
organizations.

The Communist Party's transformation of the country in the
years after the Second World War – the nationalization of industries
and banks and large and small businesses and the grouping of professionals, notably lawyers and doctors, into cooperatives – struck
at the very foundations of the Jewish community. So did the dissolution of Jewish schools, a consequence of new laws making the
state solely responsible for education. The response of the Jewish
community was massive emigration. The establishment of the State
of Israel in 1948 provided an additional incentive to leave, as they
could now become part of a national Jewish homeland. Emigration
took place continuously during the Communist period at varying
rates, depending on shifts in policy of the Communist Party and
the nature of financial arrangements with Israel. Evidence of the
mood in the Jewish community was the departure of 118,000 emi-
grants between 1948 and 1951. By 1977 the Jewish community in
Romania had dwindled to 25,000, and by 1992 to 9,000.

The Gypsies were a special object of attention during the first
years of the People's Republic, as the Communist Party undertook
to integrate them into the new economic and social structures and
thus mobilize them for the building of socialism. It aimed to eliminate nomadism, provide employment and housing, and ensure a
proper education for children. But the party did little to involve the
Gypsies themselves in creating a new life, and for long periods it
all but ignored them. Then, in the late 1970s and early 1980s, the
Ceauşescu regime resumed the earlier policies with some success, as
a certain number of Gypsies became integrated into Romanian society. Their numbers also increased. According to the census of 1956,
the Gypsy population was 104,000, and by 1977 it had grown to
230,000, an increase due to the Ceauşescu regime's prohibition on

abortions and other measures to raise the birthrate. But the latter figure is challenged by a secret official report of 1983, which set the number of Gypsies at 540,000, a suggestion of how serious an issue the Gypsy minority had become. By now, because of the shrinking Saxon and Jewish populations, the Gypsies had become the second largest minority after the Hungarians. But they remained on the lowest rung of the social scale.

TURNING POINTS

The decade between 1960 and 1971 exhibits certain characteristics that set it somewhat apart from the decade that preceded it and the two that followed. These characteristics did not emerge suddenly and full-blown, but had their sources in the 1950s, if not earlier. Yet they endowed the sixties with a distinctive style and even, perhaps, a sense of unreality, when viewed from the perspective of what came later. A national Communism, even if not so designated, was proclaimed as party doctrine and was imposed in every sphere of activity. This change of emphasis imbued the decade with a style of its own. Related to the new self-assertiveness and partly inspired by it was open defiance by the party elite of continued Soviet political and economic dominance. The elite discovered in their anti-Soviet (and anti-Russian) stance a welcome means of enhancing their own popularity and rallying public support for their policies. A modest unity of thought and purpose between the elite and the populace based on hostility to the unwelcome outsider gave rise to another phenomenon specific to the period: a détente with society at large. An unprecedented relaxation, at least since the Communists had come to power, set in that affected almost all areas of public and private life. All these events were accompanied by a resumption of economic and cultural relations with Western Europe and the United States. To many Romanians it seemed like a return to Europe, and to the historians among them it recalled the opening to the West in the early nineteenth century. But none of this was on the minds of the Communist elite; their ambitions were practical, not sentimental. Then, at the end of the decade and, in some sense, extinguishing the flickers of renewal, were the so-called "July Theses" of 1971 of Nicolae Ceauşescu, who had succeeded Gheorghiu-Dej in 1965. Unsettled by a decade of "liberalization," he demanded a return to ideological conformity and party discipline.

The Communist Party elite by 1960 faced no serious opposition within the country. The interwar political, economic, and cultural elites had, in effect, been eliminated. The Communist political and economic elite was supreme. Subordinate to it was the new professional and managerial elite, which it had brought into being to take the place of the old and provide the expertise needed to run a growing and increasingly complex economy. The Communist political elite was heterogeneous, as we have seen, but despite diversity, it maintained a remarkable degree of cohesion. Its members could rally behind Gheorghiu-Dej because they agreed on two fundamental points. First, they wholeheartedly supported industrialization as the primary vehicle for economic and social transformation, and they used it as a means of asserting autonomy in dealings with the Soviet Union; and second, they could all accept the need for autonomy itself, that is, their right to make decisions about modernization free of interference from Moscow. At the same time, as the most Stalinist of elites in the East European bloc, they found their common front against de-Stalinization enormously congenial.

A measure of the party elite's cohesion and self-confidence was its inauguration of a détente with the society it had held in tight material and spiritual constraints for over a decade. Its willingness to permit a relaxation in its relations with the populace at large was self-serving: it needed to curry favor with all elements of society, especially the professional and managerial class, if it were to challenge successfully the Soviet party for dominance over the modernization project and, equally important, discourage Soviet attempts at leadership change. Yet, Gheorghiu-Dej and the more sophisticated among his inner circle had come to realize that repression, of the kind visited upon intellectuals and clergy as late as 1958–59, was no longer necessary and could even be counterproductive. More was to be gained, they reasoned, by emphasizing the fundamental bonds that united party and people.

Détente took various forms. Most striking perhaps was the effort to reconfigure the party as one of the defenders of the national interest and one of a long line of militant promoters of progressive change in the country's history. The elite's objective here was to secure legitimacy by appealing to national sentiments rather than, as before, by acting as the advance guard of Soviet proletarian internationalism. It was as though the Romanian party was giving up class struggle in favor of the ethnic nation.

National Communism, undeclared yet steadily gaining momentum, found clear expression in the elite's reconciliation with novelists and poets and historians. The party's cultural managers expanded the function of literature and re-evaluated the creative process itself. The party remained vigilant to ensure conformity to established, if now loosened, ideological norms, but dialogue tended to replace command. The conversation between Gheorghiu-Dej and George Călinescu in March 1960 is instructive. Gheorghiu-Dej expressed his own and the party's interest in literature in straightforward terms, and in the course of the conversation he provided a working definition of socialist realism. He insisted that writers had a responsibility to imbue their work with the "party spirit," and thus they had to be receptive to progressive change in society and to ideological "indications" from the party, whose task, he promised, was to help writers to understand "more justly" the reality around them. He found Călinescu's novel *Bietul Ioanide* (Poor Ioanide; 1953) particularly wanting in these qualities. He thought writers should instill in their works a "new breath," a new way of approaching the problems of everyday life, but what he found in Călinescu's novel, instead, were the old, that is, interwar literary style and "bourgeois spirit." He urged writers of genius, like Călinescu, to accept their responsibility to write for the masses, not for the "thin layer of society," to deal "faithfully" with contemporary themes, and to say plainly what they meant in order to enable the masses to grasp their thoughts and thus appreciate their art fully. To make sure these things happened, he continued, the party had established rules for writers to follow. Călinescu agreed on the writer's responsibilities to the whole society and did not challenge Gheorghiu-Dej's emphasis on ideology and the right of the party to guide the creative process. Yet, his next novel, *Scrinul negru* (The black chest of drawers; 1960), was, in effect, a statement of artistic autonomy, as he showed himself unable, or unwilling, to write in the prescribed manner. There were no dire consequences.

The socialist realism that Gheorghiu-Dej thus defined so matter-of-factly remained officially in the ascendant in the 1960s, but a new generation of writers chafed under the predominance of ideology and social criteria as the appropriate measure of creativity. In subtle ways they continually challenged the party's right to set limits to an author's field of vision and aesthetic sense. A note of defiance of party rules was evident in the volume of poems, *Sensul iubirii* (The sense of love; 1960), by Nichita Stănescu (1933–83), one of the foremost poets of the period. It served as a manifesto of the new generation of poets, who insisted on the inherent uniqueness of the creative act. Its publication marked the beginning of the ideological thaw that was to endure until the end of the decade. Notable contributions to the "spirit of the sixties" were volumes of poetry by Ana Blandiana (b. 1942), *Persoana întâia plural* (First-person plural; 1964), and by Marin Sorescu (1936–96), *Moartea ceasului* (The death of the clock; 1966), which revealed a new poetic language and proclaimed a new artistic ethics of no compromise with authority. They and their fellow poets embraced the poetic themes and sensibility of Lucian Blaga and Ion Barbu and other interwar poets, who stood as the antithesis of socialist realism.

In prose, too, the détente stimulated creativity and brought a new generation of writers to the fore. Novelists explored the psychological and moral dilemmas of individuals under stress in the prevailing regime, like Augustin Buzura (b. 1938), who described the ethical quandaries of sensitive men and women; like Nicolae Breban (b. 1934), who analyzed "strange," "distorted" individuals; and like Ştefan Bănulescu (b. 1929), who cultivated a fantastic prose. None of this fitted in with the ideological tenets or the immediate practical goals of the Communist elite. Literary criticism, too, underwent a reanimation that was spurred by the founding of many new literary journals throughout the country, among them *România Literară* (Literary Romania) in Bucharest. Critics such as Nicolae Manolescu (b. 1939) and Eugen Simion (b. 1933) dared to ignore "indications" from the party by insisting that the value of a literary work be judged on its aesthetic qualities.

A similar atmosphere of relaxation and effervescence pervaded the history profession. It is proper to use precisely that term because professional historians were supplanting the party activists who had taken charge in the late 1940s and early 1950s. Some of those historians who reaffirmed the integrity of the discipline belonged to the interwar generation, but others were at the beginning of their careers. Both generations were united in their respect for the authority of sources and their commitment to independent scholarly judgment, as they resisted the limitations imposed on research and thought by ideological sentries. They were also eager to renew full contact with Western historiography and did so through international conferences, enhanced access to publications, and research trips, all of which increased as the Communist elite pursued a rapprochement with Western Europe and the United States.

The professional historians and the party elite found common ground in the emerging tenets of national Communism. As the party challenged Soviet predominance in the political and economic affairs of the bloc, so in equal measure did historians revise the image of Russian and Soviet benevolence toward Romania crafted in the late 1940s and early 1950s. Needless to say, they could not have proceeded along such a path without the Romanian party's blessing.

Of the many products of the intertwining of the party's political ambitions with the professional historians' scholarly zeal, two in particular caught the spirit of the times. One was the four-volume *Istoria României* (The history of Romania; 1960–64), which covered the period from prehistory to the achievement of independence in 1878. At one level it marked in historiography the new stance toward the Soviet Union being pressed by the party elite, and at another level it was an attempt to recover the Romanians' identity after a decade of denial. These thick volumes also represented a significant advance in scholarship, as they presented the results of intensive research, especially on medieval and economic and social history. A second work challenged even more directly the supposed spiritual foundations on which the Soviet–Romanian relationship had been based. In publishing Karl Marx's *Însemnări despre Români* (Notes on the Romanians; 1964), the party elite sought to destroy the image of Russia as the protector of the Romanians. By emphasizing the unconcealed hostility of Marx and Engels toward tsarist Russia, the Romanians intended to justify their distancing themselves from Russia's successor – the Soviet Union – through appeals to the highest ideological authority.

The elite promoted détente with society in other ways as well. It gave more attention to the day-to-day needs of the public. Stocks of food and other consumer goods increased, and apartment construction rapidly expanded. The party maintained a social safety net, which made education and health care available to everyone at little or no cost and provided employment to all and pension benefits upon retirement. At another level it reduced the incidence of arbitrary arrests and imprisonments, so prevalent in the previous decade by limiting the reach of the Securitate. In an act of great symbolic significance the last political prisoners were released in 1964.

Despite all these appearances of moderation, the party remained fully in control, and its involvement in every aspect of social and private life was in no way diminished, a consistency completely in keeping with the nature of the regime. Nor could an organized cultural life free from party supervision develop. Still less could a vigorous press serving as a forum for open debates about vital public issues arise. Needless to say there was no liberalization of the political system at all and no move away from centralized planning and direction of the economy. It is worth remembering that détente did not come about as a response to pressure from below; it was, rather, an expression of the elite's will, of its relentless determination to maintain maximum control over society.

Détente within Romanian society was accompanied by growing tension in relations with the Soviet Union. Gheorghiu-Dej and his associates in the mid 1950s were already exasperated at their subordination to the Soviet party and were eager to take their modernization project fully into their own hands. The quest for "independence" from Moscow assumed serious proportions after Nikita Khrushchev's secret speech at the Twentieth Soviet Communist Party Congress in February 1956 denouncing Stalin's many abuses of power and after the improvement in East–West relations had begun. Several significant steps in loosening the Soviet hold on Romania followed, notably the withdrawal of the Soviet army of occupation in June and July 1958 and the continuous departure of Soviet advisers from all branches of the political and economic bureaucracy.

These successes emboldened the Romanian elite to challenge Soviet leaders openly on key matters of bloc policy. Perhaps the most contentious issue was economic. Nikita Khrushchev aimed to reinvigorate the Council of Mutual Economic Assistance, which Stalin had created in 1949 as a response to the Marshall Plan, but had left in abeyance. In the early 1960s Khrushchev decided to reinvigorate the principles behind Comecon by arranging a division of labor within the bloc and by enforcing the coordination of national economies in order both to use resources efficiently and to enhance Soviet control over the other economies. In Khrushchev's view, economic efficiency meant that some countries would concentrate on industrial production, while others would supply agricultural goods and raw materials. Discussions at Comecon meetings between 1960 and 1963 made clear that Romania's place was to be among the latter. But Gheorghiu-Dej and company stoutly rejected relegation to the level of an agricultural country and insisted on pressing ahead with their grand strategy of modernization centered on heavy industry.

The growing strain in Soviet–Romanian relations was reflected in events at a day-to-day level and could not but be apparent to the general public. In the early 1960s street names were changed, as Soviet and Russian figures, Stalin most prominently, gave way to Romanians, and the city of Braşov shed its decade-old name of Oraşul Stalin (Stalin City); all were acts of a retarded de-Stalinization. Romanian–Soviet institutions were reconditioned, such as the Maxim Gorky Institute of Russian Language and Literature, which became the School of Slavic Studies in the Institute of Foreign Languages, or they were simply dissolved, as happened to the Romanian–Soviet Institute. Russian-language instruction in schools and universities ceased to be obligatory and would henceforth have to compete with English, French, and German. The network of Russian bookstores, Cartea Rusă (the Russian book), was closed and their stocks of Russian books, much reduced, were moved to counters at large general bookstores. Much less attention was given to Soviet political news and culture in the press and on television, as Romanians turned enthusiastically to Western sources of information, literature and art, and entertainment.

As the Romanian party elite, ever so cautiously, put distance between itself and the Soviet party, it moved in equal measure to expand relations with the West. A revival of contacts had begun in the mid 1950s with agreements, first with France and then with Great Britain, on settling the financial claims of their citizens against Romania for confiscated property. Economic and cultural exchange agreements followed. The Romanian rapprochement with the United States was somewhat delayed, primarily, it seems, because the American side had to be convinced that Romania was indeed pursuing policies of its own, distinct from those of the Soviet Union, and thus could be the object of special attention. All the Western powers agreed that the opportunity should not be missed to widen whatever breach there might be between Romania and the Soviet Union.

Gheorghiu-Dej and his circle had objectives of their own. They sought normal relations with the West partly to buttress their autonomous stance toward the Soviet Union. Their main ambition was to open up advantageous economic relations. They were anxious to acquire the Western technology and manufactured goods they sorely lacked and judged essential if they were to accelerate the transformation of the Romanian economy and society. They were thus persuaded that a thriving commerce with the West – they expected to sell their own products on the European and American markets – would enable them to diminish their economic (and political) dependence on the Soviet bloc, which had shown little sympathy for their modernization project. Gheorghiu-Dej and his circle thus turned to the West in order to advance their goal of building socialism in a Romanian guise.

By no means did the Romanian party elite seek better relations with the West out of admiration for Western values. Their hostility to the "bourgeois" entrepreneurial spirit and the liberal political creed, which had defined progress in interwar Romania, was unwavering. Nor did they ever contemplate leaving the Soviet bloc. After all, their membership in it was the ultimate guarantee of their hold on power.

The Romanian elite's overtures to the West were central to a general effort to expand Romania's international contacts and thus to be seen as something other than just a member of the Soviet bloc or an agent of the Soviet Union. The increasing rancor between the Soviet and Chinese Communist parties, which broke into the open at the Third Congress of the Romanian Communist Party in

Bucharest in June 1960, offered Gheorghiu-Dej an opportunity to gain an ally in his party's own dispute with the Soviet leadership over national sovereignty. The two countries thus found a solid basis for cooperation in their shared advocacy of independent roads to socialism. But Gheorghiu-Dej did not join the Chinese camp against the Soviet Union, and his actions suggest that he intended to remain neutral. Although he indeed welcomed certain Chinese initiatives similar to his own, he was also anxious to maintain the unity of the Communist camp, upon which his own party's dominance in Romania depended. He wanted to avoid firm commitments to either side because he was experienced enough in political maneuverings to know that the Soviets and Chinese might someday compose their differences and turn on Romania. His strategy, then, was to offer his party as a mediator. His initiative was of little consequence, but it reinforced his position as an honest broker seeking to heal the breach in the international Communist front.

The culmination of this phase of the Romanian–Soviet contest was the "Declaration of the Romanian Workers' Party on Issues of the International Communist and Working-Class Movements" of April 27, 1964. It came to be known as the Romanian Communist Party's "Declaration of Independence" from the Soviet Union, but an interpretation of this kind is misleading. Such a statement had been under consideration in the Political Executive Committee of the party since February 1963, when it received reports on the Comecon meeting in Moscow, where plans were being discussed for the creation of a supra-national economic coordinating body and the unification of certain branches of industry in the bloc as a whole. These infringements of national sovereignty reinforced the determination of Gheorghiu-Dej and company to persevere in their quest for autonomy. In their April Declaration they were at pains to define the issues in dispute with unusual directness. They demanded that the principles of non-interference in the internal affairs of one state by another and full equality govern the relations of Communist states among themselves. The message to Moscow was plain: each Communist party must decide for itself on the proper means of achieving Communism without dictation from the Soviet party. But Gheorghiu-Dej and his Politburo were not aiming at reform or innovation; what they coveted was order and stability within the bloc.

Gheorghiu-Dej and his colleagues did not challenge their erst-
while mentors lightly, but the time for boldness seemed favorable.
They were, first of all, encouraged by the weakened position of
Khrushchev after the Cuban missile crisis of October 1962 and by
disharmony in the Soviet Politburo. Significant shifts in relations
between Moscow and the other members of the bloc and a thaw
in East–West relations suggested a milder reaction to defiance than
in the days of Stalin. Gheorghiu-Dej could also be certain of support at home. The party elite remained united on the crucial issues
at hand, and the populace was submissive and was attracted to
the party's new emphasis on national sovereignty. The elite indeed
intended to expand its appeal to patriotic sentiments by transforming the modernization project, that is, the drive for industrialization
and the elimination of economic and social underdevelopment, into
a struggle for national independence. They were unusually skillful
at putting national symbols in the service of their own ambitions.
But Gheorghiu-Dej was not a nationalist; he was an internationalist
Communist who discovered the value of appropriating the national
history and tradition in order to insulate himself and his group from
hostile moves by Moscow and to extend to the maximum their control over society.

A measure of how secure in the exercise of power the party elite
felt was the smoothness and rapidity with which the succession
occurred following the death of Gheorghiu-Dej in March 1965. He
had already designated Nicolae Ceauşescu as his heir, a choice that
was not seriously challenged. The saying made the rounds at the
time that a peasant (Ceauşescu) had replaced a worker (Gheorghiu-
Dej), but the thought was only partially true. Ceauşescu (1918–89)
had indeed been born in a village, and his parents were peasants
of modest standing. But he himself, after four years of elementary
school, left the village at the age of ten for Bucharest, where he was
apprenticed to a shoemaker. Although he himself said little about
his early years, he apparently joined the Union of Communist Youth
(Uniunea Tineretului Comunist) in 1933 and the Communist Party
in 1936. Because of his organizing activities, he spent much time in
jail, where he met Gheorghiu-Dej and others of the Communist elite
that would come to power after the Second World War. In the 1950s
and early 1960s he rose steadily in the party hierarchy and made

good use of his posts in the party's security and personnel apparatuses to place his own men in key positions. He was something of a hardliner and a loner. He was also enormously ambitious. When he came to power there was an agreement within the inner circle that no one of them would thrust himself forward. But Ceauşescu continually enhanced his own position as General Secretary and gradually abandoned the principle of collective leadership, and at the Tenth Congress of the party in August 1969 he laid the foundations of a cult of personality. All this time he was also busy removing Gheorghiu-Dej's men, replacing them with his own.

Yet, by and large, Ceauşescu continued Gheorghiu-Dej's policies. In domestic affairs he kept the drive for modernization on course, emphasizing industrialization; he promoted the détente with society by limiting the interventions of the security forces and by increasing the quantity and quality of consumer goods; and he furthered the rapprochement with writers by holding out hope of increased artistic freedom and of widening cultural contacts with Western countries. He took a similar tack with historians; he encouraged them to re-examine past events and leading figures, and, especially, to re-evaluate the historical role of the Communist Party and thereby give it and him legitimacy. Yet, other initiatives of his made evident the omnipotence of the party and, thus, sharply defined the limits of détente. Demographic policy revealed his real intentions and caught the spirit of the time by subordinating the interests of the individual to the party's way of building socialism. Since the population had been growing too slowly to suit central planners, he made abortion illegal by decree in October 1966 as a long-term means of increasing the workforce.

Ceauşescu was eager to provide a public measurement of the party's achievements and thereby enhance its standing, and thus in August 1965 he and his colleagues had a new constitution adopted to codify their accomplishments. They also changed the name of the country to Socialist Republic of Romania (Republica Socialistă România) to emphasize their attainment of the stage of socialism on the way to Communism. They took the occasion to restore the historical name of the party to Romanian Communist Party from Romanian Workers' Party (Partidul Muncitoresc Român; PMR), which it had borne since February 1948, when it had fused with the small Social Democratic Party.

In foreign relations, too, Ceauşescu followed the initiatives of his predecessor. Relations with the Soviet Union came first. They were tense, as Leonid Brezhnev, who had succeeded Khrushchev in 1964, repeatedly criticized the Romanian party for "being out of step" with the other countries of the bloc and for failing to coordinate its economic and foreign policies with theirs, accusations that had become familiar under Gheorghiu-Dej during the disputes over Comecon. Most disturbing perhaps for the Soviet side was Ceauşescu's establishment of diplomatic relations with West Germany in 1967, the first break in the Soviet bloc's boycott. His main objective was to expand trade and acquire German technology. In the same year he asserted his independence in international relations again by not breaking relations with Israel at the time of its brief war with the Arab states in 1967, as the rest of the bloc did. He also expanded Gheorghiu-Dej's overtures to China, and for the same reasons – to pursue Romania's self-determination in foreign policy and acquire additional leverage in dealings with the Soviet party.

Undoubtedly, the most dramatic manifestation of Ceauşescu's independence in relations with the Soviet Union was his condemnation of the invasion of Czechoslovakia by Soviet-led Warsaw Pact armies in August 1968. He denounced in unusually blunt language the crushing of the Czechoslovak Communist regime, which had been experimenting with a liberal brand of socialism, or "socialism with a human face." But his anxiety had not been aroused by the suffocation of the Prague Spring, as he had no sympathy for or understanding of the Western democratic tradition. Rather, he took armed intervention in the internal affairs of a fraternal socialist state as an ill omen for his own, independent way to socialism. At a large public gathering in front of party headquarters in Bucharest he departed from his prepared text to demand an end "once and for all" to interference in the affairs of other states and parties in the bloc. He also announced that he had taken steps to create armed "patriotic guards" to defend the "socialist fatherland" against any violation of its sovereignty by anyone, and he called on all citizens – workers, peasants, and intellectuals – to remain united behind the party and be prepared to fulfill their civic responsibilities at any moment.

Ceauşescu's defiance could not but bring heightened tension to his relations with Soviet party leaders. But at home and in the West his stand drew praise as courageous and enhanced his credentials as an innovator and an international statesman. Many intellectuals in Romania, in the enthusiasm of the moment, proclaimed their support for him as the leader of the nation, and some joined the Communist Party. Abroad, Western countries courted him mainly in order to widen the breach between Romania and the Soviet Union. There were high-level visits: in August 1969 President Richard Nixon came to Bucharest, and the following year Ceauşescu and his wife were in Washington; and there were material rewards: generous commercial and financial agreements were signed with Western countries, and in 1971 Romania became a member of the General Agreement on Tariffs and Trade (GATT) and the International Monetary Fund (IMF). Ceauşescu must have concluded that his independent course was a stunning success.

The true Ceauşescu revealed himself in a series of stern propositions he formulated in July 1971 on the nature and goals of Romanian Communism. The "July Theses" represented a crucial turning point in the evolution of the Communist elite's modernization project. It signaled a break in the decade-old experiment in détente with society and a return to a more doctrinaire approach to the creation of the new order. Ceauşescu had been aroused by what he took to be a slackening of commitment to Marxist-Leninist ideals and to the immediate tasks of building socialism. He found the cause in "ideological diversity" and the "bourgeois spirit," that is, the currents of modest social and cultural liberalization that had gained momentum since the later years of Gheorghiu-Dej's tenure.

One explanation for Ceauşescu's shift from détente to rigidity at this time has to do with his trip to China and North Korea in June 1971. According to this line of reasoning, what he saw proved to him what could be accomplished by ideological vigilance, discipline, and sacrifice, all directed by a party fully committed to revolutionary change. He was indeed impressed by the displays on all sides of zeal and commitment to the construction of a Communist society and by the massive public demonstrations in Pyongyang and Beijing that played to his vanity, but the principles he proclaimed in the July Theses had been evolving ever since he had come to power. They were a response to his own sense of how a Communist Romania should come into being. He demanded that Marxist-Leninist ideology be the guiding force throughout society: in the party at every level, in education, in youth and women's organizations, publishing, the media, and literature and history and creative endeavors of all kinds. Everywhere, he insisted, the "party spirit" must prevail, and he called again for the eradication of the "bourgeois mentality." Especially ominous was his determination to strengthen the party's "control and vigilance" in every sector of society. Such a drastic turn met no opposition in the highest party and state councils; they approved it unanimously and thereby set Communist Romania on a perilous course.

THE CEAUŞESCU REGIME, 1971–1989

From the promulgation of the July Theses in 1971 until the collapse of the Communist order in December 1989 the essence of the Ceauşescu regime remained in place: neo-Stalinism and a nationalism to promote socialism. In a sense, these had also been the features of the Gheorghiu-Dej regime in its later years. But the Ceauşescu years were different, too. Nepotism and corruption became a way of life at all levels of the bureaucracy, and, while both regimes were at heart repressive, Gheorghiu-Dej's was an oligarchy, while Ceauşescu's became a personal dictatorship. Perhaps the defining trait of the Ceauşescu dictatorship was the cult of personality, which, as it grew, knew no bounds. In the press, on television, and at public gatherings he was the center of attention, as all others, with the exception of his wife Elena (1919–89), were relegated to the background. By 1974, he held the three most important offices in the land when the Grand National Assembly proclaimed him the first president of the Socialist Republic of Romania; the other two posts were General Secretary of the Communist Party and Commander of the armed forces. As time passed, he came to rely more and more on members of his extended family to fill key positions. He raised his wife to a position of power second only to his own and seems to have been much influenced by her opinions. Together they prepared their son Nicu to succeed him. Such blatant nepotism led one Western commentator to describe the regime of these years as "socialism in one family."

Under conditions imposed by the cult of personality the Communist Party, in a sense, lost its position as the aggressive engine of change that it had been in its first two decades in power. Although membership in the party rose from 1,400,000 in 1965 to 3,800,000 in 1989, thereby making it the largest in the bloc after that of the Soviet Union, it relinquished its militant and ideological character, as it came to be composed mainly of those who had joined in order to enjoy the advantages that membership offered: career and educational opportunities and material benefits of all kinds. Activists who were committed to the building of socialism as a matter of principle were few. Although the party rituals were maintained – the national congresses, the local conferences, the choosing of officials, and the public celebrations – they became increasingly hollow, as the Ceauşescu family and its narrow circle of clients together with the security apparatus steadily overshadowed the party, usurping its powers and functions. All this was by design, as Ceauşescu was intent on making the party wholly dependent on his will and preventing any competing power base from forming within it. A most effective device, from Ceauşescu's point of view, was the so-called rotation of cadres, that is, the periodic transfer of high officials from one post to another. Especially vulnerable were party officials who held independent opinions on key issues, which suggested disloyalty to the General Secretary and thus often led to demotion. One of the unfortunate consequences of such procedures for both Ceauşescu and the country as a whole was the accumulation at the top of officials who were disposed to give Ceauşescu only the advice he wanted to hear.

The economy during the 1970s showed increasing signs of weakness, despite continued impressive growth, and from the 1980s it entered a phase of breakdown. The causes were many and complex. The drive to industrialize under Ceauşescu was unrelenting and pushed to extremes. In his vision, heavy industry was to serve multiple purposes: lay the foundations of the new Communist economic order, ensure Romania's autonomy in relations with the Soviet Union, and raise the country's international standing. Industry and its various auxiliary enterprises, then, continued to come first when allocations of investment capital were made, often at the expense of agriculture and other, seemingly less critical branches of the economy. To finance its ambitious economic plans the regime had recourse to loans from foreign governments and international financial institutions such as the IMF, thereby imposing substantial debt on the country. The strategy was to use the loans to build new enterprises and expand the productive capacity of older ones and then sell their goods on the international market, which meant primarily the West, and use the profits to repay the loans.

Events took a different course. By the later 1970s both industry and agriculture were being adversely affected by shortages of energy and raw materials, natural disasters, and poor management at the local level, but ineffectual decision-making and coordination at the highest levels were also at fault. Ceauşescu would not be deterred from the course of creating a heavy industry, even as its disadvantages became increasingly apparent. He was not perceptive or daring enough to recognize the slow disaggregation of the system he himself had put in place. He clung to his particular vision of the future and would not abandon the means he had chosen to achieve it.

In response to the mounting crisis of the 1980s Ceauşescu and the group around him rejected any serious concessions to market forces and international economic trends, as was happening in Hungary, for example. Instead, they tightened the mechanisms of central planning and control, required greater productivity from labor without offering commensurate raises in wages, reduced supplies of energy and food and other goods to the public, and found ways to increase taxes. Then came Ceauşescu's decision in December 1982 to pay off the large foreign debt as quickly as possible in order to prevent Western countries and their financial institutions from interfering with his direction of the economy. As a result, the regime subjected the populace to still greater privations. More ominously for the regime, these austerity measures tested the loyalty of the rank-and-file of the party and even some of the privileged as their living standards fell.

While the economy faltered and the suffering of the populace grew Ceauşescu initiated grandiose projects which required enormous commitments of labor and capital, but whose economic and social worthiness was doubtful. Work on the Danube–Black Sea canal, abandoned in the early 1950s as unrealistic, was revived and pushed to completion in 1986. Although it cut significantly the distance a ship would have to travel along the lower Danube to the Black Sea, traffic fell short of expectations. Undeterred, Ceauşescu planned to extend the project by having a canal dug across southern Wallachia to Bucharest, thereby making it a seaport. It was part of his grand design to transform Bucharest into a truly European capital, which he advanced by a huge construction program in the heart of the city intended to create massive public buildings, notably the Palace of the Republic, second in size only to the Pentagon in Washington. To provide space extensive areas of Bucharest, which dated from the later nineteenth century and gave the city much of its charm, were razed. Nor did rural areas escape the demolition and building frenzy. Ceauşescu's "systematization of the village," contemplated for some years, was now set fully in motion. It had as its chief objective the replacement of thousands of villages by "agro-technical centers" and the transformation of their inhabitants into proletarians. The whole scheme seems to have been intended as the final stage in the modernization process in the countryside begun in the late 1940s. Ceauşescu and his colleagues thought "systematization" was the way to destroy at last the traditional peasantry and its mentality and way of life, a success that had eluded collectivization.

The regime abandoned the détente with society. No aspect of social life escaped scrutiny, as the party imposed its will on the populace even more resolutely than before. The attainment of Communism justified, in Ceauşescu's view, both the permanent dissolution of civil society and intrusion into the most intimate areas of private life, notably through the rigid enforcement of the prohibition on abortions. The same spirit of control, the same disdain for the individual citizen, prevailed in every endeavor, public and private, in work, education, information, health care, housing, food, and entertainment.

The system had produced benefits, too. Illiteracy had been eradicated, as the party sought to expose all layers of the population to its teachings about the inevitability of Communism and thus the more easily enlist citizens in the hard work of achieving it. Education at the secondary and higher levels was open to greater numbers of students than before from the humbler ranks of society, and all received funding. In the same way medical care was available to all free of charge or at low cost, an improvement that benefited the rural population especially. Unemployment was eliminated in the sense that everyone was guaranteed a job, even though the position in question might not be one's first choice and in many enterprises more people were on the payroll than were needed. With employment came benefits such as help with housing and guaranteed pensions on retirement. The wide social safety net thus installed was of crucial importance for the majority of the population in both cities and the countryside, and, as long as it functioned adequately, it may well have softened opposition to the regime.

To those elements of society that did not fit easily into the new national Communist state that Ceauşescu was constructing he offered toleration, but he and they knew that such an arrangement could be only temporary. In dealing with the churches, for example, he followed, on the whole, the tactic initiated by Gheorghiu-Dej. To the Romanian Orthodox Church he provided material benefits and a limited sphere for the exercise of its strictly religious functions, and in return he expected its clergy to give full support to the regime's social and economic objectives at home and put its aspirations and accomplishments in the best possible light at international church conferences. The regime made it clear that the clergy could have no other public role than that which the party assigned to them. On the whole, the great majority of the clergy acquiesced.

The Ceauşescu regime, like Gheorghiu-Dej's, proclaimed the equality of women and put their "emancipation" high on the party's agenda. Indeed, from the beginning of the People's Republic massive numbers of women joined the workforce in all those places from the factory to the experimental laboratory that had previously been almost exclusively masculine. They also joined party and state bodies at all levels in accordance with appropriate quotas. They even had their own organizations. But here was another example of form without substance, since women were not masters of their own destiny. The party dealt with them as it dealt with minorities and intellectuals and clergy and all other social groups. It made decisions without true consultations with those who would be affected by its actions. The chief aim of the Communist Party was not to further the liberation of women, in the true sense of the term, but rather, first, to acquire an additional labor force with which to

19 Nicolae Ceauşescu, his wife Elena, and his son Nicu at the opening of the Danube–Black Sea canal, 1986

carry out its economic projects, and, second, to weaken the autonomy of the family and dissolve existing structures in favor of new collectivities.

During the Ceauşescu era women were declared to be "equal socialist workers," and Elena Ceauşescu, who became increasingly visible in the 1970s and who shared political power with her husband and accompanied him on all his travels, seemed the personification of the new socialist woman. But this example of the equality of the sexes hardly reflected the actual condition of women. Equality for them meant devoting themselves full time to the building of socialism, being mothers and thereby nurturing the future workforce, and contending with all the problems of daily life.

The cultural policies pursued by Ceauşescu did not deviate from the principle put in place after the Communist seizure of power in 1947: the mobilization of all creative talents in order to further the building of socialism. As in Gheorghiu-Dej's time, periods of constraints alternated with moments of liberalization, as the needs of domestic and foreign policy dictated. But under Ceauşescu the sequence of events led inexorably from the liberalization of the 1960s to the constraints of the 1980s, as he himself, rigid and dogmatic, became the obligatory center of attention. The regime's methods of cultural management are especially striking in the historiography and literature of the time. Yet, the censorship sometimes proved surprisingly porous, and writers and scholars, as usual, were immensely resourceful in contesting the boundaries of creativity it imposed.

From Ceauşescu's perspective, as he himself suggested in the July Theses, the primary function of history was to serve the party's or, as became increasingly evident, his own interests, and thus it was supposed to become one of the ideological pillars of his brand of national Communism. But historians exhibited a strong sense of professionalism.

Despite, but sometimes because of, exhortations by the regime, historians engaged in wide-ranging, fundamental research. They investigated the long-term trends of Romanian political and institutional development and made signal contributions to an understanding of economic and social change in the countryside from the Middle Ages to the twentieth century. They debated such contentious issues as the nature of serfdom and of landholding in the principalities of Moldavia and Wallachia, the effects of Ottoman suzerainty on their economic and social evolution, and peasant uprisings and workers' discontents in the early twentieth century, and in the process they produced solid and often pioneering monographs and they assembled invaluable collections of sources of all kinds. Even though the regime's ambitions often tended toward a kind of cultural autarchy, as in the economy in the later 1980s, and it was forever wary of Western intellectual and cultural currents, historians maintained and even expanded their contacts with Western scholarship.

Patriotic fervor and the cult of personality promoted incessantly by the regime inevitably led to exaggerations and distortions in historiography as it was practiced by some. Insistence on the autochthonous sources of the Romanians' political and cultural achievements focused attention on the Dacians and Thracians as the true progenitors of the modern Romanians. This "Thracomania," as critics called the current, diminished the role of the Slavs in the formation of the Romanians, an idea much in vogue in Stalin's time, and even downgraded the contributions of the Romans.

A typical example of historiographical embroidery was the attempt, with the Institute for the History of the Romanian Communist Party in the lead, to integrate the party into the broad sweep of Romanian history and give it an honored place. The objective was to enhance the party's legitimacy before public opinion by showing how it had been and continued to be the defender of the country's independence. To elaborate such a thesis and be convincing was a daunting task in view of the party's subservience to the Soviet Union in the interwar period and in the decade after the Second World War. But such inconveniences could be covered over by well-placed jabs at tsarist Russia and the Soviet Union. Bessarabia proved useful for this purpose. Several works called attention to the Hitler–Stalin pact of August 23, 1939, by which the Soviet Union's annexation of the province was tacitly agreed to. A partial rehabilitation of Ion Antonescu, who appeared in several works as the protector of the Romanian nation, was an equally daring stroke aimed at the Soviet Union and intended to arouse patriotic feelings.

In the meantime, the cult of personality around Ceauşescu grew to enormous proportions. He was presented everywhere as both the primary source of ideas and the dynamic maker of decisions. Historians of an ideological bent placed him in the long line of descent of the creators of modern Romania going back over 2,000 years and including Prince Alexandru Cuza, who had united Moldavia and Wallachia, Prince Mircea cel Bătrân, who had fought the Ottoman advance, and, ultimately, Burebista, whom party historians proclaimed the founder of the unified Romanian state.

It is not surprising that in such an intellectual climate an authentic Marxist historiography failed to develop. Marxism-Leninism was largely abandoned in favor of an interpretation of Romanian history that assigned to the Communist Party the role of leader of the nation. For the party and Ceauşescu, then, history was not the bearer of grand truths about the evolution of Romania; it was, rather, a tool for achieving practical goals of the moment.

Literature, from such a perspective, was supposed to perform a similar service. The convergence of the cult of personality and

nationalism found extraordinary expression in the doctrine of
protocronism (protochronism; first in time) in the 1970s and 1980s.
Its immediate origins may be traced to an article published by the
literary critic Edgar Papu (1908–93) in the popular literary and cultural monthly *Secolul 20* (The 20th century) in 1974. In moderate
tones he suggested that it was time to measure the originality and
merits of Romanian writers of the past against the background of
their contributions to European cultural values. Some of his com-
ments fitted in with the new nationalism and self-glorification
Ceauşescu was indulging in. Numerous supporters of the regime,
who became known as protochronists, took over Papu's ideas for
their own purposes, thereby intensifying the nationalist rhetoric.
They were convinced that the Romanians had erred in emulating
Western culture in the nineteenth and early twentieth century, since
it had imposed upon them a deep sense of cultural inferiority. Papu,
too, expanded upon the theme, and in *Din clasicii noştri* (From
our classics; 1977) he proposed to transform the Romanians' supposed feelings of cultural inadequacy into a sense of dignity and
self-worth. The protochronists now took matters to absurd lengths.
They compared Neagoe Basarab to Dante and Machiavelli, and they
pronounced Mihai Eminescu the precursor of modern European
poetry and I. L. Caragiale the indispensable innovator of modern
drama. On the other hand, the protochronists were highly critical
of Eugen Lovinescu. His doctrine of synchronism was anathema
to them because, in their view, he recognized the superiority of the
West and accorded it the decisive role in modern Romania's evolution, thereby belittling the contributions of Romanian writers and
thinkers.

At one level the controversy between the protochronists and their
critics was a continuation of the long-standing debate over identity and paths of development between liberals and conservatives,
traditionalists and Europeanists reaching back into the nineteenth
century. At another level protochronism lay at the ideological heart
of the Communists' drive for modernization, since the Ceauşescu
regime used it to foster a new cultural consciousness as part of the
original project to create the "new socialist man." But Ceauşescu
gave the matter a special twist. By adopting protochronism as his
own and thus turning away from the proletarian internationalism

of the 1950s, he served notice that the new socialist man would be Romanian.

Despite the vigilance of the censors and the ideological watch-men after the promulgation of the July Theses, poets and novelists, like historians, continued to perfect their craft and experimented ceaselessly with form and theme. Of the leading authors of the Communist era, the novelist Marin Preda and the poets Nichita Stănescu and Ana Blandiana persevered in writing in a social atmos-phere increasingly inhospitable to individual creativity. Their efforts were seconded by a younger generation of writers. Typical were the poets grouped around the literary review *Echinox* (Equinox) in Cluj in the 1970s, who created a poetry ill-suited to the regime's promo-tion of militant social themes. Instead, they cultivated a poetry of meditation that drew inspiration from the magic signs and arche-types of the spiritualized village of Lucian Blaga. In the 1980s poets and prose writers throughout the country continued to experiment, focusing especially on the writer's relation to his text and seeking new links to the readers as organizers of the text. They took a new approach to reality, as they shifted their attention from the great social issues of the time to the day-to-day problems of the ordinary person. Thus, literature as art kept evolving, in spite of the webs of ideology and censorship, but also, perhaps, because of them, as a challenge that authors readily accepted.

In foreign policy Ceauşescu gave a high priority to good relations with the United States and Western Europe as a means of expanding trade and the transfer of technology and ensuring ready access to credit. He sought to persuade them that he himself was a valuable partner in solving international problems, a form of recognition, which, he was certain, would also strengthen his position at home. At the same time, he welcomed an improvement in relations with the Soviet Union and the East European bloc, and, on the whole, he became more cooperative with the Warsaw Pact and Comecon, without renouncing his independent stance. His motives were prac-tical: he needed the East as economic partners to supply needed raw materials and provide convenient markets for Romanian goods. Then, too, they were simply more congenial politically and ideolog-ically in ways the West could never be. In relations with the United States and other Western countries in the 1980s strains developed as the authoritarian nature of the Ceauşescu regime became increasingly apparent. Not only its violations of human rights but also its growing debt, its failure to make timely interest payments, and its constant need for additional credit, all signs of economic breakdown, put the West on guard. Yet, it continued to support Ceauşescu as long as he could serve as a wedge in their contest with the Soviet Union.

Ceauşescu's dictatorship came undone in the course of ten days in the second half of December 1989. Even many around him recognized how brittle the regime had become, as he had shown none of the realism and suppleness of Mikhail Gorbachev in the Soviet Union and of Communist leaders elsewhere in the bloc. Rather than engage in even modest adjustments of old economic models, he clung to them, especially forced industrialization, and used repression and time-worn promises and slogans to hold the crumbling structure together. He treated any innovation in the existing order as a threat to his authority and an impediment to the achievement of his long-term goals. Despite increasing discontent, no one foresaw his precipitous fall from power.

Opposition had manifested itself in various forms for over a decade before the collapse. Most serious were strikes by thousands of coal miners in the Jiu Valley in 1977 and street demonstrations and attacks on party buildings by factory workers in Braşov in 1987. They had been roused to action by lowered wages, inadequate supplies of food and other goods, and hard working conditions. Negotiators for the regime made promises of improvements, and then, after calm had been restored, security police picked out the leaders of the demonstrations and moved them elsewhere in a form of internal exile. There were also acts of dissidence by intellectuals from time to time, and at the party congress in 1979 Constantin Pârvulescu, an old stalwart, criticized Ceauşescu's concentration of power in his own hands at the expense of party organizations. None of these actions, spontaneous and uncoordinated, had significant immediate consequences.

The visit of Mikhail Gorbachev to Bucharest in May 1987 failed to sway Ceauşescu from his course. Gorbachev had come expressly to persuade him to restructure his regime in order to save it, as was being done in the Soviet Union and other countries of the bloc. But

Ceaușescu would have none of perestroika and spent his time trying to convince his Soviet guests that everything was going according to plan in Romania. He made certain that Gorbachev met only those Romanians who would repeat the same assurances. After the visit relations between the two countries hardened, a turn that increased Ceaușescu's international isolation.

A further ill omen, this time from the Romanian Communist Party, was the so-called "Letter of the Six" of March 10, 1989, a protest against Ceaușescu's policies drawn up by six retired party officials, including Gheorghe Apostol, a candidate to succeed Gheorghiu-Dej in 1965, Corneliu Mănescu, foreign minister, 1961–72, and Alexandru Bîrlădeanu, who was mainly responsible for drawing up the plan for economic autonomy in the 1960s. They urged Ceaușescu to restore civil liberties, raise the standard of living of the population, return the party to its true role as the vanguard of socialist construction, and revise the project of modernization to take account of contemporary conditions. Ceaușescu did not reply directly, but had the six put under house arrest.

The causes of Ceaușescu's fall were diverse, but he was in large measure the author of his own overthrow. He had insulated himself from reality, as his lack of meaningful response to the admonitions of Gorbachev and the six party veterans and his use of force rather than dialogue in dealing with worker grievances reveal. It was thus his inability to measure the gravity of the situation he confronted in the last years of his regime and, more immediately, in the middle of December 1989 that led him to make fatal errors of judgment. Critical in bringing him down was the widespread disaffection his policies had caused at all levels of society. His obsession in the 1980s with paying back the nearly 10 billion dollars of foreign debt as quickly as possible caused severe shortages of food and other consumer goods, as exports took precedence over the population's well-being; there were also longer workdays without adequate compensation, and drastic curtailments of energy supplies, especially for heating in the winter. For the general public, then, the aggravations of daily life were multiplied. More serious was the alienation taking place between Ceaușescu and his closest supporters, on the one hand, and significant elements of the managerial and technological classes, the military, and the party membership, on the other.

Its main causes were not only the hardships to which even they had now been exposed, but also the need they had recognized for fundamental changes in the way economic and social planning was being carried out. They wanted consensus and rational decision-making to replace arbitrariness and improvisation. It was from among them that the leaders of post-Ceauşescu Romania would first come.

The Ceauşescu regime was not the victim of an organized coup. The "plotters," who belonged to the party, the military, and the bureaucratic and technological elites, had indeed prepared themselves to act if the appropriate circumstances arose, but they had neither the intention nor the capability of mounting a frontal assault on a system they themselves had done much to strengthen and perpetuate. In any case, the model for most of them was a managed reform structured by enlightened Communists as promoted by Gorbachev in the Soviet Union, not a headlong embrace of Western political values and the market economy.

A minor, local confrontation at last gave Ceauşescu's opponents in the Communist Party and others the opportunity to act. A Hungarian Protestant pastor in Timişoara (Temesvár), László Tőkés, who had for some time been delivering sermons critical of the Ceauşescu regime, defied attempts by his bishop to transfer him to a remote rural parish. When the police came to move him on December 15, several hundred parishioners surrounded his house and blocked entry to it. They were quickly joined by more inhabitants of the city, including Romanians. Unrest rapidly spread to other neighborhoods, bringing workers and young people and the general populace into the streets. It became an anti-Ceauşescu and anti-Communist movement which defied all efforts to impose order by the security forces, including the killing of numerous demonstrators.

Ceauşescu, apparently unaware of the seriousness of the situation, had gone to Iran on an official visit on December 18, but as reports from home became increasingly grim he hastily returned to Bucharest on the 20th. He tried desperately to suppress the disorders in Timişoara, which were now spreading to other cities. He ordered the army commanders in Timişoara to crush the rebellion by whatever means were necessary, but nothing decisive happened. In Bucharest his supporters organized a mass meeting in the large square in front of party headquarters on the 21st, perhaps with the expectation of repeating the exhilarating success of a similar assembly in August 1968, when Ceauşescu's denunciation of the Warsaw Pact's invasion of Czechoslovakia had won him unprecedented popularity. He began his speech by blaming the troubles in Timişoara on "hooligans" incited by "foreign elements," by which he meant Hungarian irredentists, another appeal to Romanian national sentiments, but the crowd began to boo, and, startled, he was unable to finish his speech. Violence broke out, and elements of the Securitate and the army used brute force to halt the demonstrations. Many protesters were killed.

The end came quickly. On the 22nd Ceauşescu decided to organize another rally of the party faithful in the square. It proved to be a fatal error. Already the minister of defense had withdrawn the army from direct confrontations with demonstrators. Even before Ceauşescu began his speech large crowds attacked party headquarters, and Ceauşescu and his wife fled from the roof of the building by helicopter. They were eventually set down north of Bucharest and were picked up by army units and taken to a military base in Târgovişte. The group of Communists around Ion Iliescu in Bucharest were now determined to seize power and ordered the Ceauşescus to be tried on charges of genocide. A sham of a trial ensued. On December 25 the Ceauşescus were found guilty, sentenced to death, and executed immediately. The unseemly haste with which the matter was handled suggests that Iliescu and company were anxious to eliminate the Ceauşescus as quickly as possible, lest at a regular trial they reveal too much about the inner workings of the dictatorship and its personnel. It was an inauspicious beginning for the new Romania.

7

After 1989

The some twenty years following the events of December 1989 may well be called a time of transition, although at the beginning it was not clear what direction political development would take. It was soon evident that Romania's ties to Europe, built up in the course of some two centuries, had been severely strained by the Communist experiment, and thus the 1990s and the following decade are sometimes called the era of the "return to Europe." The description is apt, if we conclude that Romania had left Europe during the Communist period. Yet, the Iron Curtain was more porous, even in the case of Romania, than is often acknowledged.

POLITICS

After an initial confusion of political tendencies, one, leading toward a European-style parliamentary democracy and membership in Western economic and security organizations, gradually became paramount. Nonetheless, Communist rule had left its mark in many areas of public life, especially on the mentality of the political and managerial class. In the early years of the transition, therefore, former Communists, as we may call them, who dominated political life, had to adjust to unfamiliar ways. The majority eventually saw the wisdom of accommodation with the West, and it was the members of the pre-1989 elite, mainly those of the second rank, who were largely responsible for the country's reconnecting with the West. The forces opposed to the former Communists also played a significant role in restoring ties to Europe, but in the nineties these parties and groups achieved unity of purpose only on rare occasions. All these ambitions and hesitations – left, right, and center – go far toward explaining the complexity of the time.

The former Communists had at hand a serviceable instrument with which to craft the new Romania and maintain themselves in power: the National Salvation Front (Frontul Salvării Naţionale; FSN). Its original purpose, as understood by its democratic and pro-European members, was to serve as a non-partisan supervisor of the restoration of a multi-party, parliamentary system that would ensure the widest possible political activity and freedom of expression. But the former Communists, who controlled the FSN, registered it as a political party on February 6, 1990 and announced their intention to take part in elections for president of the republic and parliament in May. The two "historical parties" of the interwar period – the National Peasant Christian Democrat Party (Partidul Naţional Ţărănesc-Creştin Democrat; PNŢCD), as it was now called, and the National Liberal Party (Partidul National Liberal; PNL), which had come back into existence in January, objected strenuously to such maneuvering, since the FSN would have an unfair advantage in the elections, because of its control of the governmental administrative machinery, economic institutions, and the media. They therefore withdrew from the FSN. Ion Iliescu (b. 1930), a former high Communist Party official who had emerged as its leading figure, appealed to the working class to protect the Front (and the nation) from the historical parties, which, he claimed, were intent on restoring the old order dominated by the monarchy, class privilege, and wealth. Following Iliescu's injunctions, the Communist-dominated FSN organized the transport of thousands of coal miners from the Jiu Valley to Bucharest at the end of January to intimidate and attack opponents of the FSN.

The Front indeed had a clear advantage over its opponents in the elections of the spring of 1990. It used to the full its control of the government and the media, especially television, to mount an aggressive campaign. It offered itself as the patriotic defender of Romania's independence and territorial integrity against both the Soviet Union and Hungary and promised to maintain the social safety net put in place during the Communist era. It also benefited from the disarray of the PNŢCD and the PNL, whose leaders did

20 Ion Iliescu

not immediately grasp the extent of the change that had taken place in the mental climate and in the material aspirations of the population as a whole during the preceding four decades. Rather, they thought that their parties could easily return to the prominence they had enjoyed in the interwar period. But the consequences of the Communist cleansing of the political and economic elites in both the cities and villages in the 1950s soon became evident. Opposition leaders discovered that they had lost the social constituencies that had once sustained them. Their new circumstances made cooperation between the National Peasants and Liberals imperative, but they could not set aside old rivalries and partisan ambitions.

The FSN won an overwhelming victory in the final round of the elections in May. Ion Iliescu gained 85% of the vote for president to 10% for the Liberal candidate Radu Câmpeanu and 4.3% for the National Peasant Ion Raţiu. The FSN also became the dominant party in parliament, receiving 66.3% of the vote to 6.4% for the

PNL and 2.6% for the PNȚCD. The Hungarian Democratic Union of Romania (Uniunea Democrată Maghiară din România; UDMR), which represented the Hungarians of Transylvania, received 7.2%, evidence that the Hungarians had preserved a united front, despite the considerable diversity of opinion among them. The victory of the FSN revealed how attractive certain aspects of the Ceaușescu regime – the social benefits and the nationalism – continued to be for large segments of the population, a mood that Iliescu and company recognized and efficiently exploited. The elections also brought out a sharp division between the rural population, on the one side, which had remained socially and culturally conservative and feared drastic changes, if, as the FSN warned, the "bourgeois parties" came to power, and, on the other side, the better-educated, urban dwellers, who favored an end to the close identification of party and state. The FSN also appealed to a widespread egalitarian sense, cultivated during the Communist period, that was hostile to great disparities of wealth, as the FSN itself claimed to be, whereas the historical parties did little to counteract accusations that they were intent on leading the country back to the class inequalities and social discrimination of the interwar decades.

Overt opposition to the FSN persisted after the elections. Particularly annoying to its leaders was the massive sit-in at University Square in the center of Bucharest led by students and intellectuals, who demanded a clear break with the Communist past and rejected the perpetuation of rule by "Communists." They were dubbed *golani* (vagabonds) by the new FSN government, which on June 13 had them removed by thousands of miners, who were again summoned to Bucharest from the Jiu Valley. This second *mineriada*, as opponents of the FSN called the new descent of the miners on the capital, revealed the links of the new regime to the mentality and methods of the recent past and did much to discredit it in the West.

The first FSN government after the elections took office on June 28, 1990 with Petre Roman (b. 1946) as prime minister. A university professor and the son of a Communist stalwart of the interwar period, Walter Roman, he had a reputation as a reformer who was eager to replace centralized direction of the economy with a market system and filled his cabinet with technocrats who, he hoped, would accomplish the task as smoothly as possible. But he faced resistance immediately from the President and his circle, who indeed recognized the need for change, but were not convinced of the merits of private entrepreneurship and thus intended to proceed cautiously. Ion Iliescu, in particular, seemed averse to the "return to Europe" that some of his colleagues were advocating. A secretary of the Central Committee until his falling-out with Ceauşescu in 1971 and his relegation to provincial party responsibilities, he felt comfortable with Gorbachev as his model. He was also decidedly hostile to the monarchy – he obliged the recently returned King Mihai to leave the country in December 1990 – and he expressed skepticism about whether private property was socially useful and could bring stable prosperity. The Roman government itself cast doubt on its own commitment to Europeanization by signing a treaty of friendship and cooperation with the Soviet Union and by showing its reluctance to deal forthrightly with such pressing domestic issues as minority rights, especially for the Hungarians of Transylvania, and the return to the Greek Catholic Church, which had sprung back to life, of church buildings and other property taken from it in 1948.

Divisions within the FSN, notably the disputes between Roman and the Western-educated technocrats, on the one side, and Iliescu and the Communist Party-influenced gradualists, on the other, revealed a serious contradiction in the assignment of executive powers in the new Constitution of 1991. It made the president and the prime minister, in a sense, natural competitors, even though they might belong to the same party. Thus, the president designated the prime minister, but his choice was limited to nominations from the majority party in parliament or to those made after consultations with leaders of various important parties in parliament. He had no power to dismiss a prime minister once installed, nor could he dissolve parliament, except after two failed attempts by the government to win a vote of confidence. Yet, he had considerable authority as the directly elected choice of the citizens and as the leader of the majority party in parliament. The discord between Iliescu and Roman, which grew in intensity, finally brought down the Roman government. A third intervention of the miners of the Jiu Valley in Bucharest at the end of September 1991 sealed its fate and again raised serious questions in the West about Romania's commitment to political democracy. The FSN formed a new government, which had as one of its urgent tasks convincing potential international partners that their country was indeed on the way to being a part of Europe in both in practice and spirit.

The new government had to deal with formidable challenges, as severe economic problems persisted and opposition parties organized themselves more efficiently. A sign of popular disenchantment with the slow pace of change under the FSN was its poor showing in local elections in February 1992, the first such free elections at that level in half a century. Its percentage of the vote fell from 66 percent in 1990 to 33 percent. An immediate consequence was the splitting of the party in two. Iliescu formed a new party in March 1992, the Democratic National Salvation Front (Frontul Democrat al Salvării Naţionale; FDSN), whose immediate task was to ensure his re-election as president, while Roman kept control of what remained of the FSN.

In the meantime, other political groupings and parties came to the fore. The most important was the Democratic Convention of Romania (Convenţia Democrată din România; CDR), which had been formed on November 26, 1991, but had existed in looser form since December 1990. It was a coalition of parties which adhered to Western principles of multi-party parliamentary government. The dominant partner was the PNŢCD. It had been formally reconstituted on January 11, 1990 under the leadership of Corneliu Coposu (1916–95), who had been secretary to Iuliu Maniu from 1937 until the dissolution of the National Peasant Party in 1947 and had been imprisoned by the Communist regime from then until 1964. He enjoyed high standing among his fellow Peasantists, but was little known to the general public. From the beginning his party opposed the FSN as merely the successor of the Romanian Communist Party and presented itself to the public as the leading force capable of thwarting "neo-Communism." At its first congress in September 1990 it called for a political, but also a moral, restructuring of Romanian society in harmony with the teachings of Christianity. Its two main partners in the CDR were the National Liberal Party and the Romanian Social Democratic Party (Partidul Social Democrat Român; PSDR). The first had been re-established on January 15, 1990 by old Liberals and by others with no links to the historical party. From the start it was rent by factionalism and for a decade played no significant role in political life. The PSDR, revived on January 18, 1990, undertook to carry on the traditions of democratic socialism inaugurated by its predecessor founded in 1893, but its influence on the course of events was modest.

There was also a revival, or if we include the national Communism under Ceauşescu, a prolongation, of Romanian nationalist political thought and objectives dating from the creation of Greater Romania at the end of the First World War. The most important expression of this tendency after 1989 was the Greater Romania Party (Partidul România Mare; PRM), founded and led by Corneliu Vadim Tudor (b. 1949), a modest poet and a political activist who had placed himself in the service of the Ceauşescu regime. The PRM is perhaps best viewed as a movement rather than a party, since its fortunes depended primarily on the volatile inclinations of its leader. It was hostile to Western-style democracy and favored some form of authoritarianism; it stood for an ethnically pure Romania and thus treated the ethnic minorities, especially the Hungarians, as enemies; it was anti-Semitic at a time when the Jewish population of Romania was disappearing, and in election campaigns it sought advantages by accusing its opponents of being part of the "international Jewish conspiracy," even though they were not Jewish; and it promoted a cult of personality around Vadim Tudor. The PRM thus shared many of the attributes of the Iron Guard of the 1930s, but the main source from which it drew inspiration was, in fact, the Communist regime, especially in its nationalist phase in the later years of Ceauşescu. During the nineties the PRM had a modest 4 percent of the seats in parliament, but its public visibility was much greater, because of the provocative behavior of Vadim Tudor. The other significant extreme nationalist party, the Party of Romanian National Unity (Partidul Unităţii Naţionale Române; PUNR), shared many of the goals of the PRM and, like it, owed its prominence mainly to an impulsive leader, Gheorghe Funar, the mayor of Cluj. Based in Transylvania, it appealed especially to those who thought of the Hungarians (and Hungary) as the chief threat to Romania's territorial integrity.

The only significant minority party was the UDMR. Constituted in the latter days of December 1989 as an association of political and civic groupings, it served as the principal representative of the Hungarians of Romania throughout the post-1989 period. Although its members represented diverse approaches to political and social issues, they could also close ranks when pressing for Hungarian political self-administration and cultural autonomy. The UDMR was intent on avoiding political isolation, as it found its interests best served by cooperation with the majority parties. The Saxons and Jews had so declined in numbers (119,436 and 9,107, respectively, according to the census of 1992) that they no longer played a significant role in political life as ethnic communities.

The FDSN government, which held office from November 1992 to December 1996, moved toward Europe in both its domestic policies and foreign relations with seeming reluctance until its final years. Its initial hesitations reflected the Communist backgrounds and gradualist approach to change of President Iliescu and the prime minister, Nicolae Văcăroiu (b. 1943), who had spent much of his previous career in the State Planning Commission. The influence of the recent past, then, represented by Iliescu and Văcăroiu, acted as a formidable impediment to dramatic innovations. A new oligarchy arose composed of former party officials, members of the security services, and managers of state firms, who used their political connections to obtain generous bank loans and avoid close supervision by the government. Others not so favored, especially small and medium-sized businessmen who were, in a sense, close to the Western-style entrepreneur, found it difficult to compete. The FDSN's alliance with the nationalist PRM and PUNR also affected its domestic policies. The Văcăroiu government had to take the two parties' wishes seriously, since they had enough seats in parliament to undermine its stability, and in 1995 at the height of their influence they obtained important ministries, Foreign Affairs and Interior. Still another basis for their cooperation was more spiritual – the strong nationalist sentiments they shared. Yet, the FSDN and its two partners had constantly to be on guard against the opposition parties, as they gained in strength and cohesion.

Despite the West's doubts about Romania's commitment to democracy and an entrepreneurial economy and the seeming reluctance of Iliescu and many around him to abandon the old order they had known, Romania gradually renewed its connections to Europe. Such a reconciliation with Europe was in accord with the country's evolution since the later eighteenth century, except for the interruption of the Communist years. As the Văcăroiu government became more fully engaged with Europe, so Europe's influence on its policies grew. Iliescu, Văcăroiu, and the majority of their closest supporters now moved deliberately toward close cooperation with the West, undoubtedly because they had concluded that only such a course could ensure their country's economic prosperity and international security and, hence, their own tenure in office.

They took a series of steps that indicated a turn to the West. In 1993 Romania signed the Association Agreement with the European Union, which signified a willingness on both sides to proceed with formal membership. At the same time Iliescu and Văcăroiu agreed to bring their country's economic system into harmony with European institutions and practices. They also recognized the need to conform to European standards of human and minority rights and adhered to the United Nations-sponsored Convention for the Protection of Human Rights and Fundamental Freedoms in 1994 and the Council of Europe's Convention for the Protection of National Minorities in 1995. In the same year the Romanian government formally requested admission to the European Union (EU). It was also eager to join an alliance system, which could only be NATO. Although Iliescu in his first presidency (1990–92) had been prepared to work closely with a reformed Russia, such a course had little support at any level. The suspicion of Russia as the national enemy, which had arisen in the first half of the nineteenth century, had been reinforced by the Communist experience. In any case, the Văcăroiu government signified its desire to cooperate with NATO by signing the Partnership for Peace in 1994, a preliminary step to formal adherence to the alliance.

The consequences of all these agreements on Romanian domestic and foreign policy were far-reaching. A pro-Western orientation made the continued presence of the PMR and PUNR in the government coalition incompatible with integration into a democratic Europe, and the government expelled them in 1995. Entry into the EU and NATO also required the Romanian government to reach an accommodation with one of its partners to be – Hungary – and negotiations between them resulted in the signing of a Treaty of Friendship and Cooperation in September 1996. It thus raised expectations that a mutually acceptable solution to the status of the Hungarian minority in Transylvania was finally at hand.

Yet, dissatisfaction with the government of Ion Iliescu and the PDSR grew as it showed little aptitude for solving problems of immediate concern to broad segments of the voting public. The economy gave few signs of sustained growth, and the standard of living for the majority of the population remained low; corruption was rampant, and the sense that the system operated only for the benefit of the favored few was widespread; and the social safety net of the Communist era had been seriously frayed. The PDSR itself had fallen victim to factionalism, and Iliescu seemed unable to provide his party and its allies with firm direction. Many former supporters now saw him as a president out of touch with existing realities and no longer the staunch defender of social justice they had thought him to be just a few years earlier.

In the meantime, the Romanian Democratic Convention (Convenţia Democrată Română; CDR), the successor to the earlier Democratic Convention of Romania, was gaining strength and cohesion. A coalition of the PNŢCD, the PNL, and a few smaller parties, it offered hope to those who were intent on replacing former Communists with liberal democratic reformers who would move the country briskly toward a European parliamentary system in practice. The Convention's candidate for president, as he had been in 1992, was Emil Constantinescu (b. 1939), president of the University of Bucharest in 1992, who enjoyed a well-deserved reputation for political liberalism and personal integrity. With high expectations of a turn of fortune, the majority of voters (54.4 percent) in the second round of voting elected him president and gave the CDR roughly 30 percent of the vote for members of both the Chamber of Deputies and the Senate. The prime ministers, Victor Ciorbea (b. 1954) (1996–98) and Radu Vasile (b. 1942) (1998–99), came from the leading partner of the coalition, the PNŢCD.

The record of the CDR governments in dealing with the most pressing domestic issues was, on the whole, mixed. They had little success in stemming the growing economic and financial crisis of the country until 1999, when Mugurel Isărescu (b. 1949), the Governor of the National Bank of Romania and an independent, became prime minister and lowered the inflation rate and gained the backing of the IMF. Yet, the privatization of industries and other businesses as a means of ending wasteful state subsidies and putting the economy on a market footing and thereby impressing international financial institutions made only modest progress. Corruption continued largely unchecked. On the other hand, the CDR had some success in assuring a measure of justice to those wronged by the Communist regime. It shepherded through parliament a series of measures culminating in a law of 1999 which abolished state-controlled farms, forests, and pastures and restored up to 50 hectares each to former owners. Another form of restitution it sponsored had to do with the return to the Greek Catholic Church of some of the church buildings seized and given to the Romanian Orthodox Church in 1948, but this issue as well as the disposition of Greek Catholic school buildings and other property remained in dispute between the two churches.

The CDR also made progress in fostering a rapprochement between the Romanian state and the Hungarian minority. Undoubtedly, the presence of the UDMR in the CDR coalition lent urgency to a resolution of outstanding minority issues. The Ciorbea government modified existing legislation to allow the use of Hungarian in schools which had a significant number of Hungarian children and in the local courts. Its successor took an important step in satisfying Hungarian demands for a separate university when in 1998 it agreed to the establishment of a multi-cultural Hungarian-German (Petőfi-Schiller) University with funding by the state.

The Ciorbea government, like its predecessors both before and after 1989, gave little attention to what was now the second most important minority in Romania after the Hungarians – the Gypsies or, as they were now known, the Roma. Research carried out in 1992 suggested that those who identified themselves as Roma numbered 536,000, but estimates by others put the number of Roma at 1 million, or 4.3 percent of the population of the country. In any case, despite some integration into the majority community, the majority continued to remain apart. After 1989 elements among the Roma undertook to organize their community politically in order to take advantage of their numbers and promoted a sense of ethnic feeling through enhanced schooling and sustained scholarly activity. The consequence of all this suggested eventual integration into the larger society, but, to some Roma leaders, the cost over the long term would be the loss of their own identity. If language is taken as an indicator of ethnicity, then the danger of community dissolution was far from remote, since only some 16 percent of those who considered themselves Roma still spoke their own language, Romany.

The CDR's greatest success perhaps lay in the decisive moves it made to draw closer to the West. It left no doubt about its intention to become a full partner of Europe. The first step was to join NATO, and to enhance its prospects it fully supported the alliance's intervention in Kosovo in the spring of 1999 by opening Romanian air space to NATO warplanes and by joining in the embargo against Serbia. It thus reversed the policy of strong support for Serbia maintained by Iliescu. President Constantinescu remained steadfast in his support of the NATO campaign, despite strong opposition from the Romanian public.

THE SPIRIT OF THE TIME

Cultural and intellectual life during the first decade after the fall of the Communist regime returned to something like the interwar years in atmosphere and style. A remarkable openness to the most diverse opinions on the nature and functions of literature and history and on the freedom to create, the abundance of literary and historical reviews and the variety of expression they promoted, the proliferation of publishing houses and the revival of a free marketplace for books, and the return of cultural entrepreneurs of all sorts and the retreat of the state as the omnipotent overseer of ideas and of authors and editors was exhilarating for both the younger and older generations of writers and scholars and for the reading public. Paradoxically, the dissolution of order and hierarchies after 1989 and even the disappearance of regulations imposed from above, notably the mechanisms of the censorship, caused no little confusion, especially in literature, as new genres, often of a popular kind, and new writers, many of unknown antecedents, appeared suddenly and competed with established authors. Doubts about values to be honored and a hesitation about directions to take characterized the decade. The situation resembled the uncertainties in politics. Yet, in culture as in politics, the trend toward the restoration of close ties to Europe was unmistakable. As in the interwar period, the order of the day was adaptation rather than imitation.

In history, too, the collapse of old inhibiting structures led to the same effervescence typical of intellectual life generally in the nineties. At the Institutes of History of the Romanian Academy and in the universities scholars enjoyed new flexibility in choosing themes for research and exercised unaccustomed freedom in expressing their opinions on controversial subjects. They returned to neglected subjects such as the careers of "bourgeois" politicians and the Romanians of Soviet Bessarabia and Bukovina, and they abandoned topics that had received exaggerated attention such as the Communist Party and the working-class movement. In certain respects they brought their treatment of the Romanians' historical development into line with interwar scholarly norms. But at the same time they built upon their own achievements during the Communist period: the emphasis on social and economic history, the scholarly publication of documents and critical editions of texts covering the whole range of Romanian history, and signal advances in the auxiliary sciences. As before the Second World War, they expanded foreign contacts to such an extent that research and teaching and graduate study abroad became a regular stage in a historian's career. Thus, historians took part in the general reconnecting with Europe and in the process made their own contributions to the study of the continent's history.

Among major institutions, the Romanian Orthodox Church stood out as an exception to the general embrace of Europe. Its structures had survived the Communist era intact in large part because of the accommodation Patriarch Justinian and his successors had maintained with the Communist regime. It was a stance that was subjected to wide public criticism in the period immediately after the regime's collapse in 1989. Many in the church hierarchy themselves were contrite because of their collaboration with the regime and their failure to take a stand against its unrelenting pressure on clergy and faithful. Patriarch Teoctist Arăpaşu (1915–2007; patriarch, 1986–2007), responding to deep disillusionment with his leadership, especially among clergy and theology students, resigned in January 1990 and withdrew to a monastery until summoned by the Holy Synod to return in April. In time, the acrimony and sense of crisis abated, as laymen and clergy, many reluctantly, came to accept the arrangement between the Church and the Communist Party as having been crucial to the church's survival.

The church hierarchy began the work of restoration in the early months of 1990. They sought to restore fully the place the church had had in public life in the interwar period. They insisted that it be recognized as the national church and that its privileged position be codified by law. They were thus opposed to a separation of church and state, an act, in their minds, that would be a repudiation of the church's intimate involvement in the historical development of the Romanian people. They preferred to maintain the *symphonia*, or harmony, between church and state inherited from the Byzantine tradition, a relationship in which the spiritual mission of the one complemented the worldly concerns of the other for the ultimate benefit of the faithful. But they demanded that the state cease its interference in the internal affairs of the church and recognize its administrative autonomy. The several governments of the decade seemed to accept the essence of the hierarchy's argument and gave the church preferential treatment. They thus ignored the demands of the minority churches and many secular groups that church and state be separated in accordance with the practice in many Western democracies. As for the dispute between the Orthodox Church and the restored Greek Catholic Church over the return of the latter's buildings and other property, neither the PDSR nor the CDR government was willing to intervene. By failing to act, they left the Orthodox predominant.

FORM AND SUBSTANCE

The elections for president and parliament in November 2000 seemed, at first glance, to signal a return to the neo-Communism of the early 1990s. Ion Iliescu won the presidency in the second round with two-thirds of the vote, and his party, the PDSR, and its electoral partners gained a majority of seats in both houses of parliament. Yet, the majority of voters were responding less to ideology and more to their practical experience of the preceding four years of CDR administration and to the general political climate.

Two decisive shifts in political life had occurred which opened the way for Iliescu's return. First of all was the disarray in the ranks of the CDR and its inability to satisfy the hopes of the electorate for a more prosperous and secure way of life. The CDR coalition, after four years in office, lacked cohesion and was thus ill-prepared for the election campaign. It suffered a further blow when President Constantinescu, perhaps discouraged by factionalism and his low standing in public opinion polls, yet confident that Mugurel Isărescu could rally the coalition for victory, announced in July 2000 that he would not seek re-election. The second shift had to do with Iliescu's move from the left toward the center, from Marxism to modern social democracy. He now spoke approvingly of private property as the foundation of a market economy and national prosperity and assured Western governments that he and his party would strive to carry out internal economic reform and bring Romania closer to integration into the Euro-Atlantic community. He bolstered his democratic credentials by agreeing on September 7, 2000 to unite his party with the democratic PSDR. He was thus eager to present his party to the Romanian public as different from what it had been, that is, more democratic, more European, and ready to work productively with other democratic parties. Indeed, in parliament his party promoted national reconciliation. At the same time he continued to distance the PDSR from extreme nationalist parties, especially the PRM, with which he now formally broke off relations. Reinforcing these changes was pressure from the EU, which required him to renounce all undemocratic affiliations, if Romania's negotiations for entrance into the EU were to proceed smoothly.

The elections of 2000 offered several surprises to both the public and political observers. That Iliescu and his party led all other parties in the first round and that the CDR, fractured as it was and unable to mobilize support behind a single candidate for president, did poorly were not surprises. That Corneliu Vadim Tudor, at the head of the PRM, came in second was, however, unexpected. He polled 3,178,000 (28.3 percent) votes to Iliescu's 4,076,000 (37 percent). Large numbers voted for him not because they had been won over by his authoritarian political stance or his hostility to minorities. Rather, they were expressing disenchantment with the entire political class and were thus voting against the system itself. They had been discouraged especially by the performance of the centrist parties of the CDR, which had let them down by failing to deal effectively with crucial issues and by offering no hope of improvement in the foreseeable future. But, now, those who had turned their backs on the CDR were thoroughly alarmed by the prospects of a PRM government with Vadim Tudor as president. In the second round, therefore, they voted solidly for Iliescu and the new PDSR; he received 6,697,000 votes (66.8 percent) to 3,324,000 (33.2 percent) for Vadim Tudor. The PDSR won enough seats in parliament to be able to govern, but Iliescu concluded an informal alliance with the UDMR and won the support of the PNL, thereby assuring himself of a comfortable majority. One of the casualties of the elections was the PNŢCD, which failed to enter parliament and fared badly in local contests, winning only the mayor's office in Timişoara. It disintegrated in 2001 and ceased to be a significant player in political life.

The new PDSR government was headed by Adrian Năstase (b. 1950) as prime minister and, as a result of a decision of the party congress in early 2001, he also became president of the party. Trained in international law and before 1989 a younger member of the Communist Party elite, he was determined to be a promoter of multi-party politics and a Europeanist and thereby remove any remaining stigma from his party as the successor of the Communist Party. A forceful statement about the direction in which he intended to take the party was the formal union he and Iliescu brought about with the Romanian Social Democratic Party (PSDR) in June 2001. Although small, the PSDR was affiliated with the Socialist International and thus enabled its larger partner to join the European family of democratic parties, an event of great moral significance for the newly renamed Social Democratic Party (Partidul Social Democrat; PSD). In a sense, the fusion of the two parties represented the culmination of the general trend toward the unification of Romanian social democracy underway for a decade.

As prime minister and president of the PSD Năstase vigorously pursued his goal of making Romania more European and, hence, capable of carrying out its responsibilities as a reliable regional power and contributor to Europe's international stability and economic development. In domestic policy he sought to bring the Romanian economy into harmony with Western Europe's by pressing forward with the privatization of large state-run enterprises and by making the economy in general conform to the requirements of a market-oriented system. He also continued the reconciliation with the minorities. Besides cooperating in parliament with the UDMR, his government sponsored a law on public administration in April 2001 which granted minorities the right to use their languages in local government and in the judiciary in those areas where they constituted at least 20 percent of the population. Năstase also made an effort to reduce the incidence of corruption, which pervaded all sectors of the public administration, but, short of a drastic and disruptive intervention, little could be accomplished against the practices of patronage and favoritism that had become a way of life. Năstase himself depended on the so-called "barons," oligarchies of the politically connected and the wealthy in many cities and districts, which ensured crucial electoral and financial support for the PDS.

Despite the heavy material and moral baggage of the Communist era, Romania thus moved toward integration into Europe. Both Iliescu and Năstase entertained no doubts that the future of the country was linked to the establishment of a mutually beneficial working relationship with NATO and the EU. In a sense, they continued the foreign policy of Emil Constantinescu. The pursuit of this crucial objective in large measure shaped the policies adopted by the PDS. It even led the party to sponsor significant changes in the constitution in 2003 to bring the fundamental law of the land into conformity with European legislation. Admission to both NATO and the EU, then, was a powerful incentive to change, to be more European. In foreign affairs it fully supported the United States after September 11, 2001, and as the United States became involved in Iraq and Afghanistan the strategic value of Romania grew. Its willingness to provide bases and troops hastened accession to NATO, and on March 29, 2004 Romania formally became a member of the alliance. At the same time Prime Minister Năstase pressed forward with negotiations to join the EU, which the majority of politicians endorsed. The process had begun with Romania's signing of an association agreement with the EU in 1993, and in

December 1999 the Council of Europe had decided to begin formal negotiations with Romania for adherence to the EU. During the ensuing complex negotiations between 2000 and 2004 major issues were resolved. But the final steps in reaching this long-cherished goal were taken under another government, as Năstase lost popularity because of economic policies that caused widespread hardship and a level of corruption that reached into the cabinet itself.

A new political coalition, the Justice and Truth Alliance (Alianţa Dreptate şi Adevăr), formed by the National Liberal Party and the center-left Democratic Party (Partidul Democrat; PD) and headed by Traian Băsescu (b. 1951), the mayor of Bucharest from 2000 to 2004, came to power in national elections in November 2004. Băsescu won the presidency in the second round with 51 percent of the votes, and the Alliance gained sufficient strength in parliament to be able to form a government with the help of smaller parties. The new administration, with Călin Popescu-Tăriceanu (b. 1952), the head of the PNL, as prime minister, made final accession to the EU its primary task. It signed the formal Accession Treaty on April 25, 2005, and in the next year and a half it negotiated with the European Commission in Brussels to bring Romanian institutions and procedures into full conformity with EU standards. The long-awaited accession took place on January 1, 2007.

Perhaps the above date may be taken as the end of the post-Communist transition period. Romania was again formally linked to Europe politically and economically, as it had been in the interwar decades and before. Spiritually, that link had never been broken for the majority of educated Romanians. Now it had been reaffirmed. A longer historical perspective will suggest what lasting effects the Communist experience may have had on the Romanians' worldview and how substantial their new embrace of Europe will be.

It is worth noting at the end of this extended exploration of Romania between East and West that the overthrow of the Ceauşescu regime did not bring an end to the debate over identity and models of development. Indeed, the continuity of discourse is striking, since it revolved around the same two seemingly contradictory notions – integration into Europe and the ethnic nation. On the one side stood the nationalists, who, as we have seen, clung to the image of a traditional Romania for Romanians guided by the virtues of a simpler existence before modernization, and on the other side were those who remained convinced that the country's future could only be in a Europe that was democratic and pluralistic. There were also those who admired the West, but were reluctant to be part of a Europe that disregarded, so they thought, the individuality of ethnic nations. This debate after 1989 is by no means extraordinary. It has been of long duration and has played a crucial role in the foundation of modern Romania. If the history of the past two centuries is any guide, then even after integration into the EU the controversy over who the Romanians are and how they should thus shape their destiny will not have ended.

FURTHER READING

Only works in English are cited.

GENERAL

Achim, Viorel. *The Roma in Romanian History* (Budapest, 2004)

Boia, Lucian. *History and Myth in Romanian Consciousness* (Budapest, 2001)

 Romania: Borderland of Europe (London, 2001)

Călinescu, George. *A History of Romanian Literature from Its Origins to the Present Day* (Milan, 1988)

Hitchins, Keith. *The Identity of Romania*, 2nd edn. (Bucharest, 2009)

Mârza, Radu. *The History of Romanian Slavic Studies: From the Beginnings until the First World War* (Cluj-Napoca, 2008)

Mitu, Sorin. *National Identity of the Romanians of Transylvania* (Budapest, 2001)

Stahl, Henri H. *Traditional Romanian Village Communities* (Cambridge, 1980)

Verdery, Katherine. *Transylvanian Villagers: Three Centuries of Political, Economic, and Ethnic Change* (Berkeley, 1983)

ANCIENT TIMES

Brezeanu, Stelian. *Daco-Romanian Continuity: Science and Politics* (Bucharest, 1984)

Crişan, Ion Horaţiu. *Burebista and His Time* (Bucharest, 1978)

Glodariu, Ioan. *Dacian Trade with the Hellenistic and Roman World* (Oxford, 1976)

Pârvan, Vasile. *Dacia: An Outline of the Civilizations of the Carpatho-Danubian Countries* (Cambridge, 1928)

MEDIEVAL, TO 1774

Andreescu, Ştefan. *Vlad the Impaler (Dracula)* (Bucharest, 1999)

Cernovodeanu, Paul. *England's Trade Policy in the Levant and Her Exchange of Goods with the Romanian Countries under the Later Stuarts (1660–1714)* (Bucharest, 1972)

Duţu, Alexandru. *European Intellectual Movements and Modernization in Romanian Culture* (Bucharest, 1981)

  Romanian Humanists and European Culture: A Contribution to Comparative Cultural History (Bucharest, 1974)

Hitchins, Keith. *A Nation Discovered: Romanian Intellectuals in Transylvania and the Idea of Nation, 1700–1848* (Bucharest, 1999)

Iorga, Nicolae. *Byzantium after Byzantium* (Iaşi, 2000)

Papacostea, Şerban. *Stephen the Great, Prince of Moldavia, 1457–1504* (Bucharest, 1996)

Prodan, David. *Supplex Libellus Valachorum or the Political Struggle of the Romanians in Transylvania during the 18th Century* (Bucharest, 1971)

Spinei, Victor. *Moldavia in the 11th–14th Centuries* (Bucharest, 1986)

MODERN, 1774–1947

Bucur, Maria. *Eugenics and Modernization in Interwar Romania* (Pittsburgh, 2002)

Drace-Francis, Alex. *The Making of Modern Romanian Culture: Literacy and the Development of National Identity* (London, 2006)

Eidelberg, Philip G. *The Great Rumanian Peasant Revolt of 1907: Origins of a Modern Jacquerie* (Leiden, 1974)

Georgescu, Vlad. *Political Ideas and the Enlightenment in the Romanian Principalities (1750–1831)* (New York, 1971)

Haynes, Rebecca. *Romanian Policy toward Germany, 1936–1940* (New York, 2000)

Hitchins, Keith. *Ion I. C. Brătianu: Romania* (London, 2011)

  A Nation Affirmed: The Romanian National Movement in Transylvania, 1860–1914 (Bucharest, 1999)

Orthodoxy and Nationality: Andreiu Şaguna and the Rumanians of Transylvania, 1846–1873 (Cambridge, MA, 1977)

The Romanians, 1774–1866 (Oxford, 1996)

Rumania 1866–1947 (Oxford, 1994)

Iordachi, Constantin. *Charisma, Politics and Violence: The Legion of the "Archangel Michael" in Interwar Romania* (Trondheim, 2004)

Jelavich, Barbara. *Russia and the Formation of the Romanian National State, 1821–1878* (Cambridge, 1984)

Kellogg, Frederick. *The Road to Romanian Independence* (West Lafayette, 1995)

Livezeanu, Irina. *Cultural Politics in Greater Romania* (Ithaca, 1995)

Marinescu, Beatrice. *Romanian-British Political Relations, 1848–1877* (Bucharest, 1983)

Michelson, Paul E. *Romanian Politics, 1859–1872: From Prince Cuza to Prince Carol* (Iaşi, 1998)

Mitrany, David. *The Land and the Peasant in Rumania: The War and Agrarian Reform (1917–1921)* (London, 1930)

Munteanu, Basil. *Modern Rumanian Literature* (Bucharest, 1939)

Ornea, Zigu. *The Romanian Extreme Right in the 1930s* (Boulder, 1999)

Petreu, Marta. *An Infamous Past: E. M. Cioran and the Rise of Fascism in Romania* (Chicago, 2005)

Riker, T. W. *The Making of Roumania* (London, 1931)

Roberts, Henry L. *Rumania: Political Problems of an Agrarian State* (New Haven, 1951)

Spector, Sherman D. *Rumania at the Paris Peace Conference: A Study of the Diplomacy of Ioan I. C. Brătianu* (New York, 1962)

Torrey, Glenn E. *Romania and World War I: A Collection of Studies* (Iaşi, 1998)

The Romanian Battlefront in World War I (Lawrence, 2011)

Turnock, David. *The Romanian Economy in the Twentieth Century* (London, 1986)

THE COMMUNIST ERA

Deletant, Dennis. *Communist Terror in Romania. Gheorghiu-Dej and the Police State, 1948–1965* (New York, 1999)

Fischer, Mary Ellen. *Nicolae Ceauşescu: A Study in Political Leadership* (Boulder, 1989)

Gabanyi, Anneli Ute. *The Ceauşescu Cult: Propaganda and Power Policy in Communist Romania* (Bucharest, 2000)

Gilberg, Trond. *Modernization in Romania since World War II* (New York, 1975)

　Nationalism and Communism in Romania: The Rise and Fall of Ceauşescu's Personal Dictatorship (Boulder, 1990)

Hlihor, Constantin and Ioan Scurtu. *The Red Army in Romania* (Iaşi, 2000)

Jowitt, Kenneth. *Revolutionary Breakthrough and National Development: The Case of Romania, 1944–1965* (Berkeley, 1971)

Kideckel, David. *The Solitude of Collectivism: Romanian Villagers to the Revolution and Beyond* (Ithaca, 1993)

King, Robert R. *A History of the Romanian Communist Party* (Stanford, 1980)

Kligman, Gail. *The Politics of Duplicity: Controlling Reproduction in Ceauşescu's Romania* (Berkeley, 1998)

Kligman, Gail and Katherine Verdery. *Peasants under Siege: The Collectivization of Romanian Agriculture, 1949–1962* (Princeton, 2011)

Levy, Robert. *Ana Pauker: The Rise and Fall of a Jewish Communist* (Berkeley, 2001)

Montias, John Michael. *Economic Development in Communist Romania* (Cambridge, MA, 1967)

Negrici, Eugen. *Literature and Propaganda in Communist Romania* (Bucharest, 1999)

Shafir, Michael. *Romania: Politics, Economics and Society. Political Stagnation and Simulated Change* (London, 1985)

Siani-Davies, Peter. *The Romanian Revolution of December 1989* (Ithaca, 2005)

Tismaneanu, Vladimir. *Stalinism for All Seasons: A Political History of Romanian Communism* (Berkeley, 2003)

Verdery, Katherine. *National Ideology under Socialism: Identity and Cultural Politics in Ceauşescu's Romania* (Berkeley, 1991)

POST-1989

Gallagher, Tom. *Modern Romania: The End of Communism, the Failure of Democratic Reform, and the Theft of a Nation* (New York, 2005)

Stan, Lavinia and Lucian Turcescu. *Religion and Politics in Post-Communist Romania* (Oxford, 2007)

Verdery, Katherine. *The Vanishing Hectare: Property and Value in Postsocialist Transylvania* (Ithaca, 2003)

INDEX

Page numbers in *italics* refer to figures.